Transforming Wisdom

Transforming Wisdom

Pastoral Psychotherapy in Theological Perspective

Edited by

Felicity B. Kelcourse

and

K. Brynolf Lyon

CASCADE *Books* • Eugene, Oregon

TRANSFORMING WISDOM
Pastoral Psychotherapy in Theological Perspective

Cascade Books
An Imprint of Wipf and Stock Publishers
199 W. 8th Ave., Suite 3
Eugene, OR 97401

www.wipfandstock.com

ISBN 13: 978-1-4982-0895-6

Cataloguing-in-Publication data:

Transforming wisdom : pastoral psychotherapy in theological perspective / edited by Felicity B. Kelcourse and K. Byrnolf Lyon.

xiv + 254 p. ; 23 cm. Includes bibliographical references.

ISBN 13: 978-1-4982-0895-6

1.Pastoral psychotherapy 2. Pastoral counseling. 3. Pastoral psychology. 4. Pastoral care. I. Title. II. Kelcourse, Felicity Brock. III. Lyon, K. Byrnolf, 1953–.

BV4012.2 T71 2015

Manufactured in the U.S.A.   10/08/2015

Grateful acknowledgment is made to Shinzen Young for permission to use his figure from chapter 9, The Full Grid, p. 103, in *Five Ways to Know Yourself* (2011). http://www.shinzen.org/Retreat%20Reading/FiveWays.pdf-1.59 Created: 3/11/2011 • Modified: 6/15/2011.

To our students, colleagues, and mentors in the field
of Pastoral Theology and Psychology

Contents

List of Figures and Tables

Acknowledgments

THIS WORK IS DEEPLY indebted to the community of scholars and practitioners whose lives and work has touched our own. Our thanks to colleagues in the Society of Pastoral Theology and the Psychology, Culture,
and Religion group of the American Academy of Religion. We recognize
that the field of pastoral care and counseling could not exist without the
leaders and mentors of the American Association of Pastoral Counselors
and the Association for Clinical Pastoral Education, whose guidance of
past, present, and future practitioners in the field is irreplaceable. We also
thank the American Group Psychotherapy Association, the American
Association for Marriage and Family Therapy, Blanton-Peale Graduate
Institute, the Center for Religion and Psychotherapy of Chicago, and
other such professional development and training organizations for
the work they do promoting development at the personal/professional
boundary.

More personally, we want to thank Ann Ulanov and to honor the
memory of Don Browning and Randy Mason. They provided crucial mentorship to us at significant periods in our lives. Likewise, the past and present faculty of Christian Theological Seminary (including especially former
colleagues Sue Cardwell, Ursula Pfafflin, Lowell Colston, and Brian Grant)
have helped nurture a community sustaining and encouraging the difficult
work of pastoral psychotherapy. We are especially indebted to the contribu-
tors to this volume, including both new and established leaders in our field,
whose patience and hard work has made this possible.

Finally, we want to thank Maureen Sweeney for her editorial resilience
and precision. Without her generous help and the help of the editorial staff
of Cascade Books, this work would be much the poorer.

Contributors

Matthias Beier is Associate Professor of Pastoral Theology and Mental Health Counseling at Christian Theological Seminary in Indianapolis, Indiana. A nationally certified and licensed psychoanalyst, licensed Mental Health Counselor, and AAPC Diplomate, he is the author of *A Violent God-Image* and *Gott ohne Angst.*

Pamela Cooper-White is Christiane Brooks Johnson Professor of Psychology and Religion at Union Theological Seminary, New York. She is a psychoanalytically trained psychotherapist, AAPC clinical Fellow, and a licensed and NBCC Board Certified Counselor. Her publications include *Many Voices: Pastoral Psychotherapy in Relational and Theological Perspective*; *Shared Wisdom: Use of the Self in Pastoral Care and Counseling*, and *The Cry of Tamar: Violence against Women and the Church's Response*, 2nd edition.

Suzanne Coyle is Associate Professor of Pastoral Theology and Marriage and Family Therapy at Christian Theological Seminary, Indianapolis, Indiana. An AAPC Diplomate and AAMFT Fellow and Approved Supervisor, she has a Post-Graduate Diploma in Narrative Therapy and Community from the Dulwich Centre in Australia. Her publications include *Re-storying Your Faith* and *Uncovering Spiritual Narratives: Using Story in Pastoral Care and Ministry.*

Carrie Doehring is Associate Professor of Pastoral Care at Iliff School of Theology, Denver, Colorado. She is a licensed psychologist, is ordained in the PCUSA, and is an AAPC Diplomate. Her publications include *The Practice of Pastoral Care: A Postmodern Approach* (revised and expanded).

James Furrow is Evelyn and Frank Freed Professor of Marital and Family Therapy at Fuller Theological Seminary in Pasadena, California. He is an AAMFT Clinical Fellow and Approved Supervisor. His publications include *The Emotionally Focused Therapy Casebook*; *Becoming an EFT Therapist: The Workbook*; and *Preparing Couples for Love and Marriage*.

Steven S. Ivy is Senior Vice President for Values, Ethics, Social Responsibility, and Pastoral Services at Indiana University Health, Indianapolis, and Affiliate Professor at Christian Theological Seminary in Indianapolis. He is an ACPE Supervisor, an AAPC Fellow, and a Member of the American Society for Bioethics and Humanities. His publications include *The Promise and Pain of Loneliness*.

Felicity Kelcourse is Associate Professor of Pastoral Care and Counseling at Christian Theological Seminary, Indianapolis, Indiana. A licensed Mental Health Counselor, AAPC Diplomate, and AAMFT Supervisor, she is the editor of *Human Development and Faith*, second edition and the coeditor (with Kathleen Greider and Debora Van Deusen Hunsinger) of *Healing Wisdom: Depth Psychology and the Pastoral Ministry*.

Ryan LaMothe is Professor of Pastoral Care and Counseling at Saint Meinrad Seminary and School of Theology in Saint Meinrad, Indiana. He is a licensed Mental Health Counselor, an AAPC Fellow and a Diplomate in the American Psychotherapy Association. His two most recent books are *Heresies of the Heart*; and *Missing Us: Psychoanalysis and Community*.

Insook Lee is Associate Professor of Pastoral Care and Counseling at New York Theological Seminary, New York. She is a certified Fellow in AAPC. Her published articles include "Asian American Women's Agency and Postcolonial Theory," "Aggression in Korean American Women: Cultural Adaptation and Conceptual Reformulation," and "Zen and Pastoral Psychotherapy: A Reflection on the Concept of No-I."

K. Brynolf Lyon formerly served as Lois and Dale Bright Professor of Christian Ministries at Christian Theological Seminary in Indianapolis, Indiana. He is now in private practice of psychotherapy and Co-Executive Director of Indygroupwork. He is a licensed Mental Health Counselor, a Diplomate and Clinical Mental Health Specialist in trauma counseling with AMHCA, and a Certified Group Psychotherapist. He is the coauthor (with Dan Moseley) of *How to Lead in Church Conflict: Healing Ungrieved Loss*.

Joretta L. Marshall is Professor of Pastoral Theology, Care, and Counseling and Executive Vice President & Dean at Brite Divinity School in Fort Worth, Texas. She is an AAPC Diplomate whose publications include *Counseling Lesbian Partners* and *Forgiveness and Abuse: Jewish and Christian Reflections*. She is a coauthor of *Practicing Care in Rural Congregations and Communities*.

Christopher F. J. Ross is Associate Professor in the Psychology of Religion at Wilfred Laurier University in Waterloo, Ontario. He is a clinical psychologist. His publications include "Buddhism, Healing and Pastoral Care," in *Psychotherapy: Cure of the Soul*, and "Type-wise: Using Jung's Theory of Psychological Types in Teaching Religious Studies," in *Teaching Jung*, edited by Kelly Bulkeley and Clodagh Weldon.

Chris R. Schlauch, Associate Professor of Counseling Psychology and Religion and Psychology of Religion at the School of Theology and the Graduate School of Arts and Sciences at Boston University (since 1985), is the author of *Faithful Companioning: How Pastoral Counseling Heals* and coeditor (with W. W. Meissner) of *Psyche and Spirit: Dialectics of Transformation*.

Phillis Isabella Sheppard is Associate Professor of Religion, Psychology, and Culture, at Vanderbilt University Divinity School and Graduate Department of Religion in Nashville, Tennessee. She is a practical theologian, psychoanalyst, and a licensed Clinical Professional Counselor. Her publications include *Self, Culture, and Others in Womanist Practical Theology*; "Black, Beautiful and Good: Gender, Sexuality, and Race in Practical Theology"; "Religion—It's Complicated: The Convergence of Race, Class, and Sexuality in Clinicians' Reflections on Religion"; and *Tilling Sacred Ground: Explorations in a Womanist Cultural Psychology of Religion*, forthcoming.

Ann Belford Ulanov is Christiane Brooks Johnson Memorial Professor Emerita of Psychiatry and Religion at Union Theological Seminary, New York. She is Emerita, Diplomate, American Association of Pastoral Counselors and a Certified Jungian Analyst and member of the Jungian Psychoanalytic Association. Her many publications include *Spiritual Aspects of Clinical Work; The Unshuttered Heart: Opening to Aliveness/Deadness in the Self;* and *Knots and Their Untying: Essays on Psychological Dilemmas;* and, with her late husband Barry Ulanov, of *Religion and the Unconscious; The Healing Imagination: The Meeting of Psyche and Soul,* and *Cinderella and Her Sisters: The Envied and the Envying.*

—————— 1 ——————

Prelude: Why This Book Now?

K. Brynolf Lyon

When you want to awaken, I am that wanting.[1]

—Rainer Maria Rilke, *The Book of Hours*

PASTORAL PSYCHOTHERAPY IS AN expression of the life of faith in conversation with contemporary psychotherapeutic disciplines.[2] It is an effort to understand and live the faith in the midst of the concern to meliorate human emotional suffering. This book is an effort to provide a comprehensive introduction to the practices of pastoral psychotherapy so understood. While single-authored volumes have addressed important perspectives on various aspects of, or clinical approaches to, pastoral psychotherapy and handbooks have provided brief discussions of the individual issues involved, this book invites the reader to take a broad, multi-theoretical perspective on the practice of pastoral psychotherapy in the second decade of the twenty-first century.[3]

1. Rilke (2005) 81.

2. What *faith* means in this context is itself contested terrain. People ascribe many different meanings to that term, which carry divergent moral, emotional, and theological interests and sensibilities, as the reader will see in the chapters that follow. For now, I mean merely to suggest by *faith* leaning into experience in ultimate trust and loyalty. The life of faith is, then, the way life is shaped by one's efforts to live out authentically that ultimate trust and loyalty.

3. For recent single-volume treatments of psychodynamic perspectives on pastoral psychotherapy, see Schlauch (1995); Grant, (2001); and Cooper-White (2007).

Pastoral psychotherapy today must be situated between two significant cultural developments. First, the landscape of modern secularity conditions the situation of pastoral psychotherapy in important ways. On the one hand, after an extended time during which the psychotherapeutic disciplines in general disparaged the life of faith, those very disciplines have rediscovered the importance of spirituality with a vengeance. What is happening is a land shift from the time of Freud's (1927/1964) declaration that religion was a neurosis and Skinner's (1948) claim that religion represented a mere behaviorally maintained superstition. A great number of psychologists, psychiatrists, and psychotherapists have now published books and articles on "spirituality" as essential to emotional health.[4] Unfortunately, many of these books imagine that spirituality can be talked about in the abstract, apart from any particular religious tradition or community that nurtures and develops the beliefs and practices associated with that way of life. Often the argument is made that "religion" is concrete, particular, and institutional whereas "spirituality" is universal. There are profound philosophical problems with this way of divvying up the language of faith. Whatever language of spirituality is used has its origins somewhere, in some particular way of construing and living in the world in faith. To imagine that it does not is simply license to import someone else's beliefs and core assumptions under the guise of the "universal."

A less cynical way to see this development within the secular clinical disciplines, of course, is to notice that it is a kind of reenchantment of the world, a sleight of hand suddenly harvesting seemingly fallow ground. While the secular disciplines understand themselves to be offering objective accounts of the various expressions of spirituality, as Don Browning (1987) suggested many years ago and as Marie Hoffman (2011) has argued more recently, these accounts are always embedded within normative and larger narrative, mythic structures that give shape to the experience they intend merely to describe. This has the effect of reenchanting human experience, imbuing its newly charged spirited sensibility with the air of a nonetheless falsely claimed objective truth. The inevitably constructive character of such descriptions of spirituality most certainly does *not* mean the therapist has license to impose their beliefs on others. It does, however, point to the problem that there is no simple, neutral place to stand in addressing and assessing spiritual issues. Given that this is the case, one ought to be accountable somewhere. Pastoral psychotherapy attempts to recognize that

---

4. See, for example, Pargament (2007); Schermer (2003); Winer & Anderson (2007); West (2000); Sperry and Shafranske (2004); Walsh (2010).

accountability, calling its practitioners toward clarity regarding their theological sensibilities.

On the other hand, another side to the challenge of secularity to pastoral psychotherapy has less to do with the secular clinical disciplines and more to do with the great shifts in Western culture itself. The world in which pastoral psychotherapy must function is dramatically different from that which gave birth to the movement at the beginning of the last century. The increase in secularity itself presents us with a vastly transformed world. Many of our clients hold the increasingly widespread belief that, as the philosopher Charles Taylor (2007) has noted, they can give a perfectly fine account of their lives without reference to the religious beliefs of a historic religious community. So what *is* the relationship of the language of faith to the practice of therapy? What difference does our rootedness and commitment to a particular religious community mean to the therapy we practice?

The second significant cultural development facing pastoral psychotherapy in our time is the emergence of a powerful conservative Christian movement, which promotes so-called Christian counseling. While this is a very diverse group of professionals, some within this group have far less difficulty answering the questions above. Some self-described Christian counselors, for example, believe that the Scripture is the inerrant or infallible word of God, the final authority for all matters within its purview. These professionals endorse some version of what is called biblical counseling: counseling as the application of biblical principles to life's problems. While Christian counselors also have clinical theories from which they practice, it is quite clear that for some such persons final authority resides with the Bible rather than with clinical theory or mutually critical dialogue. Or it is simply asserted, perhaps on the claim of revelation, that good clinical theory obviously could not contravene the Bible. Curiosity and exploration threaten to give way to judgment. Singularity erases multiplicity. Human experience, from this perspective, must finally fit or be formed to whatever one takes to be "the Biblical witness."

Pastoral psychotherapy as understood in this volume takes a different position with regard to human life and the ways the resources of the faith might be helpful to struggling persons. In effect, it appeals to a different family of theological and psychological accounts of authority in general, and of authority in relation to the shaping of human life in particular. No straightforward application of religious beliefs (wherever they are derived from) is sufficient to the complexity of human life and the richness of the divine presence. Interpretations of human experience from the human sciences have their own authority that must be brought into mutually critical conversation with the claims of faith. As the reader will see in the chapters

that follow, there are many different ways of allowing clinical theory and
the resources of the faith to enrich one another outside of a reductionist
paradigm. Part of the importance of this book, we think, is reclaiming the
richness of the conversation between clinical theory and faith in the practice of psychotherapy.

To what does our profession witness in a world that is both increasingly secular and increasingly religiously polarized? Pastoral psychotherapy, in
the main, affirms the importance of both particularity and plurality. It will
show evidence of being firmly rooted in a distinctive theological perspective
even as it embraces religious and cultural diversity. In this sense, as we conceive it, pastoral psychotherapy stands between secular appropriations of a
universalizing language of spirituality on the one hand and more religiously
absolutistic appropriations of certain kinds of clinical language on the other.
It seeks to be faithful to the spiritual life as a critical and imaginative lived-
conversation between the resources of a religious community and the languages and practices of contemporary clinical theory. It resists the uncritical
imposition of preordained truths (whether religious or secular) on the human struggle even as it seeks to stand creatively at the boundary between
the community of faith and the community of clinical accountability.

Another way to say all this is that pastoral psychotherapy sees its work
as clinical *and* theological. It is an effort to understand, apply, and rethink
or extend the best we know about therapeutic practices. It is an effort to
understand, apply, and rethink or extend the best our historical religious
community believes about that Mystery in which life and the created universe is embedded. The clinical encounter is, therefore, an occasion for psychological reflection and an occasion for theological reflection. In pastoral
psychotherapy our vocation lies in both directions.

Of course, pastoral psychotherapy must finally speak and enact these
things in its own idiom. It must find its voice in that peculiar language of
faith open and compelling to it. There is no single, authorized tongue here.
Abundance abounds. A commitment to pluramentalism, even here plurally
held, shapes its work and frames its broader sensibility. Such abundance
can sometimes provoke silence, timidity, or confusion. Dare we speak at
all? It might also provoke an outspoken certainty that misshapes the abundance, an underjustified confidence that we know more than in fact we do.
Yet, amid the temptations and the ways we will get it wrong, we are invited
to have the courage and audacity to speak. We are called to risk getting it
wrong gloriously, to make the mistakes necessary to be alive.

As John Caputo (2006) might have it, pastoral psychotherapy happens
in the vulnerability and uncertainty of the event the word *God* names. It
does its work seeking, surprised by, and in response to that which is "astir"

in the event to which the name *God* refers. It is an event that is forever slipping from view, buried beneath the density of suffering and disappointment, the mirrors of language and speech. Sometimes it is the very language of God itself that obscures the event. We often use language about God to fashion golden calves to manage our anxiety or distress, to create and maintain the suffering of some in order to safeguard the dominance and insecurity of others.[5] The language of God may corrode God; that is, it may corrode the event the name of *God* discloses. Indeed, we would say that the language of God *inevitably* enthrones in our lives something other than the "God beyond God," to use Tillich's (1952) words (p. 188)—some idolatry obscuring the event our language about God is meant to disclose. Suffering and language, vulnerability and sin, obscure the wonder, love and hope that calls from beneath and beyond it all. Pastoral psychotherapy does its work, therefore, with a confident lack of certainty, living always amid the faintly heard murmurings of and about God that thrive in the margins or crevices of language and breath, suffering and joy.

Indeed, if psychotherapy is "transforming suffering into speech," a bodied speech, a speech that finally speaks itself in and into relation with another's bodied speech, pastoral psychotherapy is the alchemy that occasionally turns such bodied speech into prayer or, perhaps, reveals that it has been prayer all along.[6] In pastoral psychotherapy this "Eucharistic reversal," the transubstantiation of flesh into word, will, one hopes, in faith and love, return to flesh anew and renewed.[7] In such hope resides the invitation to dare to know and address the More that is the longing to be alive to, with, and for the world from the pain and love and hope that is one's life.[8] There the event the name *God* discloses is elusively and graciously revealed: the event that beckons us to life, to life within ourselves and with others, to life that beckons others into life, that beckons others into a community that calls to all that exists to take as much waking as it can stand.

Such waking is dangerous. It is infused with the danger that accompanies liberation and compassion, the power to upend and subvert. The principalities and powers within and outside us are opposed to such waking, for

5. See, for example, the recent work of our colleague Beier (2004). See also his chapter in this collection.

6. The phrase "turning suffering into speech" is drawn from the discussion of D. A. Luepnitz (2002, p. 19). While the relational character of psychotherapy has been a topic of great interest over the past several years, it was clearly anticipated by the great pastoral psychotherapist A. Smith Jr. (1982).

7. On the "Eucharistic reversal" as mediating the relation between secularity and the sacred, see Kearney (2012).

8. This is a slight variation on Santner, 2001.

the waking demands that the lowly be elevated, that what has been excluded be found, that the captive be freed, that what has been oppressed and made weak be empowered and made strong. This kind of waking does not, therefore, leave dreaming behind but rather recognizes that to be fully awake one must live in one's dreams *while* awake. Pastoral psychotherapy works in hope, and invites others to dare to hope, that the terrors and misrecognitions to which our lives conform might yet be nudged in a direction more humane.[9] The thriving of the world is the glory of God, the magnificence of the event the name of God discloses.

The event to which the name of God refers is always More and always Other, whatever ground we must stand on in the meantime. For pastoral psychotherapy, of course, it is always "in the meantime," always not yet, however much it is already. The depth of suffering and joy that is the warp and woof of its daily practice keeps it always at the boundary between the lived apophasis (the being undone unto speechlessness, the unrepresented and unbearable states that shape our lives) and the lived cataphasis (the re-finding of words, and selves, and relationships).[10]

Pastoral psychotherapy, therefore, to whatever degree it is true to the Call or Invitation or Lure to which it responds, resists the exhaustion of meaning, the collapse of possibility in absolutist or reductionist appropriations of faith and science. It must resist. As Richard Kearney (2012) has put it, "The absolute requires pluralism to avoid absolutism" (p. xiv). If it does not, it trades the dangerous promises of God for the more proximate securities of idolatry, indulging the narcissistic conceit that God has of course favored me and mine; that it is, after all, only others whose lives are upended. In this sense, both large and small, as Freud the great ironic atheist knew, the work of therapy (and, we would add, especially pastoral psychotherapy) is interminable, its endings always more or less arbitrary and ambiguous, pointing to other beginnings awaiting the right time, and taken up by those who hear, or long to hear, the disturbance and solace of the Murmurings.

References

Beier, M. (2004). *A violent God-image: An introduction to the work of Eugen Drewermann.* New York: Continuum.

Browning, D. S. (1987). *Religious thought and the modern psychologies: A critical conversation in the theology of culture.* Philadelphia: Fortress.

Caputo, J. D. (2006). *The weakness of God: A theology of the event.* Indiana Series in the Philosophy of Religion. Bloomington: Indiana University Press

9. See the discussion of Keller, 2008, p. 122.

10. This is discussed a bit more fully in Russell and Lyon, 2011.

Cooper-White, P. (2007). *Many voices: Pastoral psychotherapy in relational and theological perspective.* Minneapolis: Fortress.

Freud, S. (1961). *The future of an illusion.* In J. Strachey (Ed. and Trans.), *The standard edition of the complete psychological works of Sigmund Freud* (Vol. 21, pp. 5–58). London: Hogarth Press. (orig. publ. 1927).

Hoffman, M. T. (2011). *Toward mutual recognition: Relational psychoanalysis and the Christian narrative.* New York: Routledge.

Kearney, R. (2010). *Anatheism: Returning to God after God.* Insurrections. New York: Columbia University Press.

Keller, C. (2008). *On the mystery: Discerning divinity in process.* Minneapolis: Fortress.

Luepnitz, D. A. (2002). *Schopenhauer's porcupines: Intimacy and its dilemmas.* New York: Basic Books.

Pargament, K. (2007). *Spiritually integrated psychotherapy: Understanding and addressing the sacred.* New York: Guilford.

Rilke, R. M. (2005). *Rilke's book of hours: Love poems to God.* (A. Barrows & J. Miller, Trans.). New York: Riverhead.

Russell, H. T., and Lyon, K. B. (2011). Positioning practical theology: Diversity, contextuality, and otherness. *Encounter 72*(1), 11–30.

Santner, E. L. (2001). *On the psychotheology of everyday life: Reflections on Freud and Rosenzweig.* Chicago: University of Chicago Press.

Schermer, V. L. (2003). *Spirit and psyche: A new paradigm for psychology, psychoanalysis, and psychotherapy.* London: Jessica Kingsley.

Schlauch, C. R. (1995). *Faithful companioning: How pastoral counseling heals.* Minneapolis: Fortress.

Skinner, B. F. (1948). 'Superstition' in the Pigeon. *Journal of Experimental Psychology, 38*, 168–72.

Smith, Jr., A. (1982). *The relational self: Ethics & therapy from a black church perspective.* Nashville: Abingdon.

Sperry, L., & Shafranske, E. (Eds.). (2004). *Spiritually oriented psychotherapy.* Washington DC: American Psychological Association.

Taylor, C. (2007). A *secular age.* Cambridge: Belknap.

Tillich, P. (1952). *The courage to be.* The Terry Lectures. New Haven: Yale University Press.

Walsh, F. (Ed.). (2010). *Spiritual resources in family therapy* (2nd ed.). New York: Guilford.

West, W. (2000). *Psychotherapy and religion: Crossing the line between therapy and religion.* Perspectives on Psychotherapy. London: Sage.

Winer, J. A., & Anderson, J. W. (Eds.). (2007). *Spirituality and religion: Psychoanalytic perspectives.* Annual of Psychoanalysis 34–35. Catskill, NY: Mental Health Resources.

2

Introduction: Pastoral Psychotherapy in North America

Felicity Kelcourse

For the glory of God is the human person fully alive.

—Irenaeus[1]

HOW IS THE PRACTICE of pastoral psychotherapy different from that of other psychotherapeutic disciplines? Does theological reflection influence counselor training and professional priorities in treatment? What distinguishes pastoral psychotherapy in particular from pastoral counseling in general?

The term *pastoral psychotherapy*, as opposed to *pastoral counseling*, is used here deliberately, to distinguish the brief counseling practiced in pastoral settings by congregational ministers, lay leaders, or chaplains from the more in-depth, usually longer-term therapeutic work effected in the contexts of individual, couple, family, or group therapy by therapists with extensive clinical training who bring theological and faith perspectives to their work.[2] The editors and authors represented in this volume recognize

1. Irenaeus of Lyon, *Against heresies*, book IV, 20, 7.

2. Throughout this book there will also be instances in which *pastoral counseling* does in fact refer to the work of clinically trained or licensed professionals. We consider pastoral counseling here as a type of healing practice distinct from the work of pastoral care, yet allied to the work of pastoral caregivers and faith communities by virtue of shared historical and contemporary faith commitments.

the importance of thoughts and feelings that often lie below one's conscious awareness as potentially powerful determinants of both worldviews and actions. Theories and theorists that consider the "unthought known" significant, as opposed to those that consider only conscious thought and observed behavior, can be grouped as theories or theoriests of *depth psychology* (Bollas, 1987; Ulanov A. B., & Ulanov, B., 1982). And because embedded theologies, whether consciously affirmed or repudiated, have the power to influence the search for meaning for good or ill, deliberative theological reflection matters (Stone & Duke, 1996; Miller-McLemore & Gill-Austern, 1999). These are the types of therapeutic, theoretical and theological commitments, including the expectation that one would explore one's own "unthought known" in personal therapy, that generally set pastoral psychotherapists apart from pastors or chaplains on the one hand and secularly oriented psychotherapists on the other.

The work of many pastoral psychotherapists and theological educators is also informed by the systemic analysis of families and larger systems, particularly the intergenerational work of Murray Bowen (1978/1993) and Edwin Friedman (1985). Systems theories recognize that persons never exist in isolation, but are profoundly influenced by their interpersonal contexts, from birth to death (McGoldrick et al., 2011; Kelcourse, 2015). And the field of pastoral care and counseling, as represented by the Society for Pastoral Theology, has progressively broadened its scope to include sociological critiques of cultural and economic systems that negatively affect individuals and communities.[3] Biblical visions of *shalom* as peace established through justice, and a compassionate respect for the interdependence of all Creation, offer hope for redemption in the face of violence and loss (McFague, 1987).[4]

To provide an historical context for the ethos of pastoral psychotherapy as it exists in North America,[5] this chapter offers an overview of the pastoral care and counseling movement. It begins with a brief look at premodern

3. "SPT began in 1985 in order to create a forum for conversation among theological educators and others interested in critical reflection on the theology, theory and practice of care in ministry." (SPT mission statement, http://www.societyforpastoral-theology.com/aboutspt.html).

4. Pastoral psychotherapist Howard Clinebell pioneered work in "ecotheology" and it is now abundantly apparent that human well-being is intimately connected to the health of local environments and the earth as a whole (Clinebell, 1996).

5. Pastoral counselors are trained beyond the USA and Canada, particularly in Korea. An International Council on Pastoral Care and Counseling (ICPCC) "exists for education, equipment and empowerment of persons and groups in the theory and practice of pastoral care and counselling . . . The intention is to promote intercultural and community care; to be engaged in interdisciplinary and interreligious networking within diverse socio-political contexts" (http://www.icpcc.net/).

approaches to healing, noting the historic lectures delivered by Freud and
Jung in 1909, which introduced depth psychology to North America. Next,
this chapter considers the foundation and evolution of twentieth-century
organizations dedicated to clinical training in ministry. Finally, it culminates with the recent legislative, multicultural, interreligious and postmodern concerns currently redefining the practice of pastoral psychotherapy.
Identifying points of consensus and dissent throughout the evolving practice of pastoral counseling and psychotherapy illuminates both avenues for
dialogue and obstacles to the integration of psychological and theological
perspectives. Criteria for psychologically adequate approaches to theology
and theologically adequate approaches to psychology are proposed.

Sociohistorical Contexts:
Premodern, Modern, and Postmodern

The discipline of pastoral psychotherapy invites the ancient wisdom of faith
traditions and the modern wisdom of the social sciences to collaborate in
the service of healing. Pastoral psychotherapists approach healing in relation to the whole person—self, psyche and soul. Defined as our primarily
conscious sense of individual identity, *self* includes personal agency and
will. *Psyche* is defined as embodied mind, which includes the unconscious;
and *soul* is understood as embodied spirit, the *imago dei,* or "that of God in
us" to which both religious traditions and subjective religious experience
attest (Kelcourse, 2008).[6]

The perspective of pastoral psychotherapy is also postmodern as it
takes seriously the inner wisdom of individuals, weighing the personal truth
of subjective experience against the best available knowledge of religious
and secular communities. While pastoral psychotherapists typically lack
the medical training of psychiatrists or psychiatric nurses, the testing and
research expertise of psychologists, or the community-based contextual orientation of social workers, pastoral psychotherapists *are* uniquely equipped
to consider questions of ultimate meaning as opposed to cultural accom-
modation, with compassionate respect for each individual as a beloved child
of God. Profoundly aware of the interaction of self, psyche, and soul, mind,
body, and spirit as fictive yet descriptive distinctions made within whole
persons, pastoral psychotherapists recognize that all human existence is
interconnected. We each depend from infancy on family, communities of

---

6. Note that small-*s self* is usually synonymous with "ego," while capital-*S Self* is
more comparable to "soul."

faith (if any), temporal sociocultural contexts, creation as a whole, and ulti-mately, divine presence as Ground of Being (Tillich, 1951–1963).

The wisdom of faith requires us to look beyond the personal wants and needs of our ego selves to find purpose and meaning in the deeper knowing of the soul, the Self Jung identifies as the center of our being and source of wholeness (Jung, 1951/1968), wisdom comparable to James Fowler's high-est stage of faith (Fowler, 1981/1995). Just as the ego-self looks primarily to its own survival, so the soul looks to the good of all. This is the wisdom of faith to which clinically trained pastoral psychotherapists are equally accountable.

Historically, many pastoral counselors have also been dually certified by the Association for Clinical Pastoral Education (ACPE). The influence of clinical pastoral education (CPE) is significant since many religious groups either require or strongly encourage CPE as training for ordination. The clinical training provided by CPE, generally undertaken in hospital settings, promotes awareness of the mind-body-spirit connections that can result in physical illness for persons suffering various kinds of loss. The clinical train-ing CPE provides promotes interreligious theological reflection and offers vivid experiential evidence of the value of pastoral presence in liminal pub-lic settings (Leas, 2009; King, 2007; Hall, 1992; Thornton, 1970).

Theological concerns that have evolved over centuries cannot be read-ily shrunk to fit a particular psychological lens, any more than the ongoing work of psychological discovery should be limited by understandings of personhood that fail to take those discoveries into account. Bilingual sensi-bilities that do not privilege one language over another, but that accept each on its own terms, are necessary to transform the wisdom of each perspec-tive—the domains of faith, religion, theology, and spirituality on the one hand; and those of anthropology, sociology, economics, ecology and psy-chology on the other—into a more complete appreciation of what humans beings are and what we may become.[7]

Premodern Therapies, Healing Rituals, and Faith

Shamanism is an ancient healing tradition that predates organized religions and is still practiced in many parts of the world today. It exists in a cul-tural context that holds faith in the efficacy of liminal spaces and wounded healers to effect healing. Both psychotherapy and modern medicine bear vestiges of these origins (Winkelman, 2000).

7. Pastoral theologian Pamela Cooper-White (2007) has argued that dimensions of multiplicity may in fact offer a more realistic appreciation of personhood than the binary conversation suggested here.

In the increasingly secular societies of North America, and particularly in Europe, many persons no longer find support for their personhood in communities of faith. How will they answer the question of faith: "On what or whom do you set your heart?" (Fowler, 1981/1995, p. 14). Faith, as the basic trust we place in someone or something that sustains us in being, continues to be a relevant category for secular scientific communities, given the fact that new prescription drugs must beat the 30 percent effective "placebo effect" (a faith cure by any other name) in order to be commercially marketed (Frank & Frank, 1993). Studies have linked participation in faith communities to improved physical health and psychological resilience (Gow et al., 2011; Pargament, 2011).

Many North Americans put their faith in Western medicine for healing and only to a lesser extent in contemporary practices of psychotherapy. In most communities it is still more socially acceptable to take a variety of pills or to end up in the hospital when one has become physically and emotionally ill from anxiety, depression, or grief than it is to darken a therapist's door. For members of faith communities, the pastor is often the first person approached in times of need. Seminary training includes pastoral care for the life transitions of marriage, birth, and death, celebration, and loss; but few pastors are able to respond effectively to acute psychological crises, including suicidal depression, posttraumatic stress, paranoia, or psychosis without additional clinical training, a robust network for referrals, or both. As a result, many persons in psychological distress do not receive optimal care by consulting either their doctor for the physical dimensions of stress or their minister for periodic pastoral and spiritual support, when sustained psychotherapeutic work may in fact be required for healing.

Both shamanism and modern medicine heal in a ritualized community context. There is an implied loss of identity as patients surrender their clothing and personal belongings to enter the liminal space of the hospital (Turner, 1967). The hospital becomes the sacred precinct where healing is expected. Transformative healing can be effected in these liminal moments if care for the spirit as well as the body is provided by chaplains and other pastoral caregivers (Fichette, 2002).

For some the crisis support available in liminal hospital settings is sufficient. For others, psychological struggles persist that are not amenable to the types of care hospitals or faith communities can provide. Some Christians feel guilty acknowledging that their religious beliefs alone may not suffice in all instances to provide the psychological healing they need. Pastoral psychotherapists, trained in theological reflection in concert with their clinical training, are uniquely positioned to support persons in emotional distress to find new meanings that restore a sense of wholeness.

Depth psychologies recognize that we can be healed or harmed both through our conscious beliefs and through the unconscious dimensions of our faith. In *Healing the Family Tree* (McAll, 1982) a Presbyterian psychiatrist records seemingly intractable cases of psychological distress that were ameliorated through the ritual of communion services offered on behalf of loved ones who had died without burial, as when lost at sea. In another context, hospital staff members who had experienced perinatal loss became healers for others by providing a loss hotline so that callers could share their loss with a peer. Virtually all callers stated that their sense of loss was exacerbated by the lack of community rituals. When there is no body to be buried, how can a death be acknowledged? Even in contemporary society where religious rituals do not typically carry the cultural and emotional weight they have for past generations, many persons find they need a ritual to be healed. Particularly for those without current faith communities, and those who have felt limited or wounded by the beliefs with which they were raised, the ritual of coming weekly to the sacred precinct of the therapist's office becomes a healing rite. The little motorized fountains and potted plants often found in a therapist's office hark back to the temple fountains and gardens of Asclepius (Meier, 2003).

Pastoral psychotherapists are uniquely qualified to serve three groups of persons: members of faith communities; those without faith communities, seeking meaning in their lives; and those damaged by toxic religion, seeking to be healed. For members of faith communities, pastoral psychotherapists have the advantage of being identified as persons of faith themselves; those who come to see them trust that their faith concerns will be treated respectfully, as potential sources of strength, not as extraneous or suspect. In relating to believers and seekers alike, the pastoral psychotherapist learns to practice discernment. Nonordinary experiences that counselees claim as positive and life-affirming are not dismissed under the heading of psychosis. Profound faith concerns can be uttered without reference to religious language while destructive beliefs may be presented under the guise of religious orthodoxy. For those wounded by "bad religion" (Morse, 2009), the therapist who has faith that "God is love" affirms of each belief "by their fruits ye shall know them" (Matt 7:16). We can each be healed or harmed by our beliefs. Ultimately it is our faith in the best we know and hope for that makes us whole.

Twentieth-Century Theologians
and Founders of Depth Psychology:

In *The Discovery of the Unconscious* Ellenberger (1970) suggests that "the emergence of dynamic psychiatry can be traced to the year 1775, to a clash between the physician Mesmer and the exorcist Gassner" (p. 53). From a twenty-first-century perspective the cures Mesmer effected by hypnotic means and the faith healings produced by Gassner might appear equally suspect. Yet the question posed by their public conflict—"which approach to healing is more powerful and reliable, science or faith" (p. 53)—presumes a false dichotomy between matter and spirit, which continues to be played out in the present day between a reductionist scientism that understands all human experience in terms of fluctuations in biochemistry, on the one hand, and the denial of matter in favor of spirit, advocated by some religious groups, on the other hand.

Sigmund Freud (1856–1939) proclaimed himself to be a "Godless Jew" in response to the anti-Semitic prejudice of fin-de-siècle Vienna and the Catholic nanny who molested him as a toddler (Marcel, 2005; Goldwert, 1992). As a modernist trained in neurology, he was overtly invested in the scientific method, yet he founded psychoanalysis on the study of dreams at a time when both scientific and faith communities ascribed little or no importance to dreaming (Savary et al., 1984). Oskar Pfister, a Swiss pastor interested in applying psychoanalytic methods to his practice of pastoral care, became a lifelong friend of Freud and his family (Freud & Pfister, 1963). The term *Seelsorge*, translated as "psychotherapy" in the *Standard Edition* of Freud's works can also be translated as the "cure of souls."[8]

Carl Jung (1875–1961) was the son of a Swiss amateur linguist who became a country pastor by default and served as a chaplain in psychiatric settings (Bair, 2001). Jung criticized his father for religious doubts, which the elder Jung would not address. Given this inheritance, it was natural for Jung to become a psychiatrist interested in the "religious instinct." When asked by a BBC interviewer towards the end of his life if he believed in God, Jung famously replied, "I don't believe, I know."[9] In the course of his correspondence with Freud, Jung mentioned being "the victim of a sexual assault by

---

8. The American Psychiatric Association invites those who have advanced the dialogue between religion and psychiatry to deliver the Oskar Pfister lecture. Recipients of this award include many prominent pastoral theologians and clinicians, among them Wayne Oates, William Meissner, James Fowler III, Ann Belford Ulanov, and Don Browning.

9. BBC, *Face to Face* interviews Carl Gustav Jung, October 22, 1959; see https://www.youtube.com/watch?v=FPGMWF7kU_8/.

a man I once worshipped" (McGuire, 1979, p. 44).[10] While Jung's *Answer to Job* was criticized by Martin Buber, Jung maintained a long friendship and correspondence with Victor White, a Dominican priest (Lammers, 1994). In short, Jung's approach to religion and spirituality as a depth psychologist can be characterized as one of ambivalent fascination, as distinct from Freud's stance of outright rejection.

I mention these two wounded healers as founders of twentieth-century depth psychology since each has exerted an influence on the practice of pastoral psychotherapy. Said founders engaged theologically trained interlocutors from the beginning. Their efforts to find healing for their patients and themselves support methods of self-observation still valued in pastoral care and counseling training.

Twentieth-Century Pastoral Psychotherapy in North America

Anton Boisen (1876–1965), recognized as the father of clinical pastoral education (CPE), brought experiential training to the historical connection between faith and mental health. He is known for using the case method as a hermeneutic for theological reflection in relation to persons as "living human documents" (Asquith, 1982). Like Freud and Jung, who initially developed their approaches to psychology as a means of understanding and healing their own woundedness, Boisen's suffering, which included four psychiatric hospitalizations, became the basis for his lifelong quest to understand mental illness in the context of faith. Unlike the founders of depth psychology, he sought a predominantly theological and pastoral approach to healing.[11] True to its founder, CPE to this day gives priority to theological reflection over psychological understandings of persons, in the manner favored by Pruyser's *The Minister as Diagnostician* (1976) and church-related educational institutions such as the Association of Theological Schools (ATS). In contrast to therapeutic disciplines emphasizing logic and behavior, yet comparable to Viktor Frankl's logotherapy (2006), theological reflection in dialogue with suffering persons supports the discovery of hope and meaning in the face of loss. Pastoral diagnosis gives priority to questions of faith.[12]

10. McGuire (1979), 49J, 10, 28, 1907.

11. Reading Boisen's autobiography, *Out of the Depths* (1960), one imagines that an analysis with Freud or Jung would have done him good.

12. Like ministers, CPE-trained chaplains are salaried in their institutional settings to provide pastoral care and do not ordinarily accept fees as in the therapeutic model.

Helen Flanders Dunbar (1902–1959), a foremother in the pastoral care and counseling movement, was Boisen's first CPE intern at Wooster State Hospital in the summer of 1925. H. Flanders (who avoided the use of her first name in publication to avert gender stigma) was a brilliant scholar credited with founding the discipline of psychosomatic medicine in America (Dunbar, 1947/1955; Stokes, 1985). Dunbar, who suffered from childhood illness, seemed driven to compensate for her 4'11" stature with towering accomplishments. In the span of three years she completed a BD at Union Theological Seminary in New York (1927); a PhD in comparative literature at Columbia University, with a dissertation on "Symbolism in Medieval Thought and Its Consummation in the *Divine Comedy*" (1929); and an MD at Yale (1930). She spent her last year of psychiatric training as an assistant at the Burghölzli mental hospital in Zurich and met with Jung during that year. She also undertook psychotherapy (as opposed to psychoanalysis) with Helene Deutsch, a member of Freud's circle, and by all accounts returned from her year abroad transformed, armed with the self-confidence to match her abilities. Allison Stokes in *Ministry after Freud* (1985) says of Dunbar:

> Through her ground-breaking articles and books, written for professional colleagues in the early years and the general public later, she provided a link between the worlds of medicine, theology, and popular culture. Her concern for the whole person—psyche and soma, mind and body—helped pave the way for holistic health care (p. 71).

Like Rollo May (1901–1994), Dunbar was a theologically trained psychiatrist and as such a valuable ally in establishing interdisciplinary dialogue between the wisdom of psychiatry and psychotherapy on the one hand, and the wisdom of theological reflection on the other. Despite her theological education, Dunbar is rarely claimed as a cofounder among the predominantly white male mainline Protestant ministers who figure prominently in twentieth-century histories of the pastoral care and counseling field.

Be that as it may (and, as noted below, Dunbar was not the only pioneer to be slighted in the histories) Union graduates Boisen and Dunbar, along with Bostonians Richard Cabot and Philip Guiles (the latter another early student of Boisen's) founded the Council for Clinical Training of Theological Students (CCTT) in Boston, in January 1930. In 1931 Andover-Newton became the first seminary to teach pastoral theology, with Guiles as the first full-time professor in the field. Disagreements between Dunbar

---

Contemporary chaplains and CPE supervisors have clearly embraced social-science research methods to demonstrate the effectiveness of pastoral care (Fitchett, 2002).

and Guiles caused Dunbar to move the CCTT headquarters to New York in 1932. Cabot sought to distance himself from Boisen following Boisen's second psychiatric hospitalization in November 1930, and questioned whether *mental* hospitals were the most appropriate venue for clergy training.

Boisen, hardly incompetent or inactive despite his breakdowns, had been teaching at Chicago Theological Seminary since 1926, and in 1932 moved the training program he supervised from Wooster State Hospital to Elgin State (Mental) Hospital, where he supervised until his death in 1965. For all his struggles it is Boisen who, to the extent of his knowledge, advanced the "vision of pastoral competence *through* clinical, psychodynamic insight," in concert with "theological reflection on the basis of empirical observation" (Stokes, 1985, p. 53).

In New York, as well as Chicago, the influx of psychoanalytically trained European refugees beginning in the 1930s had a transformative influence on theological appropriations of depth psychology. In 1933 Paul Tillich taught Rollo May at Union. In 1937, the Religio-Psychiatric Clinic, precursor of the present Blanton-Peale Graduate Institute, was inaugurated by Norman Vincent Peale and Dr. Smiley Blanton, a psychiatrist who had been analyzed by Freud (Blanton, 1971), as a free service of Marble Collegiate Church in Midtown Manhattan. In 1941 the New York psychological discussion group was formed, with Eric Fromm, Hiltner, May, and Tillich as members.

Seward Hiltner, who taught at Princeton Theological Seminary, was a leading proponent of the idea that pastoral counseling should be practiced by congregational leaders in church settings. Over against this idea, Fred Kuether, director for the Council for Clinical Training from 1947 until 1954, advocated for pastoral counseling to become a clinical specialization in its own right, allowing pastoral counselors to charge fees for service in private practice independent of the church. Howard Clinebell, founder of the Clinebell Institute in Claremont, California, attempted to mediate between these opposing views, but tensions were such that no professors of pastoral care and counseling were invited to the 1963 organizational meeting of a hundred practicing pastoral counselors out of fear that "they might outnumber us, God forbid" (Wagner, Hand & Stokes, 1992, p. 4).

Specialized Training in Pastoral Care and Counseling Today

The fact that the one hundred practicing pastoral counselors assembled in 1963 were afraid that theological educators might outnumber them attests to the rapid growth of pastoral theology, care, and counseling. Posttraumatic stress was recognized as a community issue following World War II, the Korean War, and the Vietnam War, as it is today, when more returning veterans die from suicide postdeployment than die in combat (Kemp & Bossarte, 2012).[13] Pastors serving congregations, on the front lines of community need, routinely encounter the negative effects of depression, anxiety, addiction, undigested trauma and loss, as well as developmentally induced and genetically inherited mental illness.

Despite the clear need for collaboration between congregational leaders, chaplains, and pastoral psychotherapists—to say nothing of the need to holistically integrate these sources of care with other psychological, medical and social services—pastoral psychotherapists, as specialists in spiritual care and psychotherapy, remain on the boundaries of both congregations and mental health communities. Charles Wagner and his coauthors, in a history of the American Association of Pastoral Counselors from 1963 to 1991, note that in addition to facing opposition from the church, pastoral psychotherapists also face skepticism from secular psychotherapists. Some secular therapists "tend to see pastoral counselors as ministers who have a smattering of knowledge of psychology and are passing themselves off as therapists. The history reveals how seriously (almost to a fault) the organization [the American Association of Pastoral Counselors] has taken training and supervision, and how pastoral counselors have learned from the major streams of psychological thought throughout the years" (Wagner et al., 1992, p. vii).

In 1964, the year before Boisen and Tillich died, the American Association of Pastoral Counselors (AAPC) was founded in St. Louis as an organization for pastoral care specialists and psychotherapists; it was still opposed "by persons fearing that by giving up teaching and conducting worship, clergy would become indistinguishable from psychotherapists or social workers" (Stokes, 1985, p. 185). The Association for Clinical Pastoral Education (ACPE), as direct heir to Boisen's legacy, incorporated in 1967. At the present time most seminaries and many denominations require a unit of CPE (four hundred supervised hours of clinical training) as an element of training for ministry. AAPC general membership is now open to those without theological training and claims interreligious members, but the leadership tends to be dominated by ordained ministers, both female and male, from mainline Protestant and Catholic groups. From this standpoint,

---

13. The estimated number of veterans' suicides in the U.S.A. is twenty-two a day. This figure was released by the VA in February, 2012 based on data from 21 states from 1999 through 2011. With only 40 percent of the U.S. population covered in the report the actual figure is certain to be higher.

the fear that AAPC would alienate ministers from the church has been unfounded. Most members do continue to serve and support congregations. Ambivalence about the separation between church and state has caused AAPC to eschew state licensure in most instances, making dual credentialing a necessity for practicing pastoral psychotherapists.[14] Though AAPC has historically invested in professional formation through the standards it sets for clinical membership, training for certification and service centers, the future of AAPC certification is currently uncertain.

Diversity for the Twenty-First Century[15]

Though the initial membership of AAPC was dominated by white male ministers from mainline Protestant denominations who had met the standards for certified membership (350 supervised client hours with an approved body of knowledge), early outliers included Ann Belford Ulanov (2004), a theological educator, Jungian analyst, and Episcopal laywoman, and Catholic women religious, including Sister Marie McCarthy (Anderson et al., 1995). The early membership was about 10 percent Catholic, but, lay and otherwise, Catholics did not always find an easy path to membership due to the ecclesial "endorsement" requirement (Janet Foy, personal communication). Sue Webb Cardwell (Cardwell & Hunt, 1979) became the first female president of AAPC in 1986, and Alice Graham (2004), who joined AAPC in 1981, served as the first president of color at the fiftieth-anniversary celebration in 2014. Gender diversity in AAPC is now well established. With

14. The six states that license pastoral counselors are Arkansas, Kentucky, Maine, New Hampshire, North Carolina, and Tennessee. In other states AAPC members are typically licensed as mental health counselors or marriage and family therapists. "Membership in AAPC is open to all who support AAPC's mission to bring healing, hope, and wholeness to individuals, families, and communities. The primary benefit of membership is to be a formal participant in the dialogue on the integration of spirituality and one's professional practice." (www.aapc.org/membership/).

15. Due to space limitations, only one relevant publication per leader is included. Since publication dates may not indicate seniority, leaders have been named in alphabetical order. Some of those cited are best known for their institutional leadership. Many more ACPE supervisors and AAPC pastoral psychotherapists could be named. Listed names were assembled primarily in consultation with members of the Society for Pastoral Theology. The author acknowledges with regret that this listing is necessarily partial and incomplete with respect to the age and weighted influence of those identified. It includes only pastoral care and counseling professionals serving in North America, not those in the wider international community. Yet it is hoped that even a partial listing will encourage others to explore the diversity of leaders and voices serving in the field of pastoral theology and psychology today.

the 2008–2010 presidency of Joretta Marshall (1997), AAPC established an open and affirming identity.

For AAPC, as for ACPE and SPT, growth in diversity through the addition of African American, Latino and Asian (mainly Korean) members was slow, despite the pioneering initiatives of leaders like Thomas Pugh (Pugh et al., 1998), father of African American pastoral care and professor at the Interdenominational Theological Center (ITC) in Atlanta, who earned his doctoral degree from Boston University in 1955. Edward Wimberly, also a professor at ITC (1979) joined AAPC in the '70s and SPT in the '80s. Additional early leaders include Homer Ashby (1988), Henry Brooks (1964), Caroll Felton (1980), Vergel Lattimore III (1984), Carolyn Aka L. McCrary (1989), Clinton McNair (1978), George Polk (1985), and Archie Smith Jr. (1982). Steve Sangkwon Shim (2003), a PhD graduate of Claremont School of Theology, was the first Korean Diplomate in AAPC qualified to offer supervision of counseling supervisors. Caroll Watkins Ali (1997), Urias Beverly (2003), Marsha Foster Boyd (1992), Lee Butler (2000), (1992), Toinette Eugene (1998), Horace Griffin (2006), Linda Hollies (1992), Emmanuel Yartekwei Lartey (2003), K. Samuel Lee (2010), Arthur Pressley (2011), Rebecca Radillo (2009), Daniel Schipani (2003), Teresa Snorton (2004), Angella Son (2013) and Charles Taylor (1992) continue in leadership and mentor roles. For the benefit of Korean-language counselors, Samuel Lee (Claremont School of Theology) consults with pastoral counseling training programs in Korea, and Angella Son (Drew University) directs a bilingual training program at the Blanton-Peale Graduate Institute in New York.

In the 1980s a Racial Ethnic Multicultural Network (REM) was formed within the memberships of ACPE responsible for supervisory training in chaplaincy. REM has provided a model for groups subsequently formed within the SPT and AAPC to support the professional development of persons of color. Cameron Byrd, Claudette Copeland, J. Edward Lewis, Carolyn McCrary, Clinton McNair, and George Polk founded REM. Early mentors included Calvin Banks, Carlos Bell, Henry Brooks, Delores Daniels Brown, Dalton Downs, Thanda Ngcobo, Patrick Persaud, Gale Kennebrew-Poindexter, Hallie Lawson Reeves, Eugene Robinson, Harry Simmons, Benson Thomas, and Cecelia Williams (Wilson-Cone, 2003). Urias Beverly was the first African American CPE Supervisor to serve as president of ACPE, and Teresa Snorton recently held the position of Executive Director of ACPE for twelve years, the first African American woman to serve in that capacity.[16]

16. A more comprehensive listing of ACPE founders and leaders can be found in the ACPE archives in Atlanta, Georgia.

If AAPC is to remain relevant for the twenty-first century it must nurture connections with vibrant faith communities, including especially communities of color. With mainline denominations losing members (as the closures of mainline seminaries and related faculty layoffs attest), AAPC will need to find a balance between its progressive heritage, including commitments to the leadership of women and the affirmation of Gay, Lesbian, Bisexual, Transgender, Intersex, and Queer (GBLTIQ) persons of faith on the one hand, and the typically more conservative theologies of African American, Asian, and Latino congregations on the other. An additional challenge is the desire to become a more interreligious body, despite the fact that Christian theologies remain the preferred language for most members. Matthias Beier (2004, a contributor to this volume) has urged AAPC to seek a membership fully reflective of the regional communities its members serve.

There is currently no lack of potential leadership and mentorship to meet these challenges. Space does not permit more than a cursory additional mention of current leaders, a list that includes seminary faculty, pastoral counselors and ACPE supervisors, persons with both theological and clinical training. We can hope that the students and colleagues of these mentors will carry forward the vision of a clinically trained, theologically informed, progressive, and inclusive interreligious therapeutic presence as a resource for congregations, individuals and families in need of healing.

Readers are encouraged to consider the current and future legacies of those listed here, in addition to those already cited above: Trina Armstrong, Esther Acolatse, Finbar S. Benjamin, Daphne Brown, Martha Brown, Samuel Brown-Dawson, Robin Brown-Haithco, Carrie Buckner, Peter Yuichi Clark, Michael Lee Cook, Stephanie Crumpton, Monica Cummings, Christina Davis, Gregory Ellison, Laurie Garrett-Cobbina, Willie Goodman, Julie Hanada, Koji Hayashi, Cedric Johnson, Yoke-Lye Lim Kwong, Insook Lee, Oliver Lee, Frances Rivers Meza, Hellena Moon, Tapiwa Mucherera, Fulgence Nyengele, Kirsten Oh, Heidi Park, Samuel Park, Sophia Park, Jay Orlando Perez, Renato Santos, Phillis Sheppard, F. Keith Slaughter, Reynard Smith, Siroj Sorajjakool, Mica Togami, Yuko Uesugi, Elizabeth Walker, Beverly Wallace, and Myounghun Yun. [17] Elizabeth Walker (2010) is researching a forthcoming history of African American pastoral counselors and psychology of religion scholars. Patricia Wilson-Cone has assembled contributions from ACPE's Racial Ethnic Minority group members, *Theologies from REM's Women* (2003) illustrating the practice of clinically informed theological reflection. The work of additional female leaders appears in *Women out of*

17. The author, speaking from outside the racial-ethnic groups that have formed to support diversity within AAPC, ACPE, and SPT, hopes that new generations of diverse leadership will continue to be documented by her colleagues.

order: Risking change and creating care in a multicultural world (Stevenson-Moessner & Snorton, 2010).[18]

Conclusion

Just as Anton Boisen defined the proper focus of pastoral theology and clinical pastoral education as the "living human document" (Asquith, 1982) and subsequent scholars have lifted up the "living human web" (Miller-McLemore, 2008), so the twenty-first century brings with it the challenge of understanding human existence in the context of creation, the web of life, of which humanity is a self-aware but dependent part. It has never been more essential for individuals and communities to find wisdom and healing that can bring an end to destructive consumerism, poverty, injustice, warfare, and the potential of nuclear genocide. Preachers, prophets, peacemakers, and social activists seek to lift the moral imagination of communities, addressing wounds perpetuated in society. To address the needs of wounded persons the quiet, redemptive work of pastoral psychotherapy generally takes place behind closed doors, self to self, psyche to psyche, soul to soul. Pastoral theologians also draw on the wisdom of faith communities to create community rituals for healing.[19] This book, directed as it is to pastoral psychotherapists in training, focuses primarily on traditional therapeutic contexts, while acknowledging that the support of faith communities is essential to pastoral formation. These communities serve to spiritually sustain the psychological labors of psychotherapists who must periodically "descend into hell" as companions on the path to redemption and resurrection.

In response to the questions posed at the beginning of this chapter, pastoral psychotherapists seek spiritual and relational wholeness as criteria for healing. The transforming wisdom of pastoral psychotherapy companions persons desiring to be whole in relation to their loving acceptance of self and others. Therapeutic goals, as articulated by clients—typically Freud's "to love and to work" criteria—are seen in the larger context of ultimate meaning. Individual understandings of well-being and self-worth are balanced against the demands of family and society to promote attachment to that which is truly life-giving for the client (LaMothe, 2005). The formation and professional priorities of pastoral psychotherapists are such that respect for intersubjective communication and honesty is ever valued,

18. See also an anthology of Asian voices in Christian ministry edited by Lee and Son (1999).

19. See particularly the work of Wimberly (2006); Lartey (2003); Butler (2000); Johnson (2010); Ramshaw (1987); and McAll (1982).

recognizing the worth of all persons as loved by God, without disdain for even the most broken. Pastoral psychotherapy, as opposed to a more general understanding of pastoral care and brief counseling, appreciates the depths of suffering, spoken and unspoken, as well as the heights of wholeness in the gathered multiplicity of *perichoresis* to which seekers can aspire (Cooper-White, 2007; Nyengele, 2004).[20]

Theologically adequate approaches to psychology take the long view of human experience, not limiting our understanding of persons to the standards and definitions supplied by contemporary science but appreciating the limits of our current knowledge as it may be illuminated by past or anticipated future wisdom. Psychologically adequate approaches to theology recognize that not all beliefs or statements of faith are created equal. Those that lead to fear, distrust, oppression, abuse and sadistic attacks upon the other objectively fail the criteria for goodness to which persons of ethical integrity can attest. Whatever is life-giving, hopeful, freeing, releasing the best in persons, families and communities, is to be desired. In short, there is "good religion" and "bad religion"—by their fruits you shall know them (Matthew 7:20).

In the practice of pastoral psychotherapy, theological reflection informs psychological understandings of value and meaning, while psychological and sociological understandings of health promote normative expectations for individual and community well-being. Though every society has the potential to be blinded by its own *Zeitgeist*, God's lure towards wholeness for each and all offers hope for transcendent wisdom.

References

Ali, C. A. W. (1999). *Survival & liberation: Pastoral theology in an African American context*. St. Louis: Chalice

Anderson, H. et al. (1995). *Promising again*. Louisville: Westminster John Knox.

Armistead, M. K. (1995). *God-images in the healing process*. Minneapolis: Fortress.

Ashby, H. U., Jr. (1988). Pastoral counseling and the black experience of otherness. In C. A. Wise et al. (Eds.), *At the point of need: Living human experience; Essays in honor of Carroll A. Wise*. (pp. 107–20) Lanham, MD: University Press of America.

Asquith, G. (1982). Anton T. Boisen and the study of "Living Human Documents." *Journal of Presbyterian History (1962–1985)*. 60, 244–65.

Bair, D. (2001). *Jung: A biography*. Boston: Little, Brown.

Beier, M. (2004). *A violent God-image: An introduction to the work of Eugen Drewermann*. New York: Continuum.

20. Trinitarian and feminist/womanist theologies understand *perichoresis* as the sacred relational dance central to God as Being and Becoming. God is not One alone, but always One with Others.

Beverly, U. (2003). *The places you go: Caring for your congregation Monday through Saturday*. Nashville: Abingdon.

Blanton, S. (1971). *Diary of my analysis with Sigmund Freud*. New York: Hawthorn.

Boisen, A. T. (1960). *Out of the depths: An autobiographical study of mental disorder and religious experience*. New York: Harper & Brothers.

Bollas, C. (1987). *The Shadow of the object: Psychoanalysis of the unthought known*. New York: Columbia University Press.

Bowen, M. (1993). *Family therapy in clinical practice*. Lanham, MD: Aronson. (Orig. publ. 1978).

Boyd, M. F., & C. S. Bohler (1999). Womanist-feminist alliances: Meeting on the bridge. In B. J. Miller-McLemore & B. L. Gill-Austern (Eds.), *Feminist and womanist pastoral theology* (pp. 189–210). Nashville: Abingdon.

Brooks, H. C. (1964). *The concept of God in the analytical psychology of Carl Gustav Jung.* (Unpublished doctoral dissertation). Boston University.

Butler, L. H., Jr. (2000). *A loving home: Caring for African American marriage and families*. Cleveland: Pilgrim.

Cardwell, S. W., & Hunt, R. (1979). Persistence in seminary and ministry. *Pastoral Psychology, 28*, 119–31.

Clinebell, H. J. (1996). *Ecotherapy: Healing ourselves, healing the earth; A guide to ecologically grounded personality theory, spirituality, therapy and education*. Minneapolis: Fortress.

Cooper-White, P. (2007). *Many voices: Pastoral psychotherapy in relational and theological perspective*. Minneapolis: Fortress.

Dunbar, H. F. (1955). *Mind and body: Psychosomatic medicine* (2nd ed.). New York: Random House. (Orig. publ. 1947).

Ellenberger, H. F. (1970). *The discovery of the unconscious*. New York: Basic Books.

Eugene, T. M., & Poling, J. N. (1998). *Balm for Gilead: Pastoral care for African American families experiencing abuse*. Nashville: Abingdon.

Felton, C. M. (1980). *The care of souls in the Black Church: A liberation perspective*. New York: Martin Luther King Fellows Press.

Fichett, G. (2002). *Assessing spiritual needs: A guide for caregivers*. Guides to Pastoral Care. Lima, OH: Academic Renewal Press.

Fowler, J. W. (1995). *Stages of faith: The psychology of human development and the quest for meaning*. New York: HarperOne. (Orig. publ. 1981).

Frank, J. D., & Frank, J. B. (1993). *Persuasion and healing: Comparative study of psychotherapy*. Baltimore: Johns Hopkins University Press

Frankl, V. (2006). *Man's search for meaning: Foundations and applications of logotherapy*. Boston: Beacon.

Freud, S., & Pfister, O. (1963). *Psychoanalysis and faith: The letters of Sigmund Freud and Oscar Pfister.* H. Meng & E. Freud (Eds.). New York: Basic Books.

Friedman, E. H. (1985). *Generation to generation: Family process in church and synagogue*. The Guilford Family Therapy Series. New York: Guilford.

Goldwert, M. (1992). *The wounded healers: Creative illness in the pioneers of depth psychology*. Lanham, MD: University Press of America.

Gow, A. J. et al. (2011). A stairway to heaven? Structure of the religious involvement inventory and spiritual well-being scale. *Journal of Religion & Health. 50*(1), 5–19.

Graham, A. (2015b). Identity in middle and late adolescence. In F. B. Kelcourse (Ed.), *Human development and faith: Life-cycle stages of body, mind, and soul* (pp. 223–35). St. Louis: Chalice.

Griffin, H. L. (2006). *Their own receive them not: African American lesbians and gays in black churches*. Cleveland: Pilgrim.

Hall, C. E. (1992). *Head and heart: The story of the clinical pastoral education movement.* Decatur, GA: Journal of Pastoral Care Publications.

Hollies, L. H. (Ed.) (1992). *WomanistCare: How to tend the souls of women.* Joliet, IL: Woman to Woman Ministries.

James, W. (1982). *Varieties of religious experience: A study in human nature.* New York: Penguin (Orig. publ. 1902).

Johnson, C. (2010). Resistance is not futile: Finding therapeutic space between colonialism and globalization. In K. Grieder, D. Hunsinger & F. Kelcourse (Eds), *Healing wisdom: Depth psychology and the pastoral ministry* (pp. 157–175). Grand Rapids: Eerdmans.

Jung, C. G. (1963). *Memories, dreams, reflections.* A. Jaffe (Ed.), R. Winston & C. Winston (Trans.). New York: Pantheon.

Jung, C. G. (1968). The Self. In W. McGuire (Series Ed.), H. E. Read et al. (Eds.), R. F. C. Hull (Trans.), *The collected works of C. G. Jung Vol. 9, part II: Aion* (2nd ed., 23–35). Princeton: Princeton University Press. (Orig. publ. 1951).

Kelcourse, F. B. (Ed.) (2015). *Human development and faith: Life-cycle stages of body, mind and soul* (2nd ed.). St. Louis: Chalice.

Kelcourse, F. (2008). A Phenomenology of Self, Psyche, and Soul: What Can We Learn from a Name? Metanexus Institute Conference 2008, http://www.metanexus.net/archive/conference2008/articles/Default-id=10484.aspx.html/.

Kemp, J., & Bossarte, R. (2012). Suicide data report, Department of Veterans Affairs, Mental Health Services Suicide Prevention Program, http://www.va.gov/opa/docs/suicide-data-report-2012-final.pdf/.

King, S. (2007). *Trust the process: A history of clinical pastoral education as theological education.* Lantham, MD: University Press.

Lammers, A. (1994). *In God's shadow: The collaboration of Victor White and C. G. Jung.* New York: Paulist.

LaMothe, R. (2005). *Becoming alive: Psychoanalysis and vitality.* New York: Routledge.

Lartey, E. (2003). *In living color: An intercultural approach to pastoral care and counselling* (2nd ed.). Philadelphia: Kingsley.

Lattimore, V. (1984). *Pastoral care strategies of black pastors.* (Unpublished doctoral dissertation). Northwestern University.

Leas, R. D. (2009). *Anton Theophilus Boisen: His life, work, impact, and theological legacy.* Denver: Journal of Pastoral Care Publications.

Lee, I. S., & Son, T. (1999). *Asian Americans and Christian ministry.* Seoul, Korea: Voice Publishing House.

Lee, K. S. (2010). Much depends on the kitchen: Pastoral practice in multicultural society. In K. Greider et al. (Eds.). *Healing wisdom: Depth psychology and the pastoral ministry* (pp. 34–54). Grand Rapids: Eerdmans.

Marcel, M. (2005). *Freud's traumatic memory: Reclaiming seduction theory and revisiting Oedipus.* Pittsburgh: Duquesne University Press.

Marshall, J. (1997). *Counseling lesbian partners.* Counseling and Pastoral Theology. Louisville: Westminster John Knox.

McAll, K. (1982). *Healing the family tree.* London: Sheldon.

McCrary, C. (1989). *Interdependence as a norm for an interdisciplinary model of pastoral counseling,* (Unpublished doctoral dissertation). Interdenominational Theological Center.

McFague, S. (1987). *Models of God: Theology for an ecological, nuclear age.* Philadelphia: Fortress.

McGoldrick, M. et al. (2011). *The expanded family life cycle: Individual, family and social perspectives* (4th ed.). Boston: Allyn & Bacon.

McGuire, W. (Ed.). (1979). *The Freud/Jung letters.* Princeton: Princeton University Press.

McNair, C. (1978). *The effect of pastoral counseling on the patient's adjustment to hemodialysis.* (Unpublished doctoral dissertation). Northwestern University.

Meier, C. A. (2003). *Healing dream and ritual: Ancient incubation and modern psychotherapy.* Einsiedeln, Switzerland: Diamon.

Miller-McLemore, B. (2008). Revisiting the Living Human Web: Theological Education and the Role of Clinical Pastoral Education, *Journal of Pastoral Care & Counseling* 62 (1–2), 3–18.

Miller-McLemore, B., & Gill-Austern, B. (Eds). (1999). *Feminist and womanist pastoral theology.* Nashville: Abingdon.

Morse, C. (2009). *Not Every Spirit: A Dogmatics of Christian Disbelief* (2nd ed.). New York: Continuum.

Nyengele, M. F. (2004). *African Women's Theology, Gender Relations and Family Systems Theory: Pastoral Theological Considerations and Guidelines for Care and Counseling,* American University Studies. Series 7: Theology and Religion 229. New York: Lang.

Nyengele, M. F. (2006). Gender injustice and pastoral care in an African context: Perichoresis as a transformative theological resource. *Journal of Theology 110,* 45–56.

Pargament, K. I. (2011). *Spiritually integrated psychotherapy: Understanding and addressing the sacred.* New York: Guilford.

Polk, G. (1985). *Pastoral care and minorities.* Care Cassettes 12(3) Schaumburg, IL: College of Chaplains.

Pressley, A. L. (2011). *Approaches to African American pastoral care psychology.* Nashville: Abingdon.

Pruyser, P. W. (1976). *The minister as diagnostician: Personal problems in pastoral perspective.* Philadelphia: Westminster.

Pugh, T. et al. (1998). Studies of personhood in African American pastoral care and counseling in honor of Thomas J. Pugh. *Journal of the Interdenominational Theological Center 25(3).* Atlanta: ITC Press.

Radillo, R. (2009). Pastoral care and counseling. In M. Torre (Ed.). *Hispanic American religious cultures.* (Vol. 2). Santa Barbara, CA: ABC-CLIO.

Ramshaw, E. (1987). *Ritual and pastoral care.* Philadelphia: Fortress.

Savary, L. M. et al. (1984). *Dreams and spiritual growth: A Christian approach to dream work.* New York: Paulist.

Schipani, D. S. (2003). *The way of wisdom in pastoral counseling.* Elkhart, IN: Institute of Mennonite Studies.

Shim, S. (2003). Pastoral counseling with Asian Americans. In R. J. Wicks et al. (Eds.), *Clinical handbook of pastoral counseling* (77–100). (3rd ed.). Integration Books. New York: Paulist.

Smith, A., Jr. (1982). *The relational self: Ethics & therapy from a Black Church perspective.* Nashville: Abingdon.

Son, A. M. P. (2013). *Spirituality of joy: moving beyond dread and duties.* Seoul, Korea: Jeyoung Communications.

Stevenson-Moessner, J. & Snorton, T. (Eds.). (2010). *Women out of order: Risking change and creating care in a multicultural world.* Minneapolis: Fortress.

Stokes, A. (1985). *Ministry after Freud.* New York: Pilgrim.

Stone, H. W., & Duke, J. O. (1996). *How to think theologically.* Minneapolis: Fortress.

Taylor, C. W. (1992). Black experience as a resource for pastoral theology. *Journal of Pastoral Theology,* 2, 27–34.

Thornton, E. E. (1970). *Professional education for ministry: A history of clinical pastoral education.* Nashville: Abingdon.

Tillich, P. (1951–1963). *Systematic theology,* Vols. 1–3). Chicago: University of Chicago Press.

Turner, V. W. (1967). Betwixt and between: The liminal period in *Rites de Passage.* In *The Forest of Symbols* (pp. 93–111). Ithaca, NY: Cornell University Press.

Ulanov, A. B. (2004). *Spiritual aspects of clinical work.* Einsiedeln, Switzerland: Daimon.

Ulanov, A. & Ulanov, B. (1975). *Religion and the unconscious.* Philadelphia: Westminster.

Wagner, C. et al. (1992). *The AAPC: A history of the American Association of Pastoral Counselors, 1963–1991.* Fairfax, VA: American Association of Pastoral Counselors.

Wilson-Cone, P. (Ed.). (2003). *Theologies from REM's Women of Color.* Owings Mills, MD: Watermark.

Wimberly, E. P. (1979). *Pastoral care in the Black church.* Nashville: Abingdon.

Wimberly, E. P. (2006). *African American pastoral care and counseling: the politics of oppression and empowerment.* Cleveland: Pilgrim.

Winkelman, M. (2000). *Shamanism: The neural ecology of consciousness and healing.* Westport, CT: Bergin & Garvey.

3

On Listening: Taming the Fox

Pamela Cooper-White

"You must be very patient," replied the fox. "First you will sit down at a little distance from me—like that—in the grass. I shall look at you out of the corner of my eye, and you will say nothing. Words are the source of misunderstandings. But you will sit a little closer to me, every day . . ."

—Antoine de Saint Exupéry,
The Little Prince

What, then, are the basic requirements as to the personality and the professional abilities of a [therapist]? . . . The psychotherapist must be able to listen.

—Frieda Fromm-Reichmann,
Principles of Intensive Psychotherapy

FRENCH PILOT AND AUTHOR Antoine de Saint Exupéry (1943) tells in his now famous modern fairy tale of a "little prince" who sets out from his tiny planet on an interplanetary voyage to see the universe, leaving his beloved, a rose, behind. On earth, the little prince grows lonely for his flower, and learns the meaning of true relationship from a wise fox (pp. 78–88). This story serves as an apt fable for contemplating the art

28

of empathic listening, and the value of attentive stillness.[1] Above all, *"the psychotherapist must be able to listen"* (Fromm-Reichmann, 1960, p. 7).

Perhaps you have decided to train as a pastoral psychotherapist because you were told you are a good listener. Or perhaps you have longed to be listened to, and you have discovered that by listening to others, you also listen to yourself. Perhaps you have already engaged in some form of skilled listening—through ministry, youth work, teaching, law, nursing, medicine, journalism, social work, or some other field—and you want to integrate this with a focus on *cura animarum,* the ancient spiritual practice of the "cure of souls." Perhaps there is simply something about the practice of pastoral psychotherapy that beckons you to explore further. Whatever your reasons, you probably already know or intuit a few things that this chapter will be about:

First, that listening (by which I mean *attending with all of one's self—mind and heart, body and soul, conscious and unconscious*) is the central practice of all pastoral care and psychotherapy. Second, that professional listening is both an art and a skill, and as such, it is not entirely natural or spontaneous. And third, that much of what both you and I may have once thought a pastoral psychotherapist ought to do for a patient[2] is probably wrong! As with most beginning counselors, we may believe that we must be actively and concretely helpful to the patient by doing certain scripted things: make wise comments, ask penetrating questions, share deep insights that will bring the patient to new awareness, and dispense sage advice. This script is mostly false, and sometimes even harmful. But the expectation that we should always know *what* to do, and always be *doing something* is hard to unlearn.

Misconceptions about what it means to be a good therapist are also embedded in larger questions of who we are as persons, and the social settings in which we listen. The matter of who is the listener and who is the listened-to is far more complex than counselors used to imagine, even well into the twentieth century. The selfhood or subjectivity of persons—both as we experience ourselves internally, and in relation to one another—is now understood as a question of deeper mutual influence, multiplicity, and

1. One caveat should be noted at the outset: I am using this metaphor "to tame," in the sense it is described by Saint-Exupéry in the fox's words—"to establish ties." (p. 80). By no means should this be taken literally, or in the sense of taming savages, or considering our patients to be "primitive," cf. C. Brickman's (2003) excellent critique of the implicit racism in the concept of "primitivity" as it is so frequently (mis)used in psychoanalytic theory.

2. I use the word *patient*, with its etymological roots in the Latin word *passio* ("to suffer") and its associations with healing, rather than the word *client*, with its connotations of economic and contractual exchange. Both words, however, represent legitimate aspects of the therapeutic relationship.

empathic sensitivity (both conscious and unconscious) than previously imagined. Further, we and our patients do not relate to one another as an isolated dyad, but always in the context of a wider social and cultural environment that both names and distorts many unquestioned assumptions about such "basic" realities as gender, race, sexuality, class, ability/disability, age, and other aspects of identity. Finally, as *pastoral* practitioners, we place our work under the larger umbrella of ministry and spiritual care. What does God/Spirit have to do with our work as pastoral psychotherapists— and in particular, with the art and practice of listening?

Listening as Skill and Art

"What does that mean—'tame'?" . . .

"It is an act too often neglected," said the fox. "It means to establish ties." (Saint-Exupéry, 1943, p. 80)

Psychotherapy has always been a matter of one person deeply and empathically listening to another. "It is the relationship that heals" (Yalom, 1980, p. 401). People come to therapy for a variety of reasons. They come because they are experiencing emotional pain that they cannot get rid of on their own, such as depression or anxiety; they come because they are in crisis—they have become overwhelmed by circumstances for which they can see no solution, or they have experienced a psychotic break or have "hit bottom" with an addiction; they come because they are having difficulties in intimate relationships, or they have recognized that they seem to be repeating self-defeating patterns with others at home or at work; or they come because someone who cares about them has told them they need to "see someone"—sometimes, with an ultimatum that if they do not, that person will leave them. Additionally, people seek a *pastoral* psychotherapist because they recognize that their mind, body, and spirit are not separate, and they want a therapist who is not only well-trained clinically but respectful of their religious or spiritual beliefs and values.

The first step, then, in any effective therapy, is, in the fox's words, to "establish ties." We need to demonstrate that we are interested, compassionate, and respectful. We do not need to establish ourselves as experts who know everything—because, in fact, we don't (although some patients come, at least initially, hoping we have a magic wand)! We *do* need to establish from the outset that we will be honest, sensitive to their feelings, and knowledgeable enough to hear what they have to say and at times help them to clarify it and put it in a larger framework. What this requires, first and foremost, is that we are able to listen. A patient will not trust someone whose demeanor is distracted, emotionally disconnected, or superior. The therapeutic relationship requires trust, and trust requires that we quietly, respectfully listen.

Most central to these qualities is *empathy*. Empathy may be best understood in comparison to sympathy. If I have sympathy for you, I am feeling for you, but at a distance. Empathy requires not only that I can feel sympathetic toward you, but that I make the effort to enter into your own viewpoint, your own experience—a kind of "vicarious introspection" (Kohut, 1977/2009, p. 306). Obviously I can never fully enter into another person's mind. But empathy is the sustained effort to stand in the other's shoes—to share as fully as possible the patient's affect and self-state in one's own heart and mind and body. Empathy is also the bridge by which we can recognize and appreciate difference—including our patients' and our own gender, race, sexuality, and cultural dynamics. Empathy is therefore necessary to justice-making—just listening. It is the first step in breaking down walls of prejudice and the blind spots that accompany privilege.[3]

Empathic listening, then, is the foundational capacity to which we must return again and again in each and every therapy. It is analogous to the primal capacity of the "good enough" parent's provision of a "holding environment" (Winnicott, 1965, p. 145): to be fully present to the child in his or her becoming, to listen, to see, to *recognize* the child as a precious other—both separate from us and in close relation—to nurture his or her unique growth without possessiveness or excessive anxiety. As pastoral psychotherapists we would add, to recognize that child as a precious child of the God who mothers us all (Grant, 2001).

If it is difficult for me to sit still, to tolerate silence, this raises a question, why? What might be going on inside me that makes me want to pepper the patient with questions, which will end up leading him or her in the direction I am now choosing, rather than allowing his or her story to unfold organically in his or her own time?[4] Am I feeling insecure about what s/he is telling me, and do I feel that asking for more details will make me seem more on top of things? What might be causing me to feel an urgent need to

3. For more on this, see Cooper-White (2011, pp. 156–70).

4. This is not meant to say that a therapist never asks questions, but to be aware that questions are leading, and therefore should be used sparingly, like spice in the soup. Our default should be silence and mirroring—this is the broth of empathy. Even when doing an intake, the fewer questions the better, since the order and manner in which the patient's material is presented (or left out) also provides important diagnostic information.

jump in and give advice or to intervene actively when in the long run (unless there is truly an immediate danger of harm to the patient's self or others) it will be more helpful to help the patient to come to his or her own solutions? Do I feel an urge to rescue, and is this feeling familiar to me? Do I recognize in myself a need to fix things—and people? Am I more comfortable with doing than with just being? Do I understand the emotional origins of those feelings in myself, from my upbringing, my childhood, and my relationship to my parents? Feelings that leap up in us spontaneously and unbidden are what has been classically understood as our countertransference: unresolved issues that can distort our perceptions of the patient by projecting our own "stuff" onto them (Cooper-White, 2004, pp. 9–25).

Freud's (1913/2001c) "fundamental rule" for psychoanalysis was that the patient should freely share whatever came to mind (a rule he knew would meet with unconscious resistance, a sticking point to be examined, which was actually the point of the rule)—accordingly, then the "fundamental rule" of the therapist might be: When in doubt, don't say anything; *just listen.* Allow the patient room to fumble for words, and allow yourself not to know, but to be suspended for a time in wondering and reverie (Bion, 1970/1995; Bollas, 1985). More of the patient's story is likely to emerge in quiet and even in silence, and s/he will be more able to connect with her or his own feelings, than when we are filling the air with our own sounds in an effort to keep awkwardness or our own anxiety at bay. As we listen without an anxious need to know or to do something, we also show the patient a nonanxious curiosity about the patient's life and inner world. Over time, one of the central aims of therapy is to help the patient cultivate this same kind of respectful curiosity toward him- or herself (McWilliams, 2004). Consider the useful little Zen saying *Don't just do something; sit there!*

Active Listening

Closely related to silent listening is a skill commonly called "mirroring" (Rogers, 1989, p. 128) or "active listening." Active listening is sharing back to the patient a condensed, empathically accurate synopsis of what s/he has just shared. It is not parroting by any means:

> Patient: "I was so angry at my husband that I felt like throwing something! And that's not like me at all!"

> Therapist: "So you were so angry at your husband that you felt like throwing something. And that's not like you at all!"

This is not good mirroring technique—although if the therapist were to match the precise tone of voice and level of anger expressed by the patient, it might be heard as supportive. A more effective mirroring response catches the most significant aspects of what has been communicated—both feeling and factual content—and does so succinctly so as not to get in the way of the patient's flow: "Wow, you really felt rage toward him! Way more than usual!" The briefest mirroring responses should focus on the patient's *affect*, both accurately and at the right level of intensity.

Sophisticated mirroring responses may grab onto a comment that appears to be an aside by the patient, but seems at a gut level to carry important emotional freight. This is where mirroring becomes an art, drawing on the therapist's embodied felt sense of what is important—even or perhaps especially when it is given as an aside or a seemingly lighthearted parting remark (a "doorknob comment"). Sometimes repeating back a single word or phrase can capture the gist of a long statement by the patient: "*So* angry!" Sometimes a spontaneous and emotionally connected "Mmm-hmm!" or other nonverbal vocalization (though not a mechanical, perfunctory one!) can convey empathy and encourage the flow of the patient's communication. With doorknob comments, rather than extending the session, it is useful to say, "Hmm. That actually sounds pretty important. Let's talk about that again next time."

Skills related to mirroring are paraphrasing (relating back a brief recap of a longer amount of material) and summarizing (giving a recap of a significant portion of the session either during a session or at the beginning or end of a session). Paraphrasing and summarizing serve as a way of communicating that you got it right—and of allowing the patient to correct you if not. These strategies serve as a way of letting the patient hear him- or herself, which often helps the patient clarify his or her own flow of thoughts and emotions. Finally, paraphrasing and summarizing may allow for a turn in the conversation: for example, toward problem solving (led by the patient), toward deeper reflection, or toward the introduction of some new material by the patient (Egan, 2009, p. 201; see also Taylor, 1991, p. 48).

Mirroring statements should be made only after the patient has shared enough thoughts and feelings that the therapist actually has something of substance to mirror. So silent listening is the preferred, and sometimes lengthy, prelude even to making a first mirroring response. Furthermore, mirroring should usually be offered tentatively, with such openers as "it sounds like . . ."; "I wonder if . . ."; "if I am hearing you correctly," or the like. This allows the patient to correct the therapist's understanding, or sometimes to correct their own way of putting what they are trying to communicate. The above example could be improved, perhaps, by the therapist's saying, "Wow, it sounds like you really felt rage toward him! Way more than usual!" While an over-use of such phrases can begin to sound stereotypical or formulaic, it is helpful to make them a natural part of your repertoire, because they convey humility, a willingness to listen further and to be corrected. It is also sometimes useful following a mirroring statement to ask, "Did I understand that correctly?"

When It Goes Well . . . and When It Doesn't

When a patient feels heard, at both an emotional and factual level, several things often happen naturally (Weiss & Sampson, 1986): the patient's body may relax somewhat while both the therapist and the patient may feel an increase in energy, and the patient may jump in and amplify with more or deeper sharing (that is, sharing that is more personally risk taking, intimate, meaningful or affect laden). Often during an emotionally connected exchange, the patient's and therapist's posture and body language may unconsciously begin to mirror one another. We do not make these responses happen, nor should we try to manipulate the patient into producing them! But when we do observe them, we can perceive that the relationship is flowing smoothly.

When the opposite happens—when both therapist and patient are now feeling rigid, uncomfortable, and not sure how to proceed—the best response is again to mirror what just happened: "It seems that somehow my response didn't catch what you were trying to share with me. Can you help me understand where I missed the mark?" Such an honest comment lets the patient know that you want to understand, and you are able to acknowledge a break in your efforts at care-full listening (something some patients may have rarely or never had anyone tell them before). Kohut (1977/2009; 1984), in fact, considered that it is precisely such an honest inquiry at the moment of empathic rupture that can have the most therapeutic effect, as the patient internalizes the therapist's calm, nondefensive curiosity and care.

But why must we be so quiet and circumspect? What is the harm in being more active—in giving advice, offering solutions to problems, asking questions to understand a patient's problem more efficiently? Wouldn't that help both the therapist and the patient to get down to the heart of the problem more quickly and effectively?

Listening for Complexity

If we were all fully conscious of our thoughts, feelings, fantasies, memories, motives, fears, and desires at all times, the answer to the above questions might be yes. The problem is that we are not. Although Freud (1900/2001b) claimed to "discover" the unconscious—those parts of ourselves that we do not know, and cannot know much of the time—there is ample evidence that human beings have recognized an unconscious dimension of the psyche since ancient times. Saint Augustine (2008) wrote in his *Confessions*, "I myself cannot grasp the totality of what I am" (p. 187). Earlier, Saint Paul wrote "I do not do the good I want, but the evil I do not want is what I do" (Romans 7:15, 19).[5] We do not need to take the "existence" of an unconscious dimension to life simply as a leap of faith in a theory of selfhood. All we need do is remember the last time we reacted out of proportion to something someone said to us, or sabotaged ourselves. Our dreams (Freud's "royal road to the unconscious," 1900/2001b) also suggest that more is going on in our minds than our waking self knows about.

Contemporary brain science and psychoanalysis are further expanding our understanding of the complexity of what lies outside consciousness. Since Freud (1900/2001b) introduced his "topographical model" over a century ago, we have become familiar with a sort of "layer cake" model of mind, in which consciousness lies above a deeper unconscious that is repressed downward as Freud later elaborated. (The superego actively pushes unacceptable sexual or aggressive wishes of the id out of sight and out of mind, so that the ego will have to somehow straddle between these two forces—id and superego—and come up with a compromise, usually in the form of a neurotic symptom that both disguises and relieves the forbidden wish (Freud, 1923/2001a). Contemporary analysts, supported by the findings of neuroscientists, are now visualizing the mind as more three-dimensional, in which thoughts and feelings are removed from consciousness not only or even primarily via repression (of forbidden impulses) but via dissociation (of traumatic memories that were never stored in the brain/mind at all—as traces of "unformulated experience") (Stern, 2003).

Rather than a singular "I" or "ego," a person is better conceptualized as a complex network of self-states, with a variety of memories, affects, desires, and fantasies associated to each complex part of the self (Bromberg, 1994; Cooper-White, 2004, 2007, 2011; Davies, 1998). Our day-to-day and moment-to-moment sense of being a unified person is a developmental achievement—according to one relational psychoanalyst, an "adaptational

5. Biblical translations from the New Revised Standard Version, Division of Christian Education of the National Council of Churches of Christ in the USA, 1989.

talent . . . a necessary illusion of being 'one self'" (Bromberg, 1994, p. 517). We are "braided selves" (Cooper-White, 2011, pp. 151–55, pp. 195–221), deriving our sense of cohesion, not from some internal executive director (whether "ego" or "core self"), but from the continuity over time of living in one body, in relationship with others, re-membered by our ethical practices and commitments, and ultimately held by the divine Love that created us: "more valuable than two sparrows, always attended when falling, every self counted" (Cooper-White, 2011, p. 221).

Given this complexity, is it any wonder that we must be circumspect, and listen more than we speak? We should remember that at any given time, the part of the patient to whom we are listening is only one part. If we give advice, take action, or, for that matter, take sides with a particular intense feeling or idea, we may find that we have failed to listen to other parts of the same person—parts who hold a different perspective and may offer alternative wisdom. Getting to know the many parts of another person is difficult, however—especially those parts that the patient wishes s/he didn't have, or the parts s/he doesn't even know yet but perhaps only experiences in bodily sensations, strange glimmers of thought, or actions that feel foreign to the sense of self. The more dissociated or disavowed certain parts are, the more hidden they are likely to be. And if they are exposed too suddenly, they will do what all wild creatures do: they will fight or flee.

Listening as a Practice of Intersubjectivity

> " . . . if you tame me, then we shall need each other. To me, you will be unique in all the world. To you, I shall be unique in all the world" . . .
>
> One only understands the things that one tames," said the fox . . .
> (Saint-Exupéry, 1943, p. 80)

By using the words *parts, network,* and *complexity,* above, I have also already tipped my hand toward another basic tenet I hold about the nature of listening. My theoretical home base is a school of psychoanalytic thought called relational psychoanalysis and psychotherapy (Mitchell, 2004; Mitchell & Aron, 1999)[6] and a postmodern relational theology (Cooper-White, 2007), in which empathic listening echoes the "infinite conversation" (Buber, 1970, p. 114) of which the Jewish philosopher Martin Buber wrote: "Extended,

---

6. Specifically in pastoral care and counseling see also Cooper-White (2004, pp. 35–60).

the lines of relationships intersect the eternal Thou"[7] (p. 123). Just as relational theory now regards human persons as more complex and multiple than many traditional psychologies, so the pastoral relation between persons—and in psychotherapy, the relation between patient and therapist—is understood as more complex, more interpenetrating, and carrying more mutual influence.

Gone are the days (if they ever really existed) when the therapist diagnosed and then treated the patient rather like a specimen under a microscope. Absorbing the influence of multiple disciplines, including postmodern philosophy, social constructionism in social psychology, neuroscience, infant-observation research, cultural anthropology, and even quantum physics, relational psychoanalysis has posited a way of working that recognizes at once the separate, individual subjectivities of patient and therapist and a third relationship encompassing both persons and having a life of its own through "*intersubjectivity*," both conscious and unconscious. Unconscious projections within therapy (the patient's "transference" toward the therapist, and the therapist's "countertransference" toward the patient) are expanded in this understanding to encompass not only the two partners' unresolved, neurotic baggage that can spill over onto and into each other (although this is still central to the therapeutic work), but also *all* the thoughts, emotions, fantasies, bodily sensations, dreams, and impulses that each experiences—especially unconsciously—in relation to the other. (This dynamic within pastoral care and counseling is explained in detail in Cooper-White, 2004).

What does intersubjectivity have to do with listening? The reality of intersubjectivity suggests not only that we are now listening to the other person almost as if sitting apart on two poles named *therapist* and *patient*, but that we must be listening and attending at all times to the entire pool of unconscious relationship that is coconstructed by both partners, both consciously and unconsciously as the relationship deepens over time. Communication therefore is not simply coming from the patient to us, or going from us to the patient—as if we were lobbing tennis balls across a court. We are both immersed at all times in the "shared wisdom" of the intersubjective relationship and therefore must listen and be attentive to *everything* that happens between us in the room. We must expand our attention beyond the individual person sitting before us, to also pay thoughtful attention to what is going on in our own thoughts, feelings, and bodily sensations—our countertransference—because our own feelings may in this new understanding

---

7. NB: Kaufman's translation reads "the eternal You."

be more than our own personal reactions but also a container for the patient's least verbalized thoughts, feelings, and embodied memories.

We also must attend carefully to nonverbal body "language" and "enactments"—actions that spontaneously and surprisingly arise in the therapy—because these may convey communications that the conscious mind of the patient is not yet ready or able to speak. In fact, "unformulated experience" knows no other way to speak than through bodily sensations and actions (Stern, 2003). "One only understands the things one tames," said the fox: we cannot truly know another until we enter into this dance of empathy and trust, knowing that it requires our own vulnerability, our own openness to what is cocreated in the matrix of the intersubjective relationship, which is "unique in all the world." In the fox's sense of taming as "establishing ties," these ties are internal as well as external, and they go both ways. Our patients are also continually taming us!

Listening as Play

> "I cannot play with you," the fox said. "I am not tamed." (Saint-Exupéry, 1943, p. 80)

One brief note should be added regarding the importance of play in the therapeutic relationship. Winnicott's "good enough mother," by her attentive listening, recognition, and holding of the developing infant, creates a "potential space" (Winnicott, 1971) in which the child grows in knowledge of self and other, and is able to move creatively back and forth between attachment and secure separateness. Good listening, then, is not a dour, serious exercise but an openness to listen for multiple possible meanings that may be "at play" in the therapeutic encounter. Listening creates an opening for the multiplicity of self and other to engage. Such mutual recognition is at the heart of new development, and ultimately, according to Winnicott (1971), underlies all culture—including religious faith.

Making It Safe for Fox(es) to Emerge

> "You must be very patient," replied the fox. "First you will sit down at a little distance from me—like that—in the grass. I shall look at you out of the corner of my eye, and you will say nothing. Words are the source of misunderstandings. But you will sit a little closer to me, every day . . ." (Saint-Exupéry, 1943, p. 84)

While the metaphor of "taming" certainly has its limits—we are not con-querors, nor are our patients wild beasts who must be domesticated!—the art of sitting still and waiting for the more hidden, complex parts of the other to emerge is a basic foundation of trust in any relationship. In psy-choanalyst Sheldon Roth's (2000) beautiful words, "we want to behave as if excessive movement puts all of living nature into hiding, as it does at a woodland pond" (p. 441).[8]

Most seasoned therapists can recall a time when they had an agenda (sometimes referred to as "therapeutic ambition," usually prompted by the therapist's countertransference). They pushed a patient too hard to reveal something private and tender about himself, and found themselves on the receiving end of a tirade, a miserable withdrawal by the patient, or an abrupt termination of the session or the entire therapy. Such extreme "negative therapeutic reactions" (Freud, 1923/2001a, p. 49) are rare, but we can often see them in miniature in sessions when we have probed too far, too fast into a patient's most private thoughts and feelings. Patients may react to such intrusions on our part with anger, bland compliance, or withdrawal—some-times in the form of a defensive dissociation or "checking out." They cease to be emotionally present.

Key to such negative therapeutic reactions—or, I would prefer to say, *inter*actions—is shame. Shame is a basic affect, or feeling state, which infant researchers believe comes hardwired in the human personality. We all know how shame feels. There is a physiological response of flushing of the face and neck, we cast our eyes downward or to the side, there is a catch in our voice or our breath, and we wish a hole would open up in the floor by which we could escape. There is a growing literature on the phenomenon of shame, but most researchers agree that the catalyst for most shame reactions is *feel-ing exposed* (Schneider, 1992).

One reason, then, that we emphasize listening as the foundation of therapy, rather than more active interventions, is that the more we push and probe, the more likely we are to strike a raw nerve in our patient's psyche. Feeling exposed in such a way, the patient is likely to flee, or mount all his or her resistances against our knowing what we just inadvertently uncovered. Nonjudgmental and compassionate listening will elicit more parts of the patient to speak than all the questions, advice, or active exercises we could ever devise for the patient. We don't know what we don't know—but by blundering in with pick and shovel, we may uncover not only what we did not expect, but what neither we nor the patient is ready to handle. Listening is a foundation of therapy, in part, because it also establishes *safety*.

8. On silence, chaos, and therapeutic love, see Cooper-White (2007, pp. 239–48).

Safety is primarily ensured by empathy. If we are truly empathic with multiple parts of the patient, then we are much less likely to fall into enactments that violate the patient's boundaries, or severely harm the therapeutic relationship. But there are other safeguards to therapy as well. On their second meeting, the fox tells the little prince:

> "It would have been better to come back at the same hour," said
> the fox . . . "if you come at just any time, I shall never know at
> what hour my heart is to be ready to greet you . . . One must
> observe the proper rites . . ."
>
> "What is a rite?"
>
> . . . "They are what make one day different from other days, one
> hour from other hours . . ." (Saint-Exupéry, 1943, p. 84)

By setting regular meeting times and length (normally a fifty-minute hour), by maintaining a welcoming and private meeting place, and by otherwise keeping good professional boundaries, we create a "frame" for the therapy, whose structure provides firmness and solidity around the vulnerability of each therapeutic encounter (Cooper-White, 2007, pp. 142–53; McWilliams, 2004, pp. 76–85, pp. 99–131). This has sometimes been called a "container" (Bion, 1963/1984), another image for safe holding that can re-member both patient and therapist both during and between sessions.

> "You become responsible, forever, for what you have tamed [said
> the fox]." (Saint-Exupéry, 1943, p. 88)

The way we understand ethical boundaries may shift slightly in the relational paradigm from a more hierarchical concept of fiduciary responsibility to one of "asymmetry" of roles and responsibilities (Cooper-White, 2004, pp. 58–60). However, while both participants share an intimate emotional experience, the therapist retains both the authority and the responsibility to maintain appropriate boundaries—including sexual, romantic, social, legal, and financial boundaries—as well as the duty to act to prevent imminent harm. An expanded understanding of countertransference and a relational concept of intersubjectivity do not let us off the hook for our own behaviors with patients! In fact, such increased awareness of complexity and multiplicity should make us listen all the more intently for potential disruptions, temptations, and "pulls" on our capacity to remain a calm and helpful presence. While more attention is now paid to enactments and nonverbal communication in therapy, the goal is still to assist the patient to move "unformulated experience" slowly from the unconscious through symbolization to consciousness, and from mute action to thoughtful verbalization. In this way, our work is a spiritual one, of "hearing [the other] to speech" (Morton, 1985).

Listening as God Listens

So the little prince tamed the fox. And when the hour of his departure drew near—

"Goodbye," he said.

"Goodbye," said the fox. "And now here is my secret, a very simple secret: It is only with the heart that one can see rightly; what is essential is invisible to the eye." (Saint-Exupéry, 1943, p. 87)

Listening, finally then, is more than what we do with our ears. To return to the definition in the beginning of this chapter, listening is *attending*. It involves using *all of one's self—mind and heart, body and soul, conscious and unconscious*. It involves attending not only to the patient's communications (verbal and nonverbal), but to what happens inside *ourselves* as we spend time deeply immersed in the patient's reality. It involves giving heed as much as possible simultaneously to everything that is happening in this intersubjective pool of wisdom, conscious and unconscious.

Relational analyst Donnel Stern (2010) uses the term *witness* to describe this form of deeply engaged attention, in which he says "we are called into being by acts of *recognition* by the other" (p. 110). As infants, our minds are first brought into being by recognition from our parents. As adults, we continue to need witnesses—"partners in thought"—in order for the events of our lives to "fall into a narrative awareness." Without witnesses, there can be no validation, and hence no "renewal of experience."

This practice of witnessing is sacred. By serving as witness to another's story, we create space where new images, symbols, words, narratives, and meanings can emerge. Such genuine recognition promotes inner transformation—what Stern (2010) has described as listening to others in a way that allows others to listen to themselves (p. 112). This internalization of the caring witness reinstates compassion and witnessing among formerly intolerable or dissociated parts of ourselves. By listening, witnessing, deeply attending, we are perhaps most able to approximate the way God knows and loves us. For most of us, God may seem to be silent much or all of the time. Maybe this is because God is attending to us so intently and deeply. God is listening! Our faith affirms that we are made in the image and likeness of God (Gen. 1:26), and that God knows and loves us more than we can ask or imagine. Perhaps when we truly listen to another, with our mind and heart, our body and soul, we are most able to be—however fleetingly—instruments of God's own healing recognition, God's power to resurrect us, God's own infinite love.

References

Augustine, Saint [of Hippo]. (2008). *Confessions*. (H. Chadwick, Trans.). Oxford World's Classics. Oxford: Oxford University Press. (Orig. written 397–398 CE)

Bion, W. R. (1984). *Elements of psycho-analysis*. Maresfield Reprints 23. London: Karnac. (Orig. publ. 1963).

Bion, W. R. (1995). *Attention and interpretation*. London: Rowman & Littlefield. (Orig. publ. 1970).

Bollas, C. (1989). *The shadow of the object: Psychoanalysis of the unthought known*. New York: Columbia University Press.

Brickman, C. (2003). *Aboriginal populations in the mind: Race and primitivity in psychoanalysis*. New York: Columbia University Press.

Bromberg, P. M. (1994). "Speak! That I may see you": Some reflections on dissociation, reality, and psychoanalytic listening. *Psychoanalytic Dialogues 4*, 517–47.

Buber, Martin. (1970). *I and Thou*. (W. Kaufman, Trans.). New York: Scribner.

Cooper-White, P. (2004). *Shared wisdom: Use of the self in pastoral care and counseling*. Minneapolis: Fortress.

Cooper-White, P. (2007). *Many voices: Pastoral psychotherapy in relational and theological perspective*. Minneapolis: Fortress.

Cooper-White, P. (2011). *Braided selves: Collected essays on multiplicity, God, and persons*. Eugene, OR: Cascade Books.

Davies, J. M. (1998). Multiple perspectives on multiplicity. *Psychoanalytic Dialogues 8*, 195–206.

Egan, G. (2009). *The skilled helper: A problem-management and opportunity-development approach to helping* (9th ed.). Belmont, CA: Brooks/Cole.

Freud, S. (2001a). *The ego and the id*. In *The standard edition of the complete psychological works of Sigmund Freud* (hereafter: *SE.*) Vol. 19:3–66. J. Strachey (Ed. & Trans.). London: Vintage. (Orig. publ. 1923).

Freud, S. (2001b). *The interpretation of dreams*. *SE* Vols. 4–5 (entire). (Orig. publ. 1900).

Freud, S. (2001c). On beginning the treatment. *SE* Vol. 12:121–44. (Orig. publ. 1913).

Fromm-Reichmann, F. (1960). *Principles of intensive psychotherapy*. Phoenix Books. Chicago: University of Chicago Press.

Grant, B. W. (2001). *A theology for pastoral psychotherapy: God's play in sacred spaces*. New York: Haworth.

Kohut, H. (1984). *How does analysis cure?* A. Goldberg (Ed.), with the collaboration of P. E. Stepansky. Chicago: University of Chicago Press.

Kohut, H. (2009). *The restoration of the self*. Chicago: University of Chicago Press. (Orig. publ. 1977).

McWilliams, N. (2004). *Psychoanalytic psychotherapy: A practitioner's guide*. New York: Guilford.

Mitchell, S. A. (2004). *Relationality: From attachment to subjectivity*. Relational Perspectives Book Series 20. Hillsdale, NJ: Analytic Press.

Mitchell, S. A., & Aron, L. (Eds.). (1999). *Relational psychoanalysis: The emergence of a tradition.* Relational Perspectives Book Series 14. Hillsdale, NJ: Analytic.

Morton, N. (1985). *The journey is home.* Boston: Beacon.

Rogers, C. (1989). *The Carl Rogers reader.* H. Kirschenbaum & V. L. Henderson (Eds.). Boston: Houghton Mifflin.

Roth, S. (2000). *Psychotherapy: The art of wooing nature.* Northvale, NJ: Aronson.

Saint-Exupéry, A., de. (1943). *The little prince.* (K. Woods, Trans.). New York: Harcourt, Brace, Jovanovich.

Schneider, C. D. (1992). *Shame, exposure, and privacy.* New York: Norton.

Stern, D. B. (2003). *Unformulated experience: From dissociation to imagination in psychoanalysis.* Hillsdale, NJ: Analytic.

Stern, D. B. (2010). *Partners in thought: Working with unformulated experience, dissociation and enactment.* Psychoanalysis in a New Key 12. New York: Routledge.

Taylor, C. W. (1991). *The skilled pastor: Counseling as the practice of theology.* Minneapolis, Fortress.

Weiss, J., & Sampson, H. & The Mount Zion Psychotherapy Research Group. (1986). *The psychoanalytic process: Theory, clinical observations, and empirical research.* New York: Guilford.

Winnicott, D. W. (1965). Ego distortion in terms of true and false self. In *The maturational processes and the facilitating environment* (pp. 140–52). International Psycho-analytic Library 64. London: Hogarth.

Winnicott, D. W. (1971). Transitional objects and transitional phenomena. In *Playing and reality* (pp. 1–25). New York: Basic Books.

Yalom, I. D. (1980). *Existential psychotherapy.* New York: Basic Books.

4

Culture, Ethnicity, and Race: A Womanist Self Psychological Perspective

Phillis Isabella Sheppard

Introduction: Culture, Ethnicity, and Race in Pastoral Psychotherapy

... Observation has taught us that cultures and subcultures have profound effects on the social institutions through which personality is formed. Culture is the medium in which the self grows.

—Menaker, 1995, p. 87

MY APPROACH TO ENGAGING the concerns raised by a consideration of culture and pastoral psychotherapy is informed by several interlinking self realities: I am a black woman who is a lesbian, of working-class/lower-middle-class background, the product of Catholic and Baptist/Free Methodist spiritual roots and, now, a psychoanalyst, and a womanist practical and pastoral theologian.[1] My education and research is inextricably interdisciplinary. As a practical theologian, I want to stress that, first, the articulation of a theological anthropology that includes the realities of culture, ethnicity, gender, class, and sexuality is crucial to our

1. Practical theology, in this context, represents all the varied practical arts of ministry, including congregational leadership, Christian Education and counseling. Pastoral theology and pastoral counseling can then be understood as a subset of practical theology.

44

work; and, second, the explicit insertion of the psychological dimension of self is indispensable for our theological understanding of humanness. As soon as we take these areas seriously, we are graced with the reality of the varieties human difference—of experience, culture, gender, class, sexuality—*and* with the task to make them integral to clinical conceptualizations and theological reflection.

An occasion in my early clinical training illuminated my conviction that culture, gender, class, and race must be integrated into clinical work. I was presenting the clinical case of a twenty-eight-year-old Mexican American woman, Gabriela.[2] She was born in Mexico and came to the United States at the age of eight because her father had found reliable work that could support the family. Gabriela was of strong Roman Catholic religious roots and seemed to have thrived in the new environment both socially and academically. The family made regular trips back to Mexico to visit family. At the time she sought psychotherapy, Gabriela was a third-year medical student. She presented with a long-standing depression and current relationship difficulties with fiancé, sister, and parents. Gabriela complained that she felt invisible in her family, in school, and with her fiancé. In other words, her primary relational milieu was not an optimal source of support during the stresses related to her medical-school experience or her dating life.

After the fourth session, I presented in the case conference. During the presentation, my colleagues, all of whom were white graduate students in theology and pastoral psychotherapy, expressed surprise that a Mexican woman would be in medical school. Her presenting concerns were effectively dismissed—rendered invisible, as my colleagues wondered if she had received a scholarship based on ethnicity, whether she was an overachiever, and whether she had gone to a "good" undergraduate school, and how she managed to be accepted into a good medical school. My report that she felt depressed, and invisible in her classes, with the man she was seeing, and with her family was received without curiosity or comment.

Most surprising to me was that the instructor also engaged in discussion at this level. What was apparent, to me, was that these comments were entirely based on unacknowledged cultural bias. In this case discussion blatant cultural biases were evident, but given that culture, gender and ethnicity were not integrated into the curriculum, there was little room for examining how cultural biases are interferences—a countertransference, in clinical parlance. I left that case conference angry, and, in a parallel process with my patient, feeling somewhat invisible.

2. As always, details of this case and those following have been altered to honor confidentiality.

The psychological meaning of culture was a powerful force in this patient's clinical picture as well as in class but was avoided in the curriculum and clinical dialogue. This training environment was not as unusual as I thought. Christine Wiley (1991), in her dissertation on pastoral counseling with African American women, relates similar experiences as a black woman in a seminary pastoral-psychotherapy program: "Little did I realize at the outset that . . . [I would] experience the program as a culture shock . . . [I wish] I had initially known more about the history of the pastoral counseling movement, . . . that this movement, . . . was heavily oriented toward white males" (p. 45, 335–64; 355).

These issues, of course were part of a larger blind spot in clinical education. Wiley's (1991) description parallels Beverly Greene's clinical training in psychology: "In that atmosphere . . . there wasn't a lot of room for looking at issues around women, around sexual orientation, around the role of race . . . and how it changes the dialogue" (Granek, 2009). Greene (2000) observed that even when race, culture, and gender are discussed, it is without regard to the experiences of black women who are also lesbians: "While the psychotherapy with women literature gives African American women marginally more attention than the LGB or multicultural psychotherapy literature, little is said about African American lesbians at all" (p. 82). Therapists often failed to integrate "the contextual and environmental factors that interact with and shape intrapsychic structures and dynamics" (Greene, 2000, p. 82).

These kinds of experiences in pastoral and secular clinical training programs reveal something about who and what is considered normative for a client, a clinician and supervisor. In the pastoral counseling milieu, where theological reflection and clinical conceptualization are both crucial to the understanding of therapeutic endeavor, the rendering of some individuals and cultural ethnic groups, gender, and sexuality invisible, expresses an implicit and limited theological anthropology. Whether acknowledged or not, theological anthropology undergirds pastoral psychology's theories of health, healing, and transformation; being fully visible and fully seen are indispensable aspects of pastoral psychotherapy.

Toward a Psychological Theological Anthropology

The desire or longing to be seen, known, and understood while loved is, as far as we know, a distinctly human feature. We seek to be known and formed by being known by an important other. We hear it in the voice of the psalmist:

> O LORD, you have searched me and known me. You know when I sit down and when I rise up; you discern my thoughts from far away. You . . . are acquainted with all my ways . . . Search me, O God, and know my heart; test me and know my thoughts. See if there is any wicked way in me, and lead me in the way everlasting. (Psalm 139: 1a, 2, 3b, 23–24 NRSV [Anglicized Edition])

The fulfillment of this longing to be known also involves changing as a result of being known and in relationship. We open ourselves up to others because we need relationships to know ourselves, and we need relationships to help us know how we need to change. We need relationships because we need others to be with us in the process of our changing. It is as if we become perceived, grasped, and visible in the face of this met longing.

The movement toward visibility requires a radical shift toward a deep awareness, and the formation of a pastoral curiosity. By pastoral curiosity I mean an attitude[3] of receptiveness that shapes what we see and hear. Pastoral curiosity requires a stance that allows for layers of meaning, for ambiguity, and for periods of not knowing. Pastoral curiosity values meditative reflection, and it develops over a lifetime. In the deep pastoral work that is psychotherapy that touches and activates the unconscious, we are using our curiosity to evoke our clients' curiosity and interest in their interior life. We join with them in listening to what has been stirring as a background noise or force, and we give it voice, shape, and visibility. We take notice of process and form.

The shift toward visibility is a shift toward welcoming more of one's self and others' selves into pastoral encounters. Mary McClintock Fulkerson (2007) describes the necessity of such a shift in her article "A Place to Appear: Ecclesiology as if Bodies Mattered" and proposes "a place to appear" (p. 159) as an antidote to obliviousness. Obliviousness (i.e. I don't see color, gender, class; I just see people) "suggests a kind of experiential and geographical disregard that forms an *a priori* social condition . . . A not seeing that supports many disparities in well-being in the United States, obliviousness is more likely to shape white, middle- and upper-middle-class churches than overt oppression of the marginalized. A 'place to appear,' then, is intended to suggest what might disrupt and alter such disregard" (Fulkerson, 2007, p. 159). Fulkerson, in requiring an ecclesiology of a "place to appear,"

---

3. Chris Schlauch reminded me of the emphasis on the development of a clinical attitude rather than training skills in the program at the Center for Religion and Psychotherapy.

suggests a way for a psychological theological anthropology that might "disrupt, alter, critique," and transform invisibility to a visibility as a means for recognizing the breadth of humanity. My own theological anthropology emerges from reading the biblical account announcing the creation of humans as the *imago dei* and good. Since this goodness is afforded to all humanity, we have to recognize and grapple with the notion that variation is an intrinsic and intentional facet of human creation. This grappling—a deep engagement—with human variation forms us to appreciate that each of us is created to reflect, and reproduce in our relating, Goodness. But we reflect and reproduce this Goodness not just in dyadic or close relational contexts. This grappling is to be fulfilled in a "social world where gender, class and body are inextricably linked internally and in the social negotiations in which we engage daily" (Sheppard, 2011, p. 99).

A pastoral psychological theological anthropology requires us to take the contexts, where we embody our createdness, seriously. Otherwise, when we are forced into invisibility, a distorted and damaging psychological theological anthropology is operative and, as a result, we are often unwittingly complicit in reproducing the distortion. The clinical domain can be implicated if we too, as therapists, unwittingly demand partial invisibility of our clients. We can counter these distortions only if we hear them in our selves, in our clients, and in the psychologies that inform our pastoral theologies. Our work requires an awareness of the sociocultural realities we bring into pastoral clinical work, and that we ask of ourselves: what difference do our differences make in what I hear in this situation?

Womanist Practical Theology and Practice

Womanist practical and pastoral theologians are African American women theologians who begin theologizing with the experiences and concerns of black women.[4] Womanist practical, pastoral theology is an approach that is dialogical, critical, contextual, theological, and constructive. First, womanist pastoral theology is dialogical because it engages in conversations with theology and social sciences, and has multiple sites for practices. Second, womanist pastoral theology is critical because the approach opens a critical reading of the various perspectives in light of the implications these perspectives have for black women's and black people's lives. Third, womanist practical theology is contextual in that the features of social location, including race, gender, class, economics, and so forth are engaged. Fourth, womanist pastoral theology is theological because the approach considers

---

4. See Sheppard (2003) and Parker (2009).

the theological questions that emerge from an epistemology that begins with attending to black women's lives. Finally, womanist pastoral theology is constructive because womanist theologizing ultimately constructs a specific theology with its own theological categories. These foci orient womanist pastoral psychotherapists' engagement with psychological theory and clinical practice. The implications of practicing and writing from a womanist perspective mean that culture, gender, race, sexuality and also religious experiences are approached as inextricable dimensions of existence, and are therefore crucial for clinical discussion. Womanist constructive theologian and anthropologist Linda Thomas (2004) makes a nuanced and clear statement of the connection between society, culture, and gender in black women's life and experience, and in the constructive theology of womanist theologians: "Womanist theology is critical reflection upon black women's place in the world that God has created . . . Womanist theology affirms and critiques the church, the African American community, and the larger society" (p. 38). Womanist pastoral psychotherapists, then, are concerned with how the interlocking features of culture, gender, race, and sexuality affect black women's individual sense of self as well as their experience of the black and broader community. Furthermore, womanist pastoral psychotherapists are concerned with how self and community can be strengthened and transformed through psychotherapy. Therefore, womanists are concerned with the articulation and appropriation of psychological theories that allow cultural experience to interrogate psychologies in light of the cultural context. Sheppard (2011) holds that psychoanalytic theory can only be appropriated after a critical and contextual reading, and reminds us that psychological theories are cultural productions with particular commitments undergirding their development and application. Womanist pastoral psychotherapists must read for the culture embedded in theory, and need to determine if it advances a cultural perspective that privileges one set of cultural assumptions and values over most others.

Womanist-informed Self Psychology

In my approach to clinical work, I am most influenced by a critical engagement with psychoanalytic self psychology. Heinz Kohut as the initial voice of this approach, focused his clinical theory on the development of the self, and was instrumental in the contemporary emphasis on empathic understanding and a response based on this understanding, as both a clinical and developmental necessity. Empathy is crucial to the development of "cohesive self"—that is, a self, though exposed to stress, "is not prone to become fragmented, weakened, or disharmonious" (Kohut, 1984, p. 70).[5] In terms of the developmental process, it is the early caregivers' empathic responses to the child's psychological self needs, called selfobject needs, that give shape to the self and its deficits. Kohut conceptualized four basic selfobject needs: (a) the need to have one's sense of aliveness reflected back—so the need for mirroring; (b) the need to feel connected or merged to one who was experienced as calm, safe, and strong, and therefore, idealizable; (c) the need to feel like someone in terms of interests, values, hopes; thus, a twinship need; and (d) the need to feel part of a group or people or kinship. These needs must be met in a relatively reliable way in order for the development of a self that is experienced as cohesive in most situations. The development of this self, and the selfobject experiences that foster and sustain development are lifelong needs that are met in a variety of ways in different contexts based on maturation. In other words, once we have developed a cohesive self, we are basically that self, regardless of context, except during times of great stress during which we may, in the absence of empathic responses, feel "shaky" "fragmented" or not as "together" as usual. As a result, one might be temporally vulnerable to feeling depressed, hopeless, or without a sense of anchor. This state of being is largely internal and intrapsychic, though one may behave in ways that suggest to an observer that the self has been depleted of its usual vitality. From a self psychological view, one needs an empathic response that communicates an understanding of how one came to feel vulnerable in order to begin to coalesce. However, it is important to realize that the satisfaction of selfobject needs is not something that is given to someone; my point is that empathy and selfobject satisfaction are not "tools" we pull out of our pocket for use in psychotherapy. When an empathic response has met some selfobject need, the result is intrapsychic in that the self is stronger and less vulnerable to the disorienting feeling of fragmentation. Self psychology is focused primarily on the state of the self in the clinical room between clinician and patient, and secondarily on the patient's broader social context, including fluctuations in the sense of self due to experiences in the broader sociorelational milieu. The development of a more mature, flexible, and stable sense of self is the therapeutic goal.

By way of example, consider the following vignette: Karen was a thirty-four-year-old white woman in therapy for about nine months. She had been referred by a therapist she and her husband had consulted. She came into her session and began speaking in an unusually hesitant fashion. Mentioning that she had read a quotation attributed to Nelson Mandela and wanted me to hear it, she read the following: "Our deepest fear is not that we

5. See also Kohut & Wolf (1986).

are inadequate. Our deepest fear is that we are powerful beyond measure. It is our light, not our darkness that most frightens us" (quoted in Williamson, 1992, p. 190).[6]

I was curious about the meaning of the quotation for her, why she wanted to share it with me, and what it stirred in her. At some point, given her hesitancy, I wondered if she was trying to make sense of our racial differences, and communicated this to her. Karen burst into tears stating that I was saying she wasn't like me, and that I was talking about us being different when she had not noticed. In this vignette, I was not initially curious enough, which was a countertransference reaction, about the meaning of her hesitancy, and as a result, there was an empathic break in our work that was restored when I recognized that she experienced herself as like me—in a twinship transference, but that she also was shifting toward an idealizing transference where she felt bolder, greater, and as having potential to do greater things because of her tie to me. During the session I was aware of the change in her self state when I bluntly inserted race and difference in the session, and became aware of the fluctuations in her sense of self as we worked to gain understanding of what happened. Obviously, I am collapsing a great deal here, but this was, in many respects, a typical understanding of a self psychological approach. However, while I unempathically inserted race into the session, I remained internally curious about Karen's choice of Mandela's quote, her not "noticing" our difference, and the intensity of her response. I had to ask myself if racial difference was actually a part of the transference dimensions of her experience, and whether self psychology could help conceptualize this aspect of her treatment.

Through a closer reading of Kohut's (1985) essays on self psychology and culture,[7] the limitations of his self psychology in terms of taking culture into consideration are revealed. When discussing the self and its development, he is primarily discussing the nuclear-family model, and the cultural myth that it is the mother who is primary provider of early mirroring. I refer to this as myth because in many sociocultural contexts, the mothering function is met by a variety of caregivers and does not rest solely on a one-to-one dyadic child-mother relationship. Furthermore, while Kohut did consider culture in a broad sense, he primarily addressed culture through an upper-middle-class and privileged lens, with emphasis on "artists, historians, intellectuals" (Strozier, 1985, p. xxix) to the near exclusion of race, gender and

6. Though often attributed to Mandela, the quote is actually from Williamson (1992).

7. Take special note of "On the continuity of the self and cultural selfobjects" and "Idealization and cultural selfobjects."

ethnicity.[8] That said, Kohut's reflections on culture are useful because they do provide a provocative lens through which to engage culture as psychologically important, and through which to understand culture as a source for meeting selfobject needs. This understanding of cultural context led him to formulate notions such as the "group self" and the "cultural selfobject."[9] In this way, self psychology recognizes that not all selfobject needs occur within the confines of the nuclear family, and that the cultural productions such as art, music, and literature and the figures who created them, can function as selfobjects for individuals and cultural groups. Therefore the concept of cultural selfobjects is reflected both in Kohut's individual psychology and in his psychology of the group.

It is with rare exception, however, that we read in-depth discussions related to how the sociocultural context actually interferes or interfaces with cultural selfobject experiences (due to the distortions of racism, sexism, cultural bias, or/and heterosexism). For instance, let us return to my patient Karen. Over the next weeks after the empathic break, I learned that Karen had been "thinking about race a lot," and that she had some dreams that she "didn't think meant" she was "racist." Karen's dreams had been about brown-skinned women, Jewish women, and Middle Eastern women, who "were kind of brown." In her dreams they were powerless, devalued, and the opposite of the Mandela quotation. Karen did convey a twinship experience with them/me (in that she felt powerless and devalued) but was in conflict with what she thought about brown/black women in relation to me: in other words, her need for an idealizable selfobject experience was complicated by, in part, what she had been taught about black people (me) in relation to white people (her). Her racial content interfered with the developing idealizing transference. Therefore, race, hers and mine, were important features of transference and countertransference dynamics and, ultimately had to be considered as integral aspects of the treatment.

Conceptualizing culture and the implications for clinical work is not without complications. M. T. Miliora (2007) was interested in the impact of "patriarchal, sexist, familial, and cultural contexts" on the developmental arrest of the self of a young Taiwanese woman she treated, and raised many provocative questions about the familial and cultural contexts as negative and inhibiting factors in the client's development (p. 35–44). For instance, Miliora traced the development of this woman's overwhelming sense of obligation to her family's demands that included her time, space,

8. See Lang (1984); Lang (1990); Pangerl (1996); Rector (1996) and Roland (1996).

9. For the most part, Kohut restricted his consideration of these ideas to his essays and did not develop the clinical implications of these concepts.

and emotional resources. Relying on Roland's *In Search of self in India and Japan* (1988), she appropriated his concept of the "familial" and the "we" self versus the "individual" self. Unfortunately, Miliora's cultural assumptions about the nature of self in relation to important others and in relation to familial and cultural norms leans in favor of a very Western understanding of self-development that would result in a more individuated self . In my reading of her work, she presents the profile of a woman suffering from the pressures of too much of the "we" and "familial" self, but she does not help us understand what a healthy "we" and "familial" self might look like *within that cultural context.* The reader is then left with the impression that the patient's cultural context is incapable of helping form a healthy self. Ultimately, Miliora seems to compare an "Asian" self and culture to a Western autonomous self—with the Western self serving as the ideal and idealized. I may have a skewed reading of her work, but her approach to culture suggests that the aim of psychotherapy is to reproduce the Western self. Miliora left me with a question asked by others in a variety of ways: Is the (Western) 'self' universal?

In her article "Beyond Empathic Failures: Cultural Racism as Narcissistic Trauma and Disenfranchisement of Grandiosity," however, Miliora (2000) provides a nuanced examination of the impact of racism on those toward whom it is directed. Those who take the brunt of racism, she holds, experience a diminishment of their self-esteem as well as a thwarting of their ambition. Racism, then, "is a cultural trauma" (Miliora, 2000, p. 43) because the broader culture fails to mirror or reflect in a positive regard the experiences of black and other ethnic minorities. Racism in the wider culture, in fact, disenfranchises the self (Miliora, 2000, p. 49) such that, the development of a firm and realistic sense of self and a fairly regulated self-esteem is more than likely compromised.

In appropriating self psychology we are confronted with the question, is the self universal? Karen Seeley (1999), in her ground breaking work, *Cultural Psychotherapy: Working with Culture in the Clinical Encounter,* takes up this question and concludes that not only is the concept of self not universal, but the notion of a unified self is not universal either. Psychoanalytic theory, according to Seeley (1999), is culturally located because "despite their pervasive influence on clinical theory and practice . . . because psychologies are based on Western conceptions of self and the mind, they can be ill-suited to clinical work with persons from other cultures. Assuming a universality of human mind, and assuming there to be a cultural fit . . . these clinical models steer practitioners toward conventional Western meanings and interpretations" (p. 32). With regard to class and related fantasies that clinicians can impose on the therapy, Neil Altman (1995) writes that "we have ignored class, culture, and race as powerful elements in the psychoanalytic field only by being unreflectively embedded in our society's arrangements with regard to these categories . . . culture, class and race can be quite invisible if one lives in many parts of America" (p. xvii). Altman further argues that cultural biases are insidiously embedded in our theories and practices whereby "nonmainstream members of our society [are seen as] non-analyzable" (1995, p. xvii). Those designated as "non-analyzable" are also frequently those who cannot afford to pay analytic fees. As a result, conscious and unconscious material arising in the clinical domain expressing a lack of privilege or nondominant cultural themes are psychologized away or deemed pathological.

Ethnicity and the Intrapsychic Life

The impact of the cultural context on the psyche was taken up by Rafael Javier and Mario Rendon (1995) in their article "The Ethnic Unconscious and its Role in Transference, Resistance and Countertransference: An Introduction." They "offer an in-depth understanding of the complex human motivations inherent in ethnic tension, racism, and discrimination" (p. 513) and posit that psychoanalysis is able to provide insight into these concerns because of its complex theories of the mind. They also recognize that psychoanalysis has "focused in the main on the study of the individual's internal structure . . . without much concern for the influence of ethnic components of the psychic structure" (p. 514). Toward this end, they, along with others, understand the ethnic unconscious to "refer to individual's processes which can only be explained in reference to his or her specific cultural background" (p. 515) and, "repressed material that each generation shares with the next and is shared by most people of that ethnic group" (Herron as quoted in Javier & Rendon, 1995, p. 516). Obviously, these authors are also speaking of an individual's identification with one's ethnic group (and that group's values, aspirations, and concerns), and how this identification impacts one's sense of self or self-concept (p. 511). This unconscious ethnic material is to be grappled with and understood as grist for the mill of psychotherapy and psychoanalysis. Furthermore, they agree with others that systemic, interpersonal and intrapsychic dynamics are implicated in personal and societal dynamics of cross-cultural aggression. With Michael Moskowitz (1995) they argue that stereotyping is integral to cross-cultural exchanges that result in ethnic tension and aggression; " although the potential for racism is deep and universal, it can only become actualized in an atmosphere where stereotyping becomes a central component of the interaction" (Javier

& Rendon, 1995, p. 517). Stereotyping has both group and individual psychological functions: "There is no ethnicity. There is hatred and the need to deny our own badness . . . Ethnicity and race are fantasies . . ." (Javier & Rendon, 1995, p. 518).

Clinical Conceptualization Vignette: Josefina[10]

The woman sitting in my waiting room, "Josefina," was a new patient, her nutmeg colored skin looked dry, grayish and sick. Her eyes peered out from dark pools encircling her eyes. She wore old jeans, a sweatshirt, and a pair of dirty sneakers-without socks. Her hair was flattened, though short brown resistant curls hid beneath the lack of care. She cried. She followed me into the office and cried and, cried. And then she began to speak. She was articulate, intelligent, educated, and in deep suffering. She identified herself as a devout and practicing Catholic, and wore a small gold cross around her neck that I learned was given to her by her mother who harbored a deep commitment to her faith. The mother gave it to Josefina just prior to her death when Josefina was twelve.

Though Josefina was clearly a beautiful woman, she gave the impression of a self under siege. She looked at me with a desperation and terror in her eye—a suffering I had seldom witnessed in my office. When she spoke of her family background, her story was filled with loss and cultural disruptions and as she spoke, a sense of dis-ease and doubt concerning the realness of her ethnic, religious, and cultural identity emerged. As she spoke, my eyes were repeatedly drawn to the cross she wore around her neck that she would reach up and touch while she spoke.

Josefina, at twenty-eight years of age, was referred to me because of my interest in religious and cultural experience in the clinical arena. She was currently enrolled in a religious studies program at a Catholic University. Josefina had recently returned prematurely from a short-term mission trip planned by her department. During the month that she was in Peru, Josefina had reported that she suffered from severe intestinal problems and migraines. A visit to the physician found no medical cause. She did not tell the program coordinators that she was also suffering from frightening and disorienting flashbacks related to childhood violence and violation. In spite of Josefina's efforts, her past would not remain in the past. In the form of

---

10. Josefina is not the patient's actual name. Material has been altered to protect confidentiality.

disorienting flashbacks and somatic complaints, Josefina's trauma was making itself known again.

Josefina was the second oldest of five children, and born in Argentina. Her parents' history was shrouded in mystery. While Josefina knew that they were immigrants to Argentina, the circumstances related to their immigration to Argentina were unclear; the story was that they barely escaped with their lives. In Argentina, her father rose to some prominence in a government office, and her mother supported his aspirations socially and emotionally as she cared for their growing family. When the country became unbearable for "liberal" minded individuals, they managed to escape when the father was offered a professorship, and they settled in the United States in a community of Spanish-speaking exiles from various nations. The family was highly respected and the father was considered an "expert" on political and social affairs related to their community.

Barely five years after their arrival in the United States, Josefina's mother was diagnosed with cancer, and she died a slow death over the next several years. During her mother's illness, her father changed from a lively, passionate and politically engaged man to one depressed, angry and often absent. The family's life disintegrated into near chaos. The home was filled with fear. No one spoke to the children or prepared them for their mother's impending death. In the midst of this terror, Josefina tried to parent her younger siblings and care for herself. Gradually the household turned to one permeated with a danger of violence that ended one evening when Josefina's brother violently and sexually attacked her. The family did not address the attack. Since leaving for college, Josefina has been estranged from her family. She has continued however, to fervently and actively participate in a Spanish-speaking parish—so much so that many in the parish believed she would become a nun.

Josefina's narrative raised a number of questions over the course of her brief treatment. What was the nature of her religious experience? What was the relationship of her religious experience to selfobject needs? What was the relationship of her cultural background and history as conveyed via her parents to her selfobject needs and her sense of self? And finally, clinically and theologically, how might I understand the significance of the cross around her neck?

Splitting, Secrecy, Selfobjects
and Cultural Confusion

During the course of her treatment, Josefina reengaged her family around her mother's death, the sexual abuse by her brother, and the family's cultural roots. She encountered a great deal of resistance from her father and grandmother in terms of discussing culture. Josefina came to define this resistance as secrets in the family tree. The secrets, however, were known, and actually revealed the way the family dealt with any painful history. I understood Josefina and the family, to be engaged in the process of splitting. Splitting is "knowing and not knowing," as in "the left hand does not know what the right hand is doing." As one patient said, "I think this is what self psychologists mean by splitting: I know reality, but I can't accept it." There is a way in which we are not *fully aware* that there is another side to our psychic life: a parallel side with its own processes, that does recognize that it is operating against the other side of itself. In psychotherapy we have opportunity to become inquisitive, probing, and inviting about both sides and how they coexist. Kohut (1971) conceptualized this as a vertical split and distinguished it from a horizontal split (repression) because in repression one has no awareness since the unacceptable feelings or thoughts have been pushed into the unconscious.

In the case of Josefina and her family, I also understood splitting to be a response to trauma: the known traumas were the loss of the mother and the selfobject functions she provided, the disintegration of family functioning, and the sexual abuse of Josefina. The trauma that was revealed in due time was that of the loss of the family's cultural roots and history—really a loss of cultural continuity. These losses were traumatic as events but also because they were sequestered out of full awareness rather than integrated into Josefina's self-understanding.

The unacknowledged aspect of the family cultural background was the secret that included a rapid departure both from the Middle East and from northern Africa and Argentina. Until Josefina was in treatment, she was not fully conscious of her Middle Eastern roots or that their escape was because of the family's Jewish background and the anti-Semitism her parents were trying to escape. It took Josefina's desperate situation for the family to open up and provide the missing pieces to their life story. Strikingly, upon hearing her father and grandmother discuss it, Josefina realized that there had been many times when pieces of the history had "slipped out" in family discussions in her presence. However, Josefina had learned to split out of awareness what she had heard. In her family the cultural roots related to a hidden Jewish background were experienced as a dangerous narrative. The fear of danger was not just a psychological experience but a social reality that could expose them to an actual attack.

The loss of the mother was deeply, though unconsciously, tied to the loss of cultural experience. Josefina's grieving of her mother was complicated and unfinished partly because her father's mourning was compromised and he was emotionally unavailable to help manage the selfobject experiences previously provided by the mother. Therefore Josefina was left without the needed assistance in grieving her mother (Shane & Shane, 1990).

The father's inability to remain available left the whole family without an adequate selfobject environment. Thus, for Josefina, there was the loss of the mother and the loss of potential cultural experiences. Therefore, splitting, and appropriation of religious objects as compensatory selfobjects experiences were important features of her self functioning. The cross and Catholicism took on selfobject functions previously provided by her mother. The cross was a way to maintain her connection with the mother.

In the case of Josefina, one aspect of her relationship to culture and ethnicity, as transmitted via the parents, mirrored the anxiety and confusion she experienced psychically. These differences in her experiences of her self (culture/ethnicity and religion) indicated differences in her self-state. The cultural ideals she associated with Spanish and Catholic were the remnants of her earliest relationship to her mother and her once functioning family, and fostered a sense of self cohesion. The cross was a reminder of the culture and religion she had shared especially with her mother. She longed for the cross to "work" again as a soothing, self enhancing selfobject. But her actual ethnic and cultural identifies did not serve this function .

Clearly, Josefina's case illustrates the importance of considering the impact of cultural, religious, and other contextual experiences as self-enhancing as well as potentially self-fragmenting experiences. Our relationship to our cultural roots reveals quite a bit about the nature of our self or sense of self, (Gehrie, 1980, p. 381), and for Josefina, the relationship to culture and religion mirrored the anxiety and confusion she experienced psychically.

Ethnicity and race are indeed fantasies, but they are social fantasies with the power to shape the perceptions and actions of individuals, groups, and societies; they are formative; they can be death dealing. Their impact is real and makes attending to culture so crucial. If culture, "with its values, attitudes, beliefs, traditions, and general systems of collective meanings, including those regarding race . . . influences the psychoanalytic dyad," (Bonovits, 2005, p. 55), then pastoral psychotherapists cannot give short shrift to culture. Therefore, a womanist self psychological perspective makes culture (and related features) crucial to a psychologically informed theological anthropology, crucial to understanding deep self experience, essential to responding with empathy in the clinical domain, central to enhancing the ability *and desire* to reflect, essential to the formation of the pastoral clinical attitude, and crucial to theoretical conceptualization of the case.

Conclusion

These brief vignettes reveal the complexity of culture in pastoral psycho-therapy. It is clear that we need to think about the ways culture, ethnicity, race, and spirituality are implicated in our clinical theories as well as the practices of pastoral psychotherapy based on them. Pastoral psychothera-pists bring implicit theological anthropologies to clinical work, and all too frequently, their theological anthropology concerning the nature of self fails to give explicit attention to the importance of ethnicity, race, and sexuality. The invisibility of race and ethnicity in the clinical room includes clients as well as clinicians' identity and experiences in the broader cultural world. As a womanist practitioner, I strive to be aware of ethnicity, gender, race, and cultural dynamics that frame self experience. While my patients meet with me alone, in reality therapy does not occur in a vacuum.

Unless specifically addressed, psychotherapy and clinical training pro-grams, pastoral and others, actually reproduce social and cultural dynamics that privilege some cultural ways of being at the expense of valuing variety. In pastoral psychotherapy this insidiously sanctions a cultural perspective as normative and this communicates a theology of humanity as well. I am convinced that our pastoral theologies and psychological perspectives need to be transparent and in dialogue with the sociocultural realities that we encounter in the clinical endeavor because pastoral psychotherapy does not occur in a social-cultural vacuum. Ignore this, and pastoral psychotherapy becomes embedded in the dynamics of disavowal; exerts cultural power; and ultimately communicates that pastoral psychotherapy cannot include all aspects of the self . If pastoral psychotherapy is to deepen one's experi-ence of self, it has to be a genuine empathic space that welcomes all of who we are.

References

Altman, N. (1995). *The analyst in the inner city: Race, class, and culture through psychoanalytic lens*. Relational Perspectives Book Series 3. Hillsdale: Analytic.

Bonovits, C. (2005). Locating culture in the psychic field: Transference and countertransference as cultural products. *Contemporary Psychoanalysis, 41,* 55–76.

Fulkerson, M. M. (2007). A place to appear: Ecclesiology as if bodies mattered. *Theology Today, 64,* 159–71.

Gehrie, M. J. (1980). The self and the group: A tentative exploration in Applied Self Psychology. In A. Goldberg (Ed.), *Advance in self psychology* (pp. 367–82). New York: International University Press.

Greene, B. (2000). African American lesbian and bisexual women in feminist-psychological psychotherapy: Surviving and thriving between a rock and a hard place. In L. C. Jackson and B. Greene (Eds), *Psychotherapy with African American women: Innovations in psychodynamic perspectives and practice* (pp. 82–125). New York: Guilford.

Greene, B. (2009, September 11). Interview by L. Granek [Video Recording]. Psychology's Feminist Voices Oral History and Online Archive Project. New York, NY, http://www.feministvoices.com/assets/Feminist-Presence/Greene/Beverly-Greene-Oral-History.pdf/

Javier, R., & Rendon, M. (1995). The ethnic unconscious and its role in transference, resistance, and countertransference: An introduction. *Psychoanalytic Psychology, 12,* 513–20.

Kohut, H. (1971). *The analysis of the self: A systematic approach to the psychoanalytic treatment of narcissistic personality disorders.* The Psychoanalytic Study of the Child. Monograph 4. New York: International University Press.

Kohut, H. (1984). *How does analysis cure?* A. Goldberg (Ed.), with the collaboration of P. E. Stepansky. Chicago: University of Chicago Press.

Kohut, H. (1985) *Self psychology and the humanities: Reflections on a New Psychoanalytic Approach.* C. B. Strozier, (Ed.). New York: Norton.

Kohut, H., & Wolf, E. (1986). The disorders of the self and their treatment: An outline. In A. P. Morrison (Ed.), *Essential papers on narcissism* (pp. 175–96). Essential Papers in Psychoanalysis. New York: New York University Press.

Lang, J. (1984). Notes toward a psychology of the feminine self. In P. E. Stepansky & A. Goldberg (Eds.), *Kohut's legacy: contributions to self psychology* (pp. 51–70). Hillsdale, NJ: Analytic.

Lang, J. (1990). Self psychology and the understanding and treatment of women. In A. Tasman et al. (Eds.), *Review of Psychiatry, Vol . 9.* Washington DC: American Psychiatric Press, 384–404.

Menaker, E. & Barbre, C. (1995). *The freedom to inquire: Self psychological perspectives on women's issues, masochism, and the therapeutic relation.* Northvale, NJ: Aronson.

Milioria, M. T. (2000). Beyond empathic failures: Cultural racism as narcissistic trauma and disenfranchisement of grandiosity. *Clinical Social Work, 28*(1), 43–53.

Miliora, M. T. (2007). The cross-culturally disordered self: A self psychological study and treatment. *Journal of Adult Development, 4*(1), 35–44.

Moskowitz, M. (1995). Ethnicity and the fantasy of ethnicity. *Psychoanalytic Psychology, 4,* 547–55.

Pangerl, S. (1996). Self psychology: A feminist re-visioning. In A. Goldberg (Ed.), *Progress in self psychology, volume 12* (pp. 285–98). Hillsdale, NJ: Analytic Press.

Parker, E. L. (2009). Emancipatory hope reloaded, http://old.religiouseducation.net/proceedings/2009_Proceedings/23Parker_EmancipatoryHope.pdf/.

Rector, L. (1996). The function of early selfobject experiences in gendered representations of God. In A. Goldberg (Ed.), *Progress in self psychology, volume 12* (pp. 269–283). Hillsdale, NJ: Analytic.

Roland, A. (1988). *In Search of self in India and Japan*. Princeton, NJ: Princeton University Press.

Roland, A. (1996). The influence of culture on the self and selfobject relationships: An Asian-North American comparison. *Psychoanalytic Dialogue, 6,* 461–75.

Seeley, K. M. (2000). *Cultural psychotherapy: Working with culture in the clinical encounter.* Northvale, NJ: Aronson.

Shane, E., & Shane, M. (1990). Object loss and selfobject loss: A consideration of self psychology. *Ann. Psychoanalysis, 18,* 115–31.

Sheppard, P. I. (2003). A dark goodness created in the image of God: Womanist notes toward a practical theology of black women's embodiment. *Covenant Quarterly, 61*(3), 5–28.

Sheppard, P. I. (2011). *Self, culture, and others in womanist practical theology.* Black Religion / Womanist Thought / Social Justice. New York: Palgrave Macmillan.

Strozier, C. B. (1985). Introduction. In H. Kohut, *Self psychology and the humanities: Reflections on a new psychoanalytic approach.* (pp. xvii–xxx) C. B. Strozier (Ed.). New York: Norton.

Thomas, L. E. (2004). Womanist theology, epistemology and a new anthropological paradigm. In *Living stones in the household of God: The legacy and future of black theology* (pp. 37–48). Minneapolis: Fortress.

Wiley, C. Y. (1991). A ministry of empowerment: A holistic model for pastoral counseling in the African American community. *Journal of Pastoral Care 45,* 335–64.

Williamson, M. (1992). *A return to love: A course in miracles: Reflections on the principles of a course in miracles.* New York: Harper Collins.

5

Sexuality-Affirming Pastoral Theology and Counseling

Joretta L. Marshall

IN OUR WORK AS pastoral counselors we encounter human beings who bring to the counseling room their embodied experiences, assumptions, belief systems, and feelings about sexuality. Sometimes the issues people want to discuss relate to gender and the ways that we embody being female or male; at other times clients are focused on the expressions of love in the act of sexual intercourse; while at still other times there are questions about gender identity or sexual orientation. The issues are often multilayered and complex, and can create conflictual experiences within one's self, or can raise tensions with others including in one's family, with one's intimate partner, or within one's community.

Pastoral psychotherapists carry an ethical responsibility to be clear about our own theological and clinical perspectives as we relate to clients wrestling with gender or gender identity, sexuality or sexual orientation. Central to this work is the theological integration of sexuality and spirituality. The multiple and competing theological and psychological perspectives on sexuality and gender, alongside diverse definitions and norms that people use to discern what it means to live faithfully in light of belief systems or theological traditions, reflect the diversity of clinicians and clients. This chapter will not provide an overview of multiple positions. Instead, I propose an integrated sexuality-affirming pastoral clinical viewpoint that embodies three components: (1) a life-giving perspective on wholeness, (2) a desire to increase agency in decision making and to recognize the complexity of any choice, and (3) an enhancement of individual and communal justice-making relationships.

Before unpacking these dimensions, it is helpful to explore the interconnectedness between spirituality and sexuality.

Integration of Spirituality and Sexuality

Human beings are created with capacities for relating to one another through our senses, our spiritual lives, and our sexuality. Created in the image of God, we are born into a physical, emotional, and relational world. The biblical and historical traditions of the Christian faith affirm that our embodied realities open venues that deepen our relationships to God, to one another, to communities, and to the earth (Farley, 2008; Jensen, 2010; Nelson, 1978; VanWijk-Bos, 2003). Asserting the deep interconnections between spirituality and sexuality provides a starting place for theologically sophisticated pastoral clinical work.

Spirituality recognizes our yearning for, and intimate connection with, something that is both within and beyond us. Whatever language one uses to identify the Holy Other, our spirituality nurtures the relationships we desire with God, human beings, and the earth. Spirituality takes many forms through community and relational living, religious life and ritual, engagement with nature, and intimate emotional or spiritual connections with other human beings. These encounters with the One beyond us remind us that we are not only individuals who desire intimate relationships with one another, but sometimes our interpersonal worlds deepen our spiritual experiences. Everyone has the potential to be deeply and intimately connected to Something beyond us.

Sexuality refers to our capacity to relate to one another through our spiritual, sensual, physical, gendered, emotional, and mental worlds. The fluid and unfolding nature of sexuality shapes our lives over time in response to our experiences with self, others, and God. Illustrative of this is the self-understanding of one's sexual body as a six-year-old, which is quite different from that of a sixty-year-old self. While our early life experiences have a deep and abiding impact on shaping our perspectives, they are not determinative. Our sexuality invites us into intimacy with others through the multiplicity of such things as our gender expression, gender identity, sexual orientations, intimate partnerships, and a host of other complexities of human life. Pastoral counselors are often called into the midst of people's lives where spirituality and sexuality meet as we yearn for the deepest and most intimate life-giving connections and relationships.

One aspect of sexuality and spirituality often over-looked in the clinical context is the role of our senses in exploring and experiencing multiple
levels of relatedness with self, others, God, and earth. Our unique capacities
to draw upon our sensory abilities create diverse spiritual and sexual experiences. Some are keenly alert to the smell of fresh-baked bread or the very
earthy body that lies next to them. Others see the nuanced colors of a rain-
bow or the varying shades of people's skin. We taste the goodness of food
that matches our hunger or that surprises our senses. Some hear the crying
of a baby and feel the kiss of someone we love. Most can enjoy the embrace
and touch of those whom we welcome into our lives, and, precisely because
our senses are so central to our existence, many also know the overwhelming pain of touch that is harmful, destructive, and life-taking. Our sensuality is a reminder that our earthly bodies are filled with capacities for not
simply taking things into our cognitive sphere of awareness, but for relating
with and through our senses. Our diverse abilities to draw on the resources
of our senses facilitate our participation in meaningful relationships with
the Holy One, with others, with the earth, and with the world (Taylor, 2009).

What is critical for pastoral counselors is to note that any time we deal
with individuals, couples, families, or communities the issues of gender
identity, sexual orientation, or multiple ways of relating appear at the matrix
of sensuality, spirituality, and sexuality. Hence, we do well to walk carefully
and to be clear about our own experiences, perspectives, and theological
positions. Grounded and sensitive pastoral counselors carry with them a
self-awareness that increases their clinical competency. We ask ourselves
questions such as, what issues related to gender or sexuality make me uncomfortable or angry or fearful? How do the experiences or assumptions of
others challenge my preconceived notions of sexuality or gender? What impact do my own experiences, feelings, and theological positions have on my
work with clients? How do I discern the theological and psychotherapeutic
needs of individuals, couples, families, and communities? The stance of
openness we carry toward asking ourselves hard questions signals to clients
and communities that pastoral counselors are able to engage conversations
that rarely have easy resolutions.

Let us turn now to the three components of sexuality-affirming pastoral clinical work stated earlier, drawing upon concrete scenarios to help us
examine pastoral clinical perspectives. As you encounter the cases in this
chapter, pay attention to initial reactions, reflections, and feelings that are
raised in response to each one. Ask questions not only of the case but of
your own theoclinical assumptions and perspectives.[1]

---

1. All cases in this chapter are fictional, although they reflect situations that many

Life-Giving Wholeness

Affirming sexuality as part of a life-giving wholeness that counters shame and integrates spirituality and sexuality is the beginning case for this exploration.

> *A couple is referred to you by their pastor because there is concern among church leaders that their eight-year-old child needs to see a therapist. The young boy was "caught exploring a young girl's body" (the words of the parents of the young girl) in the Sunday School classroom between church services last week, and the pastor has asked that the parents "take the boy to see a therapist because he obviously has the potential to sexually abuse others" (the words of the church leaders). The parents describe feelings of anger at the church for assuming that there is something wrong with their son when "he was simply exploring his body and how it worked." At the same time they hint at a sense of shame for having a child who is now labeled as sexually deviant in some way. They feel "confused about what to do and how to respond" and "somewhat ashamed." They wonder what you think as a counselor of faith.*

This case invites a series of questions: How does a clinician interpret the parents' concerns? Is the church seeing something that the parents are unable to see, or do the parents know some truth that the church does not see? What is "normal" and "natural" for eight-year-old-boys and is it any different than for eight-year-old girls? Are there appropriate, respectful, and boundaried ways to intervene not only with this family, but perhaps also with the church as they try to articulate what they believe about sexuality? While these questions cannot be fully answered within the limitations of this chapter, it is clear that a holistic perspective offers a greater potential for producing positive outcomes for the parents, the children, and the church community. Much will depend on the presence or absence of mutuality or coercion and on how the children themselves experienced the incident prior to the reactions of parents and the church community.

By drawing on notions of wholeness we affirm that we are created in the image of a God who delights in our sensual, sexual, and spiritual capacities recognizing that they are all part of an integrative whole. This counters parts of our traditions that suggest that some aspects of our wholeness are split from others according to what is "good" or "bad." Ancient and contemporary theological messages of shame have unduly burdened our conversations about sexuality in ways that diminish wholeness (Farley, 2008; Nelson,

---

clinicians experience.

1978). Hence, challenging shame about existence as a sexual being is an important dimension of good pastoral clinical work.

Psychologist and pastor Karen McClintock defines "shame as a feeling of unworthiness in the sight of God or significant others" (McClintock, 2012, p. 14). McClintock and with other scholars and therapists note that the splitting within our Christian tradition between "body and spirit" creates a dualism that often relegates the body and our senses to the realm of shame. This creates in us a desire to hide our bodies and their senses from the world around us. Life-giving wholeness, on the other hand, understands that God's good gift is experienced in our sexuality and our sensuality, as well as in our spiritual lives. In fact, spirit and body cannot be separated from each other, as if one were "good" and the other "less good or bad" (Heyward, 2010; Kaufman & Raphael, 1996; McClintock, 2012; Nelson, 2010).

A life-giving perspective based in wholeness challenges in two ways the shame-driven cultures that we often experience in churches and communities of faith. First, such a perspective recognizes the damage of internalized shame and works to counter those messages. McClintock notes that to some "shame appears as the self-punishing voice inside your head, this is called intrapersonal shame" (McClintock, 2012, p. 15). In the words of shame experts Gershen Kaufman and Lev Raphael, "exposure is what we feel in the instant shame strikes . . . But we can never hide from ourselves, from those watching eyes *inside*, not entirely" (Kaufman & Raphael, 1996, p. 17). Such shame-feelings contribute to a sense of inadequacy and diminish our worthiness as sexual creatures. Pastoral counselors who theologically counter the internal expressions of shame with a sense of the giftedness of sensuality, sexuality, and spirituality will promote greater life-giving wholeness in the lives of others.

Second, church and cultural messages of shame can be equally damaging to individuals and their relationships. In the case above, initial responses by church leaders leaned toward a more shame-based theology. Pastoral counselors counter these messages by speaking about sexuality as a positive part of God's goodness not only in the clinical room but also in the public realm. Understanding sexuality as part of our God-given goodness must replace the shame-induced theology that is part of the daily discourse in too many churches. For example, it makes a difference whether the pastoral counselor whom this family sees talks about the eight-year-old in the case above as "normal" or "sinful" or "healthy" or "abnormal" or "simply exploring." In turn, the words the pastoral counselor uses carry interpretive power for the parents, the community, and the child in ways that can be life-affirming into the future. Exploring with the boy, with his parents, and perhaps even with the leaders of the church what they think it means theologically to be created in the image of God can be an opportunity to open a larger dialogue that offers new visions. Any intervention with the church, of course, needs to be done with the utmost respect primarily for what the clients want out of therapy and then only with their companionship in the process.[2]

While the words we use as pastoral counselors can offer a healing counternarrative to theologically-based shame, silence by trusted pastoral counselors can inadvertently be destructive. Pastoral counselors practice public theology as we challenge shame-induced concepts and languages that are culturally and theologically based. Pastoral counselors who are able to talk about the sexuality of children, teens, and adults in ways that are forthright, respectful, and appropriate will model for parents and others the value that God places on our bodies, senses, and relationships.

In addition to countering shame, pastoral counselors discourage sexual/spiritual dualism, or the unfortunate belief that spirituality is good and sacred, while sexuality is not (Nelson, 2010).

> Joseph, a forty-five-year-old male is concerned about his relationship with women. He is not married, but in the past few months he has experienced several problems with impotency during sexual encounters with his current intimate partner. He confides during therapy that his maternal aunt was sexually inappropriate with him as a child. This was never talked about in his family, although he did hint to his mother once "that things did not seem right" with his aunt. She asked him a few questions about what he meant and he was able to tell his mother that his aunt kissed and touched him. He does not ever remember being left alone with his aunt again. He remembers his mother encouraging him, as an adolescent, to keep praying in order to "take care of any sinful sexual thoughts"

Part of the staying power of our childhood experiences is that they come to us at times when we are not as emotionally, physically, spiritually, or sexually able to sort out our feelings and our physical experiences from more mature forms of love and care. Wholeness looks differently in childhood since much of our identity is experienced through our physicality and our very concrete experiences. While there is not necessarily a linear causal link between Joseph's early childhood experiences and his current challenges, a gifted clinician will wonder with him how he has come to make meaning of the messages voiced by his mother. What kind of legacy or power do these memories carry for him in his current self-understanding as a sexual being?

2. Such interventions are appropriate when working out of the larger social contexts of postmodern therapy such as narrative or collaborative (Madsen, 2007, pp. 249–83).

We need not allow the past to overly determine our work with clients in the present, yet we also are called to stay present to lingering experiences that reinforce shame.[3] In a life-giving way it is important for pastoral counselors to encourage conversation about the integration of spirituality and sexuality in order to open up and deepen ways of relating.

To develop meaningful relationships with self, others, and the Holy One we must honor our senses, emotions, spirits, and physical lives. To suggest that every human being has the capacity for relationality means more than that we can have friendships where we exchange physical embraces or some levels of touch; rather, it advocates that part of what it means to be created in the image of God is to draw upon our ability to relate at the deepest and most profound ways through sexual and physical intimacy. A sexuality-affirming pastoral counselor can encourage healing narratives that invite Joseph toward more whole ways of relating to others through sensuality, spirituality, gender, and sexuality.

Pastoral counselors who offer a vision of life-giving wholeness will alleviate shame in ways that are appropriate, and will help people faithfully integrate their sensuality, spirituality, and sexuality. In turn, clients and those around them will feel more able to act in ways that are integrative and whole as they move forward in their complex lives.

Increasing Agency as Gendered and Sexual Beings

Agency, or the ability to act on one's behalf and to participate meaningfully in the world through decision making, contributes to our sense of wholeness. A central theological goal for a sexuality-affirming pastoral counselor is that of enhancing the ability of individuals, families and communities to make choices that are life-giving rather than death dealing when it comes to issues such as gender or sexual orientation. Such therapy accomplishes three things: (1) it recognizes the complexity of decision making; (2) it honors the varying agential capacities of those involved; and (3) it works to assess the interpersonal impact of decisions.

> *Jason and Megan come to your office to talk about tensions in their marital relationship. They are active church members in a congregation that refers many individuals, couples, and families to you. Jason would like Megan to stay at home and take care of the children because he "makes enough money to take care of them." Megan, however, wants to continue to develop her career*

3. There is good clinical research on work with persons who experience sexual trauma in their childhood. See, for example, Cooper-White (2012, pp. 168–92).

in business and human resource management. Their disagree-
ment also has an impact on how they think about their two pre-
adolescent boys and one adolescent girl. Their conflicts often arise
as Jason seeks to encourage more culturally gender-conforming
behaviors and attitudes with the children while Megan encourages
their children to "express themselves in ways that are their own."
The tensions are often framed in theological and faith language.

The decisions that are made, who makes them, and how they are negotiated within this family have implications not only for how the couple embodies gender, but also for how their children experience gender-related decision-making. The decisions about gender in this family are complex and one hopes that conscious and deliberate conversations with a pastoral counselor will ultimately contribute to an integrated sense of wholeness for each individual and for the family.

Attending to the complexity of decision making requires pastoral counselors to honor the different theological and social perspectives on gender and its meaning, even if one disagrees with a particular vantage point expressed by either Jason or Megan. A good first step is reflecting with Megan and Jason about how each has come to particular understandings of gender, offering an open and safe space to speak honestly without judgment from the therapist. This does not mean the pastoral counselor has no theological commitments related to the embodiment of gender; it merely reflects the fact that the goal of counseling is not to convince either one of them to change their minds. Instead, the pastoral clinician sees here an opportunity to invite meaningful conversation about the rather fluid reality of gender in our culture, and to support complex decision-making as this family moves forward.

Gender is not a static concept or category. Some aspects of our gender evolve because we are assigned a gender at birth, creating an understanding by others and eventually by ourselves about who we are, how we are to behave, and where our agency is located.[4] While there is much disagreement about biblical interpretation, most sexuality-affirmative counselors agree that there is nothing biblically mandated or theologically predetermined about who we are based on our gender (Heyward, 2010). In a similar way, there is nothing essential about being male or female that is so strongly tied to our biological nature that one can say, all women are like this; or, all men act this way. Decisions related to our gender are made in the vortex of

4. Research continues to inform our understanding of how gender matters. Farley (2008) explores this issue and includes consideration of those who do not fall into the normative binary division of male and female, often referred to as intersex (pp. 133–59).

ever-changing familial, personal, social, cultural, and theological dynamics. This couple's decision making is complex and ought to be approached with genuine care and skill.

It is important to reflect on the varying agential capacities of each person in the family (including the children) by engaging the couple around such questions as these: Who has the power to make decisions in your family, and how is that agency influenced by a particular understanding of gender? Where are actions being limited by perceptions of others. or by some normative way of thinking about gender? How are expectations about gender communicated to the children and how does that enhance or diminish their life-giving wholeness? If one of the goals of a pastoral counselor is to increase the awareness of agency in both the husband and wife, it is clear that there will be conflict even as they discuss these questions. The tensions, however, do not have to damage the relationship. What will be most helpful to this couple and to their children is honest conversation about the meaning of gender alongside their decision making. By realizing that our self-understanding of gender changes over time we can lessen anxiety about normative perspectives and invite forth a sense of agency within each individual. This, in turn, changes the dynamics of power in the family system. Where conflicts arise, a gifted pastoral counselor sits in the midst of it, less sure of the right answer, and more aware that how decisions are made is as important as the choice itself.

Pastoral counselors help clients assess the impact of their decision making on others, not in ways that put the emphasis on a desire to keep others happy, but in a genuine effort to note the interconnectedness of one to another. Perhaps one of the goals of pastoral counseling with this couple is to help them imagine varied patterns of embodying gender and the impact those choices might have on them as individuals, as a couple, and as a family. Raising questions about what they hope is life-giving for their children offers an opportunity for them to live into alternative visions. Whatever choices this husband and wife make individually and together will have implications for them, their children, and the generations that are to follow.

Another case builds on the complexity of agency in a slightly different way.

> Liz, a sixteen-year-old client, articulates her growing awareness
> that she doesn't feel attracted to any of the guys in her class. When
> you gently indicate that you are open to talking about what it
> means to be gay, she clearly states that, "I'm not lesbian; I'm queer."
> The issue that brings her to your office relates to the fact that she
> would like to take one of her girl friends to the prom "just because

she is a good friend, and that's what prom is all about." You have
encouraged her to talk to her parents (who are also paying for her
therapy) but she doesn't want to because they "belong to a church
that gets all freaked out with the word queer."

How is a pastoral counselor to understand Liz and her decision making? One might be tempted to jump to the conclusion that Liz is in denial of being lesbian or that she is simply going through a "phase" that she will outgrow. However, pastoral counselors who have a more affirming perspective of the intersection of sexuality and spirituality will be slow to diagnose Liz or attach a label to her sexuality or her sexual behavior.[5] Instead, the goal is to assist Liz as she carefully makes choices that relate to the meaning of gender and sexuality in her life. The narrative of Liz's life is being written in the meaning she brings to the choices she makes. However, her choices are not a definitive statement about her orientation or her future.

While being able to talk with clients who are lesbian, gay, bisexual or transgendered is critical, it is equally important to allow clients like Liz to bring their own self-identifying language into the counseling room. Her use of *queer* is one of the reminders that we live in a world where language and the meaning attached to words change over time (Kundtz & Schlager, 2007; Marshall, 2009; Sanders, 2013). Once a word used as a derogative statement about gay men and sometimes lesbians, queer now communicates something quite different to this sixteen-year-old. A pastoral counselor who asks about the meaning of the word can assist Liz in claiming her own agency to define who she is. Equally important, however, is helping Liz recognize that her choices in language, much like her choice about who will accompany her to prom, invite responses from others that can lead to important conversations. As she increases her sense of agency, she will also face challenges of which she is currently unaware. The key is not to encourage the 16 year-old to do one thing over another, but to help her think about how she makes choices and how she invites others into the sacred spaces of her decision making in new ways.

One component of care might be to wonder with Liz about bringing her family or other friends into conversations with the two of you. This might open the door for Liz to imagine that the first response from family and church does not ultimately determine how the journey will move forward. Likewise, it allows Liz to experience agency about who to tell, when,

5. McClintock (2012) notes the shaming and destructive power of labels (pp. 22–25). In addition, there is a growing literature that notes the difference between behavior and self-identity. In other words, not all individuals who participate in same-gender behavior self-identify as gay, lesbian, or bisexual. Self-identity is much more nuanced and complex (Marshall, 2001).

and how (Tigert, 1996). Joining Liz as she attempts to avoid both naïve and predetermined expectations about responses to her choices will also invite her to imagine how to gather folks around her who will not shame her, and who will help her continue to assess and embody the values she holds. These aspects of care affirm for Liz and for those around her the importance of justice making in multiple kinds of relationships.

Relational Justice

The enhancement of relational justice—in intimate partnerships, in friendships and families, and in communal contexts—is central to a sexuality-affirming pastoral clinical perspective.

> *Michael and Jennifer, a young couple who live together, have decided not to participate in the structures of cultural marriage. They have offered to be youth leaders for their church, but the church is anxious about what kind of message they are sending to the youth by not being married yet living together. The church keeps talking about marriage and its importance while Jennifer and Michael would prefer that they discuss the meaning of good and healthy sexual relationships. The church is at an impasse, and they invite you, as a pastoral counselor they know, to talk with Michael and Jennifer.*

Relational justice and love have become central concepts in pastoral care and counseling (Ramsay, 2004). In the case above, it is clear that each of the multiple layers and webs of relatedness contains potential for creating, either deeper justice and love, or fragmentation and harm. The way a pastoral counselor invites conversation without judgment, encourages honesty without attacking another's integrity, and establishes norms for mutual engagement with one another will signal the value justice has in community. Four things emerge as important to pastoral counselors as they respond to this case.

First, this case highlights the importance of pastoral counselors' not limiting their work to the private discourse of counseling offices but offering their wisdom and experience to broader communities. Establishing ground rules and expectations for communication in the midst of conflict is essential, and pastoral counselors have much to offer here. The way we lead conversations with others illuminates our commitments to relationships of justice. Christian ethicist Marvin Ellison defines justice making as "the never-ending project of setting wrongs right, strengthening connections that are respectful and fair among individuals and groups, and making communities more inclusive and welcoming of difference" (Ellison, 2004, p. 36). A pastoral counselor in this context will help this community of faith discern what it means to treat one another with respect and to welcome difference, even differences between deeply held faith perspectives. The disagreements in this case are genuine, and it will be important for the pastoral counselor to provide space for conversations to unfold rather than to try to quickly alleviate any feelings of discomfort or disappointment.

Second, pastoral counselors in this context will take seriously the theology that undergirds our notions of marriage (Tigert & Tirabassi, 2010). In a changing world it is important to ponder the very different meanings about intimate relationships that people carry. In this process, not only will Michael and Jennifer have a chance to name their commitments, but the congregation will also articulate what is at stake for them as individuals and as a community. Ellison reminds readers that the concept of marriage has changed over time and is connected, in part, to our constructions of gender. Ultimately, he and others argue for a sexual justice that honors the connections of spirituality and sexuality, that avoids exploitation and violence, and that recognizes and values sexual differences, such as love between intimate partners of the same gender (Ellison & Thorson-Smith, 2003; Ellison, 2010). Pastoral counselors willing to walk with communities through these explorations can assist communities to encourage the integration of spirituality and sexuality.

Third, this conversation highlights the qualities in intimate relationships that reflect justice and love. Pastoral theologians and others have noted the importance of partnerships that embody love, justice, and mutuality (Marshall, 2007), that attempt to do no harm, and that respect free consent and commitment (Farley, 2008). Pastoral counselors can lead the way in assisting congregations and couples to reflect on the complex nature of intimate partnerships knowing that our experiences and visions change over time.

Finally, the way the conversation is engaged will communicate to couples and individuals within the church, as well as to the community overall, that partnerships are one way that God's fullness is made present in the world. At the same time, it is important to note that coupleship is not the only way God is made known to us. As part of this conversation it will become clear that intimate relationships, whether marked by legal marriage or by spiritual covenant, need the support of the communities around them. A pastoral counselor focused on relational justice can offer tools to strengthen sexual and spiritual friendships and partnerships, even in the midst of helping the church negotiate the different perspectives that are present. Contributing to meaningful conversations between individuals,

families, and couples in ways that enhance relational justice is an important
aspect of a pastoral counselor's work in this moment.

Conclusion

This chapter has attempted to look at three qualities of sexuality-affirming
pastoral clinical work, yet there are multiple issues that have not been attended to: the need for careful work with children and teens about gender,
and the various cultural distortions that invite such things as eating disorders or consumer spending on beauty; attending to women's health and re-
productive justice; speaking out against the ongoing acts of sexual violence
in intimate partnerships, such as date rapes or sexual abuse in marriage;
promoting appropriate sexuality education in the church for children, teens,
and adults; walking with women, men, and their families on journeys to
gender transformations; and so much more. Nor has this chapter wrestled
with the intersections of particularities such as race, class, and other differences that impact our understandings and experience of sexuality and
spirituality. Similarly, there is more constructive work to be done in assessing how the gender identity and sexual orientation of the therapist makes
a difference to clients. Pastoral clinicians who want to offer theologically
sophisticated and clinically competent care need to build knowledge and
understanding about these issues.

As pastoral counselors continue to offer therapy that is affirmative of
sexuality, I want to encourage the development of four concrete practices
that will keep us honest in our work. First, pastoral counselors need to do
all within our power to develop self-awareness about the ambiguities and
commitments from our own sexual and spiritual narratives that sometimes
get in the way of positively engaging clients. These might include previous
experiences that are buried in our souls, or deeply-held beliefs that make it
difficult to work with particular kinds of sexual or gender difference.

Second, as pastoral counselors nurture our public voices we will contribute to the larger conversations about sexuality and spirituality in our
culture. It is a gift to offer pastoral perspectives on a life-giving wholeness
that counters shame, enhances agency, and embodies relational justice.
Nurture your public theological voice and find meaningful ways to affirm
the gift of sexuality.

Third, we need to seek out diverse perspectives from supervisors, colleagues, peers, writers who disagree with us, and others. We ought not to be
content with what we think we know about sexuality or spirituality. Likewise, when clients bring sexual or gender differences into the clinical room,

they should not be expected to be our teacher. Our clients deserve pastoral counselors who continue to learn and hone concepts and skills.

Finally, we need to continue to refine the theological commitments that rest at the core and heart of pastoral counseling. Our clients, churches, and communities deserve pastoral clinicians who can speak articulately about theology and who can offer visions of a world where sexuality and spirituality are deeply integrated.

References

Cooper-White, P. (2012). *The cry of Tamar: Violence against women and the church's response* (2nd ed.). Minneapolis: Fortress.

Ellison, M. M. (2004). *Same-sex marriage? A Christian ethical analysis.* Cleveland: Pilgrim.

Ellison, M. M. (2010). Reimagining good sex: The eroticizing of mutual respect and pleasure. In M. M. Ellison & K. B. Douglas (Eds.), *Sexuality and the sacred: Sources for theological reflection* (2nd ed., pp. 245–61). Louisville: Westminster John Knox.

Ellison, M. M., & Thorson-Smith, S. (Eds.). (2003). *Body and soul: Rethinking sexuality as justice-love.* Cleveland: Pilgrim; reprinted (2008) Eugene, OR: Wipf & Stock.

Farley, M. A. (2008). *Just love: A framework for Christian sexual ethics.* New York: Continuum.

Heyward, C. (2010). Notes on historical grounding: Beyond sexual essentialism. In M. M. Ellison & K. B. Douglas (Eds.), *Sexuality and the sacred: Sources for theological reflection* (2nd ed., pp. 6–15). Louisville: Westminster John Knox.

Jensen, D. H. (2010). The Bible and sex. In M. D. Kamitsuka (Ed.), *The embrace of eros: Bodies, desires, and sexuality in Christianity* (pp. 15–31). Minneapolis: Fortress.

Kaufman, G., & Raphael, L. (1996). *Coming out of shame: Transforming gay and lesbian lives.* New York: Doubleday.

Kundtz, D. J., & Schlager, B. S. (2007). *Ministry among God's queer folk: LGBT pastoral care.* Cleveland: Pilgrim.

Madsen, W. C. (2007). *Collaborative therapy with multi-stressed families* (2nd ed.). New York: Guilford.

Marshall, J. L. (1997). *Counseling lesbian partners.* Counseling and Pastoral Theology. Louisville: Westminster John Knox.

Marshall, J. L. (2001). Pastoral care and the formation of sexual identity: Lesbian, gay, bisexual, and transgendered. In H. N. Maloney, *Pastoral care and counseling in sexual diversity* (pp. 101–12). New York: Haworth.

Marshall, J. L. (2009). Differences, dialogues, and discourses: From sexuality to queer theory in learning and teaching. *Journal of Pastoral Theology, 19*(2), 29–47.

McClintock, K. A. (2012). *Shame-less lives, grace-full congregations.* Herndon, VA: Alban Institute.

Nelson, J. B. (1978). *Embodiment: An approach to sexuality and Christian theology.* Minneapolis: Augsburg.

Nelson, J. B. (2010). Where are we? Seven sinful problems and seven virtuous possibilities. In M. M. Ellison, & K. B. Douglas (Eds.), *Sexuality and the sacred:*

Sources for theological reflection (2nd ed., pp. 95–104). Louisville: Westminster/John Knox.

Ramsay, N. J. (2004). Contemporary pastoral theology: A wider vision for the practice of love. In N. J. Ramsay (Ed.), *Pastoral care and counseling: Redefining the paradigms* (pp. 155–76). Nashville: Abingdon.

Sanders, C. J. (2013). *Queer lessons for churches on the straight & narrow: What Christians can learn from LGBTQ lives.* Macon, GA: Faithlab.

Taylor, B. B. (2009). *An altar in the world: A geography of faith.* New York: HarperCollins.

Tigert, L. M. (1996). *Coming out while staying in: Struggles and celebrations of gays, lesbians, and bisexuals in the church.* Cleveland: Pilgrim Press.

Tigert, L. M., & Tirabassi, M. C. (2010). *All whom God has joined: Resources for clergy and same-gender loving couples.* Cleveland: Pilgrim.

Van Wijk-Bos, J. W. (2003). How to read what we read: Discerning good news about sexuality in scripture. In M. M. Ellison & S. Thorson-Smith (Eds.), *Body and soul: Rethinking sexuality as justice-love* (pp. 61–77). Cleveland: Pilgrim, reprinted (2008) Eugene, OR: Wipf & Stock.

6

Personality, Individuation, Mindfulness

Felicity Kelcourse and Christopher Ross

Individuation does not shut one out from the world, but gathers the world to oneself.

—Jung, 1946/1969, p.226

HOW DO PERSONALITY, INDIVIDUATION, and mindfulness inform theological perspectives on pastoral psychotherapy? All three address the capacity to be self-aware, self-observing, in ways that attest to the realities of our being, essential skills for both therapist and patient if each desires to grow in wisdom. This chapter introduces concepts derived from analytical (Jungian) psychology and Buddhist mindfulness practices that serve as aids to intrapsychic (introspective) and interpersonal awareness. Compassionate self-assessment allows therapists to receptively attend to self and other, just as these capacities help careseekers more fully comprehend their own lived experience.

Essential to our present-moment awareness is an observing ego capable of noticing our existing thoughts and feelings. The ability to attend to wordless images and mute embodied sensation as components of the intersubjective, phenomenological field between analyst and analysand informs the transformative work of pastoral psychotherapy.[1] From a theo-

1. The psychoanalytic approach of intersubjectivity as elaborated by Stolorow, Atwood, Brandschaft, and Orange, as well as the philosophical stance of phenomenology have much in common with contemporary practices of Analytical psychology. Briefly,

logical standpoint, the therapist's goal is never to mold another into some preconceived image of health but rather to provide a space in which the therapist's respectful attention to all that careseekers bring encourages them to attend to their own deep wisdom, a "soul-knowing" of what is needed for abundant life.

Personality has to do with our innate sense of self, the ways that we naturally perceive and relate to those around us. Individuation, in the context of this chapter, has to do with our lifelong calling to express our true selves, with the belief that doing so not only responds to our individual need for meaning and purpose in life, but also best serves the greater good, broadly conceived. Mindfulness, as it has been appropriated for use in psychotherapy, allows us to be fully present in the now, the only moment in which change and choice are possible. In theological terms, we honor the Creator and creation by living into the full capacity of our created being. Buddhism can be viewed as a non-theistic philosophy, yet the Buddhist emphasis on compassion for all beings is fully compatible with the Great Commandment of Christianity (Matthew 22:35–40) and the aspirations of other world religions.

What is Personality?

In her youth, Charlotte felt she was "the odd person out" in her family.[2] Her brothers and parents loved to spend time together while she frequently felt the need for time alone. The rest of the family did not share Charlotte's love of fantasy and imagination, accusing her of having her head in the clouds while they attended to facts. As an adult, Charlotte trained to be a pastoral psychotherapist and learned to use the Myers-Briggs Type Indicator (MBTI) as an assessment tool. Of the sixteen possible combinations of eight paired personality factors, her personality preferences (INFP) were diametrically opposed to those of her family members (ESTJ). This discovery both confirmed her sense of being different and offered tools for understanding the perceptual and communication differences within the family.

Personality has been defined as "consistent behavior patterns and intrapersonal processes originating with the individual," where the term

intersubjectivity attends to the created field between two persons in dialogue. Phenomenology attends to "the thing itself" – noticing whatever arises in consciousness as receptively as possible. For further reading in intersubjectivity see Atwood & Stolorow (1984, 1993) and Orange et al. (2001). On Jung and phenomenology see Brooke (2009).

2. Case examples are extrapolated from actual cases with identifying information altered to preserve confidentiality.

intrapersonal includes "all the emotional, motivational, and cognitive processes that go on inside of us that affect how we act and feel" (Burger, 2011, p. 4).[3] The MBTI was developed by Isabel Briggs Myers (1897–1980), drawing on the work of her mother Katherine Cook Briggs (1875–1968). Katherine Briggs found her categorization of personality types congruent with the work of Carl Jung (1921/1971). Jung's work on typology began with his attempts to understand conflicts between Freud, Adler, and himself, particularly with regard to understandings of the unconscious which divided the early psychoanalytic movement (Jung, 1921/1971; Beebe, 2004). The MBTI was first published in 1962 and remains the most widely used personality inventory to this day (Saunders, 1991).

Jung (1875–1961) was a Swiss pastor's son who trained to be a psychiatrist and adopted Freud's psychoanalytic method as a young professional. Following nine years of service as an in-patient doctor at the Burghölzli mental hospital he experienced a "creative illness" that caused him to focus intently on his inner life (Ellenberger, 1970).[4] Towards the end of his life, he dictated an introvert's autobiography, *Memories, dreams, reflections* (1961/1989). This unusual life review assigns subjective experiences, such as dreams, fantasies and visions, greater or equal weight to external events.

Jung is known as a developmental theorist of adulthood (Crain, 2000). Following his own life pattern, he saw the first half of life as focused on building up ego strength, based on one's roles in the outer world, and the second half of life as devoted to discovering one's unique vocation or calling as an individual.

Personality and Individuation

The lifelong task of becoming the person we were created to be can be described as a journey from division to wholeness. Jung captures this aspect of human development through his concept of *individuation*, the term he chose to describe the processes of psychological and spiritual growth, which for him always went hand in hand. For Jung being an *in*dividual was a process of becoming "*un*divided," aware of and open to all aspects of one's being.

3. Personality psychologist J. M. Burger identifies six different approaches to personality, designated as psychoanalytic, trait, biological, humanistic, behavioral/learning, and cognitive (2011). Only the trait approach, as identified using the MBTI, is presented here.

4. Jung's method of psychological inquiry invites each individual to explore his or her own sense of calling, with an eye toward community responsibilities, mindful of ancestral wisdom (Stein, 2005).

Jung's psychology is based on the assumption that a dynamic and useful tension exists between opposites that form part of the human *psyche*—our psychological life. The most basic polarity in his depth psychology is that between conscious and unconscious. While he may have agreed in principle with Freud's summation of the psychotherapeutic process, "Where *Id* [the unconscious] was *Ego* [consciousness] shall be" (1962/1923), Jung added the dimension of the Self as a patterning force or *archetype* of psychological totality, more inclusive than ego-consciousness, and the closest analogy in analytical psychology to the theological concept of God. The self transforms and transcends many polarities, including those between the ego's drive to adapt to prevailing social demands, and the requirements of a wider, more embracing, sense of wholeness that many consider the purview of religion (Jung, 1951/1968; Ulanov & Dueck, 2008; Stein, 2014).

Jung found the most accessible aspect of our unconscious to be the sets of opposites foundational to his personality typology as articulated in *Psychological Types* (1921/1971). Understanding his personality typology is a starting place for the journey toward individuation, our own and that of our clients. Jung describes eight different ways of being conscious in order to correct our personal bias of thinking of other people as different versions of ourselves. Because we are used to ourselves, we may assume that other people are psychologically like us. We may also use our own beliefs about religion and spirituality as a largely unconscious diving board for exploring others' worlds. *An understanding of personality differences facilitates our provision of appropriate counseling by showing us specific ways in which using our own personality as a map for understanding and responding to others may prove misleading.*

An Introduction to Personality Types

Individuals are revitalized in different ways: some of us are energized from the inside through introversion (I), by spending time alone with opportunity for reflection; others are refreshed through extraversion (E), by interacting with others and acting on the external environment. Understanding these ways of being energized is helpful in pastoral counseling: an introverted person may take more time to open up, and it is nothing to do with you, the counselor. An extravert may be very vocal in group counseling simply because any group is stimulating, not out of a narcissistic drive to dominate!

Jung considered that there were also four key cognitive processes that he called functions, each of which may be directed in an introverted (I) or extroverted (E) direction: two contrasting perceiving functions—sensing

(S) and intuition (N)—ways of following and processing stimuli, and two contrasting ordering or assessing functions—feeling (F) and thinking (T). The sensing function focuses on specific details, whereas the intuitive function orients to patterns and meaning, cognizing wholes. When sensing is "in play" in pastoral counseling the questions asked by the counselor are specific and focused. Intuition, however, is helpful for rapid exploration when 'open ended questions' speed the therapist across many areas of life toward the situation that is most pressing. While there is no ideal type combination for counselor and client the match between client and counselor makes a difference. A counselor literate in personality differences will know when she has to adapt to clients who perceive the world differently.

Thinking (T) and feeling (F) are contrasting—yet complimentary—ways of ordering the information we gather through our perceiving processes. Thinking assesses information through detached, logical analysis with attention to consistency. Feeling orders on the basis of values, with special attention to human need. The prevalence of thinking or feeling flavors the counseling process. When both client and counselor favor feeling judgment, rapport may develop quickly, whereas when both parties have thinking preferences more time may be required. A feeling (F) client may experience the (T) therapist as less "available," but might come to trust their steadiness and perspective. Alternatively the thinking client may feel flooded by the immediate warmth of the feeling counselor, and this should not be pathologized as the client necessarily having "trust issues."

Myers considered that the core of our personality is constituted by the pairing of our preferred way of perceiving—Sensing (S) or iNtuition (N)—with our preferred way of organizing—Thinking (T) or Feeling (F). In the construction of the MBTI, Myers added a set of questions that related to a further set of opposites, which she found helpful in determining which one of the pair of preferred processes was turned outward toward the external world, and which was introverted. If a judging process was used to face the outside world, the individual was designated as having a Judging preference set (a J), and if her preferred way of Perceiving was turned outward, she was identified as having a perceiving preference and was designated a P. "Judging" (J) does not imply that a person is judgmental but does denote a preference for order, structure, and planning in daily life. A "perceiving" (P) person is able to "go with the flow," responding spontaneously in the here and now.

Type Frequency

All personality types are represented among those providing pastoral counseling and among those seeking it. However, the frequency of each dominant
type often differentiates counselors from the general population. Among
providers of counseling intuition and feeling (NF) predominate. NF's, representing only 10 percent of the general population (Kiersey, 2006) are also
disproportionately drawn to seminaries and pastoral counseling training
programs (Ross, 2011). Myers and McCaulley (1985) conclude, "Given that
the majority of the population prefers sensing, the fact that most counselors
prefer intuition creates a responsibility for counselors to learn methods for
communicating and treating sensing clients" (p. 73).

A common misunderstanding of personality typology is the idea
that one's preferred type, the preference for extraversion over introversion
for instance, evident in childhood, must remain one's preferred approach
throughout life. On the contrary, the concept of individuation as becoming *undivided* suggests that it may be important, particularly in the second
half of life, to explore one's "inferior function." So, for example, a person
generally preferring solitude to large groups, grand visions to immediate
details, human values to universal principles, planning to spontaneity, in
other words, an INFJ, might need to develop, in later life, the capacity to
spontaneously relate to groups of people with attention to immediate facts
(ESTP functions). Some persons may test as an *x* where preference is unclear. This lack of clarity is often caused by one's natural preferences' being
muted by environmental pressures from home or work.

A positive characteristic of the MBTI is that no one set of personality
preferences is more useful or better than any other. Each type has its own
characteristic strengths and weaknesses, and for this reason the MBTI is
often used to help working groups (and families) understand each other
better, given their personality differences; such a new understanding of differences enables them to rely on one another's strengths in complementary
ways.[5] Therapists mindful of perceptual differences between themselves
and their clients are equipped to adjust to clients' needs in treatment. For
example, an INFP therapist working with a couple noted in supervision
that her preferred use of metaphor to assist couples in identifying relational
impasses was falling flat. The husband was a mechanic and the wife was a
nurse. Based on clients' career choices, the supervisor suggested that this
couple might prefer a more factually oriented, structured approach to the

---

5. *Gifts differing: Understanding personality type* (Myers & Myers, 1995) provides
an introduction to types. Keirsey (2006) offers a pencil-and-paper, short version of the
MBTI and complete versions of the assessment test can be found online.

work. The therapist was then able to identify specific behaviors to support mutuality, and the couple agreed that this shift of focus to address communication style was useful.

As significant as personality may be for improving communication, there is more to individuation (the life journey of becoming the person we were created to be) than understanding personality preferences. Growing in self-awareness allows therapists, who may carry their own wounds, to become wounded healers, not wounded wounders. Pastoral psychotherapy training programs generally require individual therapy as a component of clinical training. Pastoral psychotherapists are trained to approach those who come to them holistically, balancing attention to three modes of knowing: conscious *ego* awareness, the *psyche* (which includes unconscious ways of knowing as through dreams or embodied memories), and *soul*, or Self, as represented in Jung's concept of a "religious instinct" (Jung, 1926/1954).[6] It is difficult if not impossible to approach others from this holistic perspective if one has not first learned to discern the component aspects of consciousness within oneself.

Stages on the Individuation Journey

The journey of individuation generally begins in midlife. Psychoanalytic theory frequently focuses on the conflicts experienced from birth to puberty as foundations for future functioning. A therapist informed by this theory will encourage a strong conscious sense of self, able "to work and to love" as Freud would say.[7] While Jung acknowledges the importance of developing a strong ego, his theory of individuation is future-oriented, hopeful that early deficits do not circumscribe our potential, envisioning the second half of life as our opportunity to "get a heart of wisdom" (Ps 90:12b).[8] The following is a brief review of anticipated stages on the individuation journey as one engages awareness of one's persona(s), shadow, contrasexual other, or "syzygy," and the Self.

6. "Consider religious experience . . . Can science be so sure that there is no such thing as a 'religious instinct'?" (Jung, 1926/1954, p. 83).

7. For a psychoanalytically oriented introduction to the basic tasks of ego development across the lifespan see Kelcourse (Ed.), (2015b), *Human development and faith* (2nd ed.).

8. For introductions to individuation theory in Analytical psychology see Murray Stein (1998); and Hollis (2000).

Persona

During the first half of life we may assume many roles. One can be a daughter, sister, wife, mother, pastor, chaplain, psychotherapist, teacher, spiritual director—inhabiting each of these roles in effective and reliable ways, while recognizing that one's core self transcends any given role. The need to be able to dis-identify from roles frequently presents itself for women when the "empty nest" stage of life challenges them to see themselves as something more than a mother, or for men, when fired or retiring from a job that has come to define their career. At these junctures, people may come to therapy asking, who am I, now that my services as a mother or engineer are no longer needed?

Shadow

In arriving at an undivided, holistic self-awareness, it is useful to explore one's "shadow" or "not-I" sense of self. A simple exercise brings aspects of the shadow into view: (1) Think of *one person* you would rather not encounter walking down the hall, someone you prefer to avoid. (2) Now identify *one aspect* of that person that particularly distresses you. (3) Once you have held that person and the troublesome aspect of their presence clearly in mind, ask yourself this: is there any hint, however small, of that person's troubling characteristic within you?

If your answer is, no, definitely not, then get a second opinion from your spouse or best friend. If your answer is yes or maybe, then consider the fact that it is often what we secretly dislike in ourselves that we find most disagreeable in other people (Kelcourse, 2015b). Clients who rage at a coworker may discover that distressing aspects of that coworker's personality relate not only to family-of-origin experiences but also to traits that they are prone to deny in themselves.

Anima/Animus—The Syzygy

Beyond ego, persona, and shadow Jung identified the "syzygy" as the bridge to the self (Ulanov, A. B. & Ulanov, B, 1994). This is the awareness of a contrasexual "other" within each woman or man, designated by Jung as the "anima" within men and the "animus" within women. Jung's theory is not as heteronormative as it might sound, given the fact that every human society posits expected characteristics for masculinity and femininity. Even gay, lesbian, bisexual and transgendered persons must come to terms with the social constructions of gender that their culture assumes. A woman may say, "I'm not a leader" if she thinks of leadership as a function of maleness. A man may have difficulty identifying his emotions if he has been taught that "real men" don't show their feelings. The journey into wholeness may require the female follower to become a leader and the male stoic to gain affective attunement.

A man or woman in midlife may discover a contrasexual "other" within by becoming strongly attracted to a person who represents unclaimed potential aspects of themselves. The stoic professional is attracted to the patient whose emotions are passionately displayed. The patient is attracted to the doctor who embodies all the accomplishments and wisdom that she would like to attain.[9] The difference between shadow and anima/animus contents is that while 'not-I' shadow contents repel us when we recognize them in others or ourselves, syzygy contents are powerfully alluring, calling us to discover unlived parts of ourselves. In Jung's theory, expressed in heterosexual terms, men are drawn to unexpressed anima/soul qualities (the good they see in women), and women are attracted to animus/soul qualities (the good they find in men). This is a hunger for wholeness that all persons feel if they will heed it, what Jung called our "religious instinct" (1926/1954).

The Self

As a pastor's son, Jung would have been well aware of mystical religious traditions that attest to an inner connection to the divine within all persons and all creation. Jung stated that "psychic processes seem to be balances of energy flowing between spirit and instinct'" (Jung, 1946/1969, p. 207). An infant is born as a bundle of instincts with innate personality traits around which an ego, or largely conscious sense of self, forms. But the spirit nature of each person is also present from birth as the soul, "that of God" in us, that connects us to all of life and to one another. The lifelong journey of individuation moves along the axis between ego and Self, with Self corresponding to soul, the *imago Dei*.

It takes a strong ego to engage the archetypal energies of the Self (Ulanov, 2000). Becoming increasingly more aware of one's whole ego-self, as it connects us to others and a greater Self in God, is the opposite of self-absorbed selfishness. As we grow in spiritual awareness, we are increasingly able to discern God's call for our lives, the vocation in which our gladness

9. Jung's treatment of Sabina Spielrein, a brilliant young woman diagnosed with "hysteria," may well have inspired his "anima" theory (Kelcourse, 2015a).

and the world's hunger meet (Buechner, 1993). The Self is the archetype of wholeness, and like God, it is both center and circumference for our lives. Without the centering energies of the Self, we find ourselves chronically out of balance.

Psychotherapeutic work with persons in the second half of life, or with young adults and children whose lives are foreshortened by terminal illness, must respond to the spiritual demands of the need for meaning. What purpose does my life serve? Have I lived the life God intended for me? These questions energize a fearless quest for discernment, what John Wesley understood as sanctification, a perfection in love (2007). Through a discerning sense of self and others, we find ourselves more able to live out the great commandment to "love the Lord your God with all your heart, and with all your soul, and with all your strength, and with all your mind; and your neighbor as yourself" (Luke 10:27).

The journey of individuation requires ego strength, spiritual hunger and clarity of purpose. But what if one finds oneself hopelessly confused, mired in depression, anxiety, endless recriminations directed towards oneself or others? Painful emotions, nagging fears and doubts afflict many persons for whom the meaning, purpose, and value of their lives is chronically clouded. How are such persons to find the inner peace and clarity that discernment and individuation require?

Faith communities are positive sources of social and spiritual support for many. But among counselors and clients alike there are those who need to heal from the effects of toxic religion, as, for example, gay, lesbian, and transgender persons who are not welcomed by their faith communities. And there is a growing trend for persons under 40 to identify themselves as "spiritual, but not religious" (Fuller, 2001). For those raised without a faith tradition, or for religious "refugees," it is helpful to know that there are spiritually based resources for healing that do not require assent to specific creeds, as in the mindfulness practices that follow. These practices offer a "how to" approach for gaining present-moment awareness that can be considered a spiritual discipline as it supports compassionate attention to self and others.

The Spiritual and Therapeutic Value of Mindfulness

Mindfulness is a resource for pastoral counselors that derives from the Theravada branch of Buddhism.[10] Jon Kabat-Zinn, author of *Full Catastro-*

10. The Theravada branch of Buddhism is prevalent in Sri Lanka, Thailand, and

phe Living, and developer of Mindfulness Based Stress Reduction (MBSR) defines mindfulness as "moment to moment awareness" (2009, p. 2). The deliberate practice of mindfulness for both practitioners and clients that has proliferated in the last decade (Davis & Hayes, 2012) is based on both solid scientific validation of its benefits (Segal et al., 2002), and central tenets of Buddhism, many of which can also be found within the Christian tradition (Thich Nhat Hahn, 1999; Wallace, 2009).

The first of what are called the Four Noble Truths in Buddhism—the starting point for the Buddhist path to healing, to Enlightenment—involves acknowledging the universality of suffering:

> It is impossible to live without experiencing some kind of suffering. We have to endure physical suffering like sickness, injury, tiredness, old age and eventually death and we have to endure psychological suffering like loneliness, frustrations, fear, embarrassment, disappointment, anger. (Dhammika, 2014)

The counterbalance to this seemingly austere belief is the Buddhist conviction that deep within *any* conscious being lies the capacity to awaken to our true nature, our inner *Buddha*, meaning someone who is truly awake.[11] This capacity for fully awakened consciousness and its fundamental healing quality is the foundation for the practice of mindfulness. Buddhist mindfulness shares common ground with the founders of depth psychology, as well as important themes of redemption and resurrection in Christianity.[12] Freud's summary of psychoanalysis as noted above, "Where *id* (the unconscious) was, *ego* (consciousness) shall be!" has the expansion of conscious awareness as its goal (1923). Jung too sought to help suffering midlife seekers along the path to individuation by making them more conscious of the archetypal patterns that were influencing their poor decisions and unmanageable relationships. In a similar spirit Kabat-Zinn (2009) affirms: "[Mindfulness] is a systematic approach to developing new kinds of control and wisdom in our lives, based on our inner capacities for relaxation, paying attention, and insight" (p. 2). The benefits of mindfulness practice extend from the original work with chronic pain sufferers (Kabat-Zinn 2009; Young 2004) to preventing relapse in the treatment of

Burma, the Southeast Asian country where some of the most prominent teachers of mindfulness in the West—Jack Kornfield (2008) and S. R. Goenka—received their original instruction.

11. Though Buddhism does not refer to a deity, the potential analogies between "Buddhahood" and "soul-knowing" are evident. Both refer to our innate capacity to access inner wisdom, what Ann Ulanov refers to in this volume as "the well" (Ch. 16).

12. Wallace (2009) cites 1 Corinthians 15:54: "Death is swallowed up in victory."

depression (Segal et al., 2002) to treating anxiety (Orsillo & Roemer, 2008), to treating obsessive-compulsive symptoms (Hershfield & Corboy, 2013), to addressing relational difficulties (Ross & Doering, 2014), to cultivating self-compassion (Germer, 2009) and fostering the therapeutic relationship (Hick & Bien, 2008). The healing power of mindfulness encourages pastoral counselors to develop this capacity in themselves and those they counsel.

Practicing Mindfulness

What are the active components of mindfulness, and how are they developed? In *Five Ways to Know Yourself* Shinzen Young (2011), a sensory phenomenologist and the developer of Basic Mindfulness, describes three attentional skills that inform the practice of mindfulness: *concentrative power, sensory clarity, and equanimity.*

- *Concentrative Power* is your ability to focus on what you want when you want. Gently holding an intention lies at the core of the attentional skill of concentration. It is the ability to focus, and remain focused, on what is held to be relevant.

- *Sensory Clarity* is your ability to untangle the elements of sensory events as they occur in your awareness, an attentional skill that traces, tracks, and monitors just *what* is being experienced in the moment.

- *Equanimity* is your ability to let experience come and go without pushing away (aversion) or pulling toward (clinging): aversion and clinging are the two "poisons" that Buddhism regards along with confusion or ignorance to be the root cause of all suffering. The core ingredient of equanimity, and of remaining in that state, is the ability to stay present to the flow of experience even as that experience changes. In Buddhism impermanence is one of the hallmarks of existence and its simple acceptance a gateway to nirvana. Nirvana, in Buddhist practice, is a state of awakening between existence and nonexistence, made possible by such freedom from clinging, aversion, and confusion that no fuel for rebirth remains.

Concentrative power and sensory clarity enable one to receive the full sensory richness of the experience—*whatever it is.* Development of equanimity provides freedom from the internal struggle to control, facilitating rest and relaxation. With concentrative power, attention becomes sustained, both *within* and *between* experiences. The three skills together produce *presence,* to one's own experience, and to another's: the starting point of sensitivity and emotional attunement that are the foundation for effective counseling: "Presence is where we meet others and mindfulness is a powerful means for constructing that house of presence" (Ross & Doering, 2014, p. 93).

Buddhist mindfulness meditation is often associated with sustained, nonevaluative attention to the breath as it moves in and out of the body. This very specific method, however, may be attractive to some individuals (kinesthetic learners) but not to others. The value of the Basic Mindfulness approach of Shinzen Young is the variety of ways through which mindfulness may be developed for Western care providers and careseekers.

Three basic strategies are used to train attention: *noting, "do nothing,"* and *"nurture positive."*

- *Noting* involves tracking sensory events over time, either with or without the help of mental labels for the kind of experience that is in awareness.

- *Do nothing* involves dropping any intention at all, releasing the individual from the need to control what is experienced in any way at all, also known as "open presence" (Nyoshul Khenpo & Surya Das, 1995).[13]

- *Nurture positive* involves intentionally holding mental images, mental talk, or pleasant emotional body sensations. *Metta*—sending love and compassion to others—is the most common form of this strategy and corresponds closely to forms of Western Christian intercessory prayer.

Young distinguishes three sensory arenas—hearing, seeing, and body sense (see Fig. 6.1)—in which each of the three attentional skills may be developed, and each sensory mode has an internal and external focus:

- *Visual experiences* includes (1) ordinary vision (regular external sights), and (2) internal vision (images—i.e., nonverbal thinking).

- *Auditory experiences* include (1) external hearing, and (2) internal self-talk (verbal thinking)

- *Somatic experiences* include (1) ordinary physical body sensations, and (2) emotionally tinged body sensations.

Each of these six modalities of experience are experienced in four different forms, and are each the focus for training concentrative power, sensory clarity, and equanimity:

13. The Quaker practice of centering prayer is similar, with the exception that one is to remain open to the leadings of the Holy Spirit that may rise into consciousness as the directed attention of the ego falls away.

- *Focus In*: Internally arising experiences are chosen as the focus of attention, including thoughts (mental images in the visual mode and mental talk in the auditory one) and emotionally tinged body sensations.

- *Focus Out*: Ordinary physical aspects of the external world are the focus of attention (sights, sounds, and physical body sensations).

- *Focus on Rest*: The restful aspects of the three sensory modes constitute the focus of attention: relaxation in the body, quietness in the hearing mode (internal as well as external), and in the visual mode internally as the "blank screen" encountered when the eyes are closed, or in the "soft focus" of the external sight when there is no fixed object of attention.

- *Focus on Flow*: With increased sensory clarity, subtle fluctuations within sensory experiences may be noted so the field of awareness is experienced as forever changing and dynamic.

Figure 6.1. Grid for Noting Sensory Experiences[14]

	In (Subjective Experience)	Out (Objective Experience)	Rest (Restful Experience)	Flow (Sensory Fluctuation)
Visual experience	Mental images	Physical sights	Visual rest (blank screen or soft focus)	Fluctuating visual experiences
Label: SEE	Label: "See in"	Label: "See out"	Label: "See rest"	Label: "See flow"
Auditory experience	Mental talk "hearing yourself think"	Physical sounds	Auditory rest (mental quiet or no audible sounds)	Fluctuating auditory experiences
Label: HEAR	Label: "Hear in"	Label: "Hear out"	Label: "Hear rest"	Label: "Hear flow"
Somatic experience	Emtional body sensations	Physical body sensations.	Somatic rest (relaxation or tranquility)	Fluctuating somatic experiences
Label: FEEL	Label: "Feel in"	Label: "Feel out"	Label: "Feel rest"	Label: "Feel flow"

14. © Shinzen Young. Taken from Young (2011), ch. 9. In this grid, each cell describes a category of sensory experience (e.g., "mental image"). The two-word phrases in quotes are the labels spoken silently as an optional aid to the more basic of "noting" experiences that are relevant to the chosen focus category (e.g., "See in").

To develop mindfulness, one needs simply to select one or more of these foci for a limited amount of time (a minimum of five minutes, and a maximum of twenty minutes at the beginning), deliberately noting what arises moment by moment in the chosen area of focus. When an experience arises that is not in your chosen focus area, for example a pain in the leg when your focus is on mental images, simply treat the pain with equanimity (let the sensation come and go) and return attention to the internal visual mode, staying vigilant for either images or rest from those internal images.

When beginning a mindfulness practice in this way it is useful for the development of sensory clarity to employ one of the two-word verbal labels found in each row of Fig. 6.1, depending on what comes into consciousness during the sensory event that one is focusing upon. This label can be a silent repetition or spoken out loud for even clearer feedback in the early stages of training, or when you are sleepy or fatigued. For instance if internal vision is the focus, when aware of an image, vocalize or subvocalize "See-in." When the image fades, "See-rest." Or "See-flow" when change is registered in the image, or when subtle change is noted within the visual rest state. When meditating using body awareness as the focus, note "Feel-out" for purely physical bodily sensations (including awareness of the breath) and the absence of such sensations as "Feel-rest"; emotion related bodily sensations are noted as "Feel-in."

The chosen area for focus may vary from session to session, depending on personal preference at the time and circumstances. For example if you live on a busy street, then choosing "hear out" as your focus might be adaptive, since cars sounds would no longer be distractions but opportunities for mindful attention! At other times or in other settings you may choose to focus on internal sounds: one's self-talk (and note "Hear in") or their absence (as "Hear rest"). After a while, when the practice is established, you can try a "Focus-out" practice when walking to work or for recreation, and note the sights and sounds, subvocalizing the labels "See-out" and "Hear-out," respectively.[15]

The natural tendency is for experience to change, including what humans evaluate as "good" and "bad" or as "not-so-good" experiences. Often it is the fear of negative experiences that leads to suffering and to individuals seeking help from a professional care provider. A mindfulness practice, while straightforward in its instructions, requires patience and support, especially at first. Pastoral counselors who would like to use this resource with others are advised to try it. A natural confidence flows from the instruction

15. "Focus out" serves as a walking meditation, deliberately remaining present in the present moment. Persons who find it difficult to pray or "center down" sitting still may find this practice particularly useful.

when counselors have experienced the benefits themselves, including the fading of "negative experience" as the attentional skill of equanimity is strengthened.

The methods of the Basic Mindfulness approach, comparable in some respects to the structured approach of Dialectical Behavior Therapy (DBT), are particularly useful for persons struggling with negative emotions.[16] Each method has a role in the development of emotional regulation. Mindfulness practice can be started within the counseling session and fairly quickly assigned as homework between sessions once the benefit has been experienced.

Here is an account of a counselor whose client struggles with depression and anger. Note the therapist tracking self-awareness as he attends to his experience of the client in the intersubjective field.

Mindfulness in Action[17]

In his first session David's downturned face and rumpled clothes suggested someone unhappy, neglecting himself. Not looking at me, he said that he had called in sick to work. He had "had it" with his colleagues and clients.

I felt myself tighten inside. Moments later I remembered to breathe, and recalled the "Feel-in" of Shinzen Young's instructions from a mindfulness retreat I had attended: "Notice body sensations that have an emotional tinge." Perhaps David heard my relaxed exhalation; as I fixed my eyes on the same part of the carpet that seemed to absorb his gaze, he abruptly raised his head. His face slackened and tears sobbed out. At forty-two he said he had just "run out of juice." I felt heaviness in my body, and a knot in my stomach. Then I realized that I was tracking my inner speech: "What had I to work with?"(noting verbal thoughts with the "Hear-in" label). With this awareness and with my eye on the clock behind his chair, I asked "Are there any *resources* you have?" He muttered: "My wife loves me but I don't know why. I've been miserable to live with ever since my father died last summer." "I don't know why" he repeated, "It's not as if we ever got on after he remarried, to that girl, while I was still in my teens!"

16. DBT was developed by Marsha Linehan, a psychologist originally diagnosed with Borderline Personality Disorder who developed this approach to support those needing skills to manage affect regulation and impulsivity (Linehan, 1993; Linehan & Dimeff, 2001).

17. This case vignette is based on an account from Robert Doering, a psychologist in private practice (see mindfulwaterloo.org/).

I felt some relief. Once I had reviewed the highs and lows of his adult life and his answers to some family-of-origin questions, I thought I could rule out a major depressive disorder.

At the end of the hour he added, "Oh! A friend told me about meditation last summer just before Dad died and I tried it and liked what it did for me. But then I just got bored with it—always focusing on the breath."

"Let's talk more about that next Wednesday then," I suggested.

By session 4, having discussed early losses and some parallels in this, his midlife passage, he confessed with a sheepish smile: "I'm feeling better!" So I thought he might now be able to consolidate some of his gains with an orientation to Basic Mindfulness. I downloaded a copy of *Five Ways to Know Yourself* (Young, 2011), and we went over some pages I had highlighted.

He showed surprising enthusiasm: "Oh great! There's some choice over what I have to meditate on. And it's really effective according to some of the studies I looked up on the web."

In David's fifth session we practiced "Focus on Rest" in the body (e.g. relaxation in the limbs), in image-space (the blank screen when eyes are closed), and in talk-space (the quietening of self-talk by noting "Hear-in"). We also covered "Focus out" in the office with both of us noting sights and sounds using spoken labels as they occurred to us, and then David alone, and then silently. At our next meeting David said he really enjoyed going out to the park each morning and practicing Focus-out. In June a local colleague offered an eight-week Basic Mindfulness training. David and his wife completed the course. I met with him monthly over the summer. A one-year follow-up visit from them both revealed that David had returned to work at his company, and that both felt better about their relationship.

Conclusion: Common Ground

Self-awareness on the part of the counselor is a necessary component of effective therapy. Understanding aspects of one's own perception, with an acquired awareness that others experience the world differently, makes it possible to remain open and responsive to the varying attunement needs of clients. Just as a teacher must read ahead of her students to effectively communicate new material, so a therapist will ideally have traveled further along on the path of individuation than the persons who come for care. Through the quality of self-awareness and the capacity for personal growth that individuation entails, both analyst and analysand will find themselves better equipped to discover meaning and purpose in life.

The redemptive work of pastoral psychotherapy includes healing from past hurts and finding rest in the present moment. At the heart of both Jungian analytical psychology and Buddhist mindfulness practices lies a deep optimism concerning the capacity of human beings to heal, given time and attention to what matters, to what has meaning. Both approaches to healing focus significantly upon suffering; their relevance for the twenty-first century relates to the transforming power of focusing courageously on what ails us. Pastoral counselors may draw on these resources both for themselves and for those for whom they care.

References

Atwood, G. E., & Stolorow, R. D. (1984). *Structures of subjectivity: Explorations in psychoanalytic phenomenology.* Psychanalytic Inquiry Book Series 4. Hillsdale, NJ: Analytic.

Atwood, G. E., & Stolorow, R. E. (1993). *Faces in a cloud: Intersubjectivity in personality theory.* Northvale, NJ: Aronson.

Beebe, J. (2004). Understanding consciousness through the theory of psychological types. In J. Cambray & L. Carter, (Eds.)., *Analytical psychology: Contemporary perspectives in Jungian analysis* (pp. 83–115). Advancing Theory in Therapy. New York: Brunner-Routledge.

Brooke, R. (2015). *Jung and phenomenology.* Routledge mental health classics editions. New York, NY: Routledge, Taylor & Francis.

Buechner, F. (1990). *Wishful thinking: A theological ABC.* San Francisco: Harper & Row.

Burger, J. M. (2011). *Personality* (8th ed.). Belmont, CA: Wadsworth.

Cooper-White, P. (2015). The power that beautifies and destroys: Sabina Spielrein and "Destruction as a cause of coming into being," *Pastoral Psychology, 64* (2)259–78.

Crain, W. C. (2000). *Theories of development: Concepts and applications,* (4th ed.). Upper Saddle River, NJ: Prentice Hall.

Davis, D. M., & Hayes, J. A. (2012). What are the benefits of mindfulness? *Psychology Monitor, 43*(6)64–67.

Dhammika, S. (2014) What is the First Noble Truth? *Good Questions, Good Answers* with Ven. S. Dhammika, http://www.buddhanet.net/ans16.htm/.

Ellenberger, H. F. (1970). *The discovery of the unconscious.* New York: Basic Books.

Freud, S. (1923). The ego and the id. In J. Strachey (Ed.) *The Standard Edition of the Complete Psychological Works of Sigmund Freud, Vol. 19.* London: Hogarth, 1962.

Fuller, R. C. (2001). *Spiritual but not religious: Understanding unchurched America.* New York: Oxford University Press.

Germer, C. K. (2009). *The mindful path to self-compassion: Freeing yourself from destructive thoughts and emotions* New York: Guilford.

Hershfield, J., & Corboy, T. (2013). *The mindfulness workbook for OCD: A guide to overcoming obsessions and compulsions using mindfulness and cognitive behavioral therapy.* New Harbinger Self-Help Workbook. Oakland, CA: New Harbinger.

Hick, S. F., & Bien T. (2008). *Mindfulness and the therapeutic relationship.* New York: Guilford.

Hollis, J. (2000). *Creating a life: Finding your individual path.* Studies in Jungian Psychology by Jungian Analysts. Toronto: Inner City Books.

Jung, C. G. (1953–1979). *The collected works of C. G. Jung* (20 volumes). R. F. C. Hull (Ed.). Princeton: Princeton University Press. (Hereafter *CW*).

Jung, C. G. (1954). Analytical psychology and education. In *The development of personality, CW 17,* pp. 63–164. (Orig. publ. 1926).

Jung, C. G. (1968). *Aion: Researches into the phenomenology of the self. CW 9 part 2.* (Orig. publ. 1951).

Jung, C. G. (1969). On the nature of the psyche. In *The structure and dynamics of the psyche, CW 8,* pp. 159–234. (Orig. publ. 1946).

Jung, C. G. (1971). *Psychological Types. CW 6.* (Orig. publ. 1921).

Jung, C. G. (1989). *Memories, dreams, reflections.* A. Jaffé (Ed.), R. Winston & C. Winston (Trans.). New York: Vintage. (Orig. publ. 1961).

Jung, C.G., Shandasani, S. & Hoerni , U. (2009). *The red book = Liber novus: a reader's edition,* by C. G. Jung. Philemon Series. New York: Norton.

Kabat-Zinn, J. (2009). *Full catastrophe living: Using the wisdom of your body to face stress, pain, and illness.* New York: Random House.

Kelcourse, F. B. (2015a). Sabina Spielrein from Rostov to Zurich. *Pastoral Psychology, 64,* 241–58.

Kelcourse, F. B. (Ed.). (2015b). *Human development and faith: Life-cycle stages of body, mind, and soul.* (2nd ed.). St. Louis: Chalice.

Keirsey, D. (1998). *Please understand me II: Temperament, character, intelligence.* Del Mar, CA: Prometheus Nemesis.

Kornfield, J (2008*). Meditation for beginners.* Boulder, CO: Sounds True.

Linehan, M. (1993). *Skills training manual for treating borderline personality disorder.* Diagnosis and Treatment of Mental Disorders. New York: Guilford.

Linehan, M. M., & Dimeff, L. (2001). Dialectical behavior therapy in a nutshell, *California Psychologist, 34,* 10–13.

Myers, I. B., & McCaulley, M. H. (1985). *Manual: A guide to the development and use of the Myers-Briggs Type Indicator.* Palo Alto, CA: Consulting Psychologists Press.

Myers, I. B., & Myers, P. B. (1995). *Gifts differing: Understanding personality type.* Mountain View, CA: Davis-Black.

Nhat Hanh, Thich. (1999). *Going home: Jesus and Buddha as brothers.* New York: Riverhead.

Noth, I. (2014). "Beyond Freud and Jung": Sabina Spielrein's contribution to child psychoanalysis and developmental psychology. *Pastoral Psychology, 64,* 270–86.

Nyoshul Khenpo, & Surya Das (1995). *Natural great perfection.* Ithaca: Snow Lion.

Orange, D. M. et al. (2001). *Working intersubjectively: contextualism in psychoanalytic practice.* Psychoanalytic Inquiry Book Series 17. Hillsdale, NJ: Analytic.

Orsillo, S. M., & Roemer, L. (2011). *The mindful way through anxiety.* New York: Guilford.

Ross, C. F. J. (2011). Jungian typology and religion: A perspective from North America. *Research in the Social Scientific Study of Religion, 22,* 165–91.

Ross, C. F. J., & Doering, R. (2014). Buddhism, healing and pastoral care. In T. S. O'Connor et al. (Eds.). *Psychotherapy: Cure of the soul; A collection of papers from the Society for Pastoral Counselling Research 2013 Annual Conference* (pp. 83–96). Waterloo, ON: Waterloo Lutheran Seminary.

Saunders, F. W. (1991). *Katharine and Isabel: Mother's light, daughter's journey.* Palo Alto, CA: Consulting Psychologists Press.

Segal, Z. V. et al. (2002). *Mindfulness-based cognitive therapy for depression.* New York: Guilford.

Stein, M. (1998). *Jung's map of the soul: An introduction.* Chicago: Open Court.

Stein, M. (2005). Individuation: Inner work. *Journal of Jungian theory and practice* 7(2).

Stein, M. (2014). *Minding the self: Jungian mediations on contemporary spirituality.* New York: Routledge.

Ulanov, A. B. (2000). *The wisdom of the psyche.* Einsiedeln, Switzerland: Daimon.

Ulanov, A., & Ulanov, B. (1994). *Transforming sexuality: The archetypal world of anima and animus.* Boston: Shambala.

Ulanov, A. B., & Dueck, A. (2008). *The living God and our living psyche: What Christians can learn from Carl Jung.* Grand Rapids: Eerdmans.

Wallace, B. A. (2009). *Mind in the balance: Meditation in science, Buddhism, and Christianity.* The Columbia Series in Science and Religion. New York: Columbia University Press.

Wesley, J. (2007). *A plain account of Christian perfection.* Hendrickson Christian Classics. Peabody, MA: Hendrickson.

Young, S. (2011). *Natural pain relief: How to soothe and dissolve physical pain with mindfulness.* Boulder, CO: Sounds True.

Young, S. (2011). *Five ways to know yourself: An introduction to basic mindfulness.* Chapter 9, The Full Grid, p. 103, http://www.shinzen.org/Retreat%20Reading/FiveWays.pdf-1.59/ (created: 3/11/2011).

----------- 7 -----------

Assessing Faith:
Beneficent vs. Toxic Spirituality

Matthias Beier

The mind is its own place, and in itself
Can make a Heav'n of Hell, a Hell of Heav'n.

—John Milton (2005),
Paradise Lost, Book I, pp. 254–55

The Church in the colonies is a white man's Church, a foreigners'
Church. It does not call the colonized to the ways of God, but to
the ways of the white man, to the ways of the master, the ways of
the oppressor.

—Frantz Fanon (2004), *The Wretched of the Earth*, p. 7

FAITH CAN HEAL OR harm, set free or oppress, propel to peace or incite to
war. This chapter argues that the primary criterion for assessing faith is
whether it builds trust or spreads fear in the existential human search for
love and justice. Simple as this may sound, it is important to consider the
particular nature of this trust or this fear, toward self or other. Consider
Anne,[1] a black Jamaican American patient studying for the ministry

---

1. To protect the identity of the patient, this example from psychotherapeutic work
has been disguised. The author has written permission from the patient to share the

in New York City, who shared the following dream in the third year of
weekly spiritually integrated, psychoanalytic psychotherapy sessions as
she sought to overcome feelings of depression: *I was in the basement, it
was golden color and bright. I walked with my father up the stairs which
were blue. On top of the stairs, I am ahead of him and face him. I feel the
inclination to push him just a little bit so that he falls down the stairs. But
I am afraid to do it, because it could also kill him. Instead I tell him that I
don't like that he wants me to do things that he really should take care of
himself. What was strange was that my father didn't look like my father. He
was a white man with a white beard. Then we go into the kitchen which
feels warm and I like it. There are so many other people and voices. And
then my father takes out a roast from the oven.*

Over the course of several sessions, Anne found in the dream expressions of faith which harmed or healed, isolated or connected, destroyed or
liberated her. The dream and the cocreated meaning of it in our therapeutic
encounter will provide a concrete, experiential backdrop for the theoretical
distinctions of beneficent versus toxic faith presented in this chapter. Following the presentation of short key therapeutic dialogues on the dream, I
will review and assess three common frameworks used today to differenti-
ate beneficent from toxic forms of faith and then present an alternative approach aiming to do better justice to the subjective dimension so essential to
faith. We will see that the very question of what faith is needs to be explored
for any assessment of the benefit or toxicity of spirituality to be possible.

Dreams, Faith, Identity, and Culture

Anne (A) and I (T) explored the meaning of her dream over several sessions. What follows is a composite of selected key portions of that therapeutic dialogue.

A1: It was so strange: I thought also of God as my father in the dream,
like the blue is like heaven [she laughs]. But it surprised me because I did
not think of God in the male gender. I don't know what to make of it. But I
have been angry at God, as you know.

T1: Your father is also white in the dream. What do you make of that?

A2: Yes [smiles], I said I did not think of God as male but I did not pick
up on 'him' being white.

T2: There is a racial dimension to the dream?

material. The case has been previously and differently disguised in Beier (2010).

A3: Yes, I think so. I had not thought of this. I think it had to do with the two clergy supervisors this year telling me what voice to have. They were both white.

T3: Did one of them have a beard?

A4: Yes [smiles], you are very perceptive. [pause] well, that's actually how I thought of God growing up. My father grew up in a different time than I did, when Jamaica was still under British rule. What he said was the law. I remember that at age 8 or 9 I thought that it was strange that the big Jesus figure in the stained glass window of our church was white. My father's God was naturally white. Wow, I never thought of that. He was trapped in this mindset just like me.

T4: Perhaps that is why you wanted to push your father down the stairs but also not?

A5: True! I think that's also what makes it difficult to study for the ministry, because there is this underlying sense that in order for me to be myself I have to come out of the basement. But then what am I going to do?
. . .

T5: What did you think your father should take care of?

A6: I really don't know. [pause] Maybe take care of his white God? [pause] Like 'roast it.' [we both laugh loudly].

T6: Roast it?

A7: Yeah, be real, don't hide behind the white God who ultimately keeps us in the basement, but have a God who is proud in me. [A tears up]

T7: Proud in you! [pause] Does this dream also say something about the dynamic between you and me in our work here?

A8: [pause] I think so. It feels here a bit like in that kitchen, warm and I like it. I guess I have liked coming out of the basement here, but now what?

T8: Are you thinking of pushing me down the stairs?

A9: No. [pause] Well, maybe yes. Because this is really intense work, and I think about stopping, maybe that has to do with it.

T9: Does my being white[2] have to do with it?

A10: Maybe. I am afraid that if I talk about race here, that I'll have to take care of your feelings, but that you should take care of it yourself. It seems irrational, because you have not given me that feeling that you can't take care of yourself. But I am afraid, because in other contexts when we talk about race and God, it seems as if I am expected to make white people feel good about their guilt.

T10: Are those the other people and voices in the kitchen?

2. Anne had previously referred to me as white. At the time, I did not question that label through self-disclosure of my own Turkish German ethnic background, staying instead with her subjective transference associations around my ethnic-racial identity.

A11: Yes, it's hard to get my own piece of meat with all these people around.

T11: How do you mean that?

A12: To have my own spirit nurtured? [tears up] And to be close to my father in a way that he can let me be the strong person I am without either of us pushing the other down.

T12: That would be heaven? [we both are moved to tears]

A13: Yeah, I guess that would be it. [pause] And I guess the same is true here. Yes, you're white and I am black. But I wish that that would not matter. Because does it really matter before God? It doesn't. But it's so hard.

T13: Well, maybe you do want to push your father, me, God – or whoever is 'on top' down from their top place because they are 'white' or 'white-minded'. But you say you are afraid you'll kill them in the dream.

A14: Yeah, nothing is gained by killing them.

T14: But maybe something is gained by you feeling how enraged you are that you were not allowed to feel you could be on the top, because of race, but also because of being a woman? [she had talked about conflicts with her father around gender previously and about seeing God as female].

A15: Yes. This is the first time I've ever allowed myself to admit all of this to myself. I never thought I would actually say these things.

T15: You thought about them sometimes?

A16: Yes, but I would suppress it. Because I was taught that 'evil thoughts' are just as bad as 'evil actions', because thinking about pushing my father down in the dream would be considered 'evil'. I'd never do it in reality.

T16: How do you feel now that you have spoken them?

A17: Actually, I feel relieved. I feel some kind of strength.

Common Frameworks for Assessing Faith

How might three common approaches to assessing faith appraise healing or harmful effects of faith in Anne's case? Our review will be guided by three questions: How does the approach define faith? How does the approach assess benefit or toxicity of faith? What are the strengths and the weaknesses of the approach? The three approaches are the paradigm of integrated versus disintegrated spirituality, by Pargament; a postmodern pastoral psychotherapeutic approach, exemplified by Cooper-White; and research on the religion/spirituality-mental/health relationship, represented particularly by Koenig and associates. Two other approaches that go beyond this chapter deserve mention: the study of attachment theory and God-images and a postcolonial theological assessment of faith. While I am appreciative of the contribution each approach makes to the study of the health or harm of uses of faith, I will argue that each is limited by the fact that it defines faith or spirituality basically in ideational (content), voluntaristic (moral), or behavioral (action) terms. The alternative, fourth approach developed here defines *faith* and *spirituality* instead in terms of the particular vicissitudes of human existential self-consciousness (spirit) about one's somebodiness or nobodiness within relationships: that is, not so much in terms of what we *think, want,* or *do* but more in terms of who we *are.*

Integrated vs. Disintegrated Spirituality/Faith (Pargament)

Kenneth Pargament (1997, 2007) is one of today's foremost clinician-researchers on the role of religion, faith, or spirituality[3] in psychotherapy, providing tools for implicit and explicit spiritual assessments (Pargament, 2007). He argues that religion helps us cope with the limitations of personal control over life, and, ultimately, with the fact of our finitude (Pargament, 1997), and defines it as a "search for significance in ways related to the sacred" (p. 32). Rooted firmly in the pragmatic tradition of William James, Pargament (1997) frames the question of health or harm of faith in terms of functionality: "Does it work?" (pp. 275–314). He answers that it works more often than not. Cognizant that faith can have helpful or harmful results, Pargament (1997) holds that harmful faith stems from problems in integration of the different parts that make up faith or spirituality. Spirituality as the search for the sacred occurs through processes of discovery, conservation, and transformation, which, in turn, involve spiritual pathways (means) and spiritual destinations (ends). Spiritual pathways are ways of feeling, thinking, acting, and relating in the search for the sacred, while spiritual destinations can be divided into a sacred core (God, divine beings, or a transcendent reality) and a sacred ring. A sacred ring encompasses "objects" sanctified through the "sacred qualities" of transcendence, boundlessness, and ultimacy. These objects are thought to be manifestations of the sacred core. They can be religious figures (e.g., Brahman or Jesus), the self, the relational, a place or a time, or possibly any other part of life that becomes sanctified. Healthy spirituality integrates spiritual pathways

3. While Pargament defines "religion" in his first book (1997, p. 4) intentionally broadly, including personal as well as institutional expressions, in his second book (2007, p. 32) he attempts to confine "'religion' or 'religiousness'" to refer to the larger social, institutional, and cultural context of spirituality." But even in his second book he can refer on a single page to "spirituality," "faith," and "religion" in very much the same way, as a way of coping. I will follow this interchangeable use here.

and destinations well, while harmful spirituality leads to a dis-integration between pathways and destinations.

> At its best, spirituality is defined by pathways that are broad and deep, responsive to life's situations, nurtured by the larger social context, capable of flexibility and continuity, and oriented toward a sacred destination that is large enough to encompass the full range of human potential and luminous enough to provide the individual with a powerful guiding vision. At its worst, spirituality is dis-integrated, defined by pathways that lack scope and depth, fail to meet the challenges and demands of life events, clash and collide with the surrounding social system, change and shift too easily or not at all, and misdirect the individual in the pursuit of spiritual value. (Pargament, 2007, p. 136)

The problem can lie either with destinations or with pathways. For instance, Pargament might say that Anne is struggling to disidentify with a "false god" (destination) of colonialism unmasked in the dream as preventing her from emerging as a self and being close to her father in a sacred way; or she might seek to overcome "sacred clashes within" where self and God are pitted against each other mercilessly, or where God or self can be seen in contradictory ways as at various times loving, punitive, detached, or demonic. In Pargament's (2007) model, Anne would be going through "spiritual disorientation," and the dream would show that she is coping with it through a "transformation" of the sacred because old pathways to and understandings of the sacred "are no longer compelling" (p. 112). Specifically, Anne would be seen as "revisioning the sacred" from a (neo)colonial oppressor "white God" who alienates her from herself and her father to a God who is not oppressive but supports her true self, voice, and close relationships.

The strength of this approach lies in its utility to analyze whether the concrete expressions of our faith line up with what we are actually spiritually seeking. However, one of Pargament's criteria for "dis-integrated" forms of spirituality is that they "clash and collide with the surrounding social system." Is the clash of Anne's internalized, oppressive God-image "harmful" to her? Taking into account oppressive realities of social systems, it would be more accurate to say that the disintegration of this God-image could lead either to healing or harm. This points to a key limitation in Pargament's functional, pragmatic criterion for the health of faith: while faith may help a person "function" well both personally and socially, it may nonetheless be harmful to the person because it alienates one from oneself. What is required is a criterion less concerned with balancing means and ends and more concerned with who one is as a human being.

A Postmodern Pastoral Psychotherapy
Perspective (Cooper-White)

Pamela Cooper-White (2004; 2007) sees faith as enabling humans to live in "fluid" "multiplicity," both internally and externally, where each person's "many self-states" as well as relational experiences are experienced without "splitting" them off. She is sensitive to the misuses of diagnostic criteria for "health and unhealth" "to impose political and social conformity" (2007, pp. vii, 97). Psychoanalytically, she suggests that "splitting is the hallmark of all psychospiritual unhealth" (2007, p. 95). "Unhealthy splitting" can take neurotic, borderline, or psychotic forms and breaks down "one's sense of self-cohesion" and capacity to relate (2007, pp. 95, 99–110). Cooper-White (2007) discusses unhealthy splitting within two classic moral-theological frameworks of "good" and "evil" in terms of "sin" (pp. 117–32; 2011, pp. 171–94): evil as lack of the good, as negative, as *privatio boni*; and evil as a force, as positive, as an ontological reality.

Evil as lack of the good is the Augustinian view that evil is lack of sufficient desire of "God" and "God's perfection"; the result is "delusory self-reliance" (Cooper-White, 2007, p. 122). One's conscious will is split into wanting to be "good" and failing to be so (Romans 7:15, 19); usually, the failure is kept out of awareness. Kohut's (1979) self psychological model of a vertical split in consciousness helps Cooper-White understand the lack of desire for the good as resulting from sense of emptiness, of "I *am* bad," due to early deprivations in mirroring by significant caregivers. This sense is defended against by compensatory archaic narcissistic inflation of the self trying to "play the role of God" instead of relying on God for growing a self.[4] The strength of this model is that it provides an empathic psycho-theological understanding of faith used for harm due to unmet legitimate narcissistic needs in those seen as "perpetrator[s]" (Cooper-White, 2007, p. 127). The second view—evil as ontological force—is dualistic and sees an active force of evil being, opposite a force of good being (Cooper-White, 2007, p. 124). Here evil, though not declared a metaphysical 'devil,' is seen as "relational and positively real" [5] and located, for instance, in traumatic, dis-empowering experiences based on gender or race resulting from systemic injustices "institutionalized in the social, political, and economic realm," (Cooper-White, 2007, p. 127). Psychologically, Cooper-White (2007) turns to an object-relations model of projective and dissociative mechanisms to

4. Schlesinger, paraphrasing Reinhold Niebuhr, as cited in Cooper-White (2007, p. 118, 121).

5. Nel Noddings, cited in Cooper-White (2007, p. 126).

understand how trauma unconsciously inserts "active, persecutory 'objects' into the child's inner landscape" (p. 128). Since a person's survival often depends on the traumatizing external figures, those objects are experienced as both "good" and "bad," and the self is correspondingly split into good and bad. Through projective identification the traumatized person may subsequently play out either the victim or the perpetrator role of the original traumatizing relationship, often in the name of rooting out evil (Cooper-White, 2007, p. 128). The strength of this approach is that it takes seriously the institutional, systemic effects of oppressive structures; avoids an individualistic perspective that blames victims; and helps explain how internalized oppressive dynamics may inadvertently turn victims into perpetrators.

The "systemic evil" (Cooper-White, 2007, p. 129) of the colonial past represented in Anne's dream and associations suggests, using Cooper-White's model, that the unhealth of faith expressed in a partly oppressive God-image is the result of an unconscious, traumatic experience of active evil. Applying an object-relations reading to Anne's dream yields the insight that Anne's sense of her father as "a white man" in the dream represents the father's inherited colonial "white" God-image, which, according to Anne, has kept him from being real and from standing up for being black. At the same time, the white God-image keeps Anne from connecting both with herself as a black woman and with her father as a black man who would be proud of her for who she is. In the projective identification dynamic, Anne wants to push her father down and (in the transference) wants to push the therapist down, just as the oppressor pushed her down. However, expressing her destructive impulses and thoughts in words through the dream and its exploration in the safe therapeutic space mitigates her fear of these impulses and thoughts, and allows her to no longer fear these "evil thoughts" in paranoid-schizoid fashion to be as bad as if they were "evil actions."

Although Cooper-White's model of assessment of the health or unhealth of faith uses psychological categories that attempt to overcome splitting and moralism, it inadvertently reintroduces moralism *theologically* by applying moral categories of good and evil to human will and desire in relation to God. By applying, within a voluntaristic model focused around free will and sin, categories of good and evil to the assessment of the health or unhealth of faith, Cooper-White's model, without intending to, tends to moralizes it. In the *privatio boni* model, humans are judged for something they are thought to be incapable of as finite beings: to love God, who is seen as an Augustinian meganarcissist, perfectly. Eventually, the best humans can do is to admit failure by relinquishing "the possibility of perfection" and, as in Klein's "depressive position," accept the "seeming inextricability of evil . . . this side of the eschaton" (Cooper-White, 2007, p. 132). In the trauma model, humans experience the effects of systemic evil, which they may unconsciously perpetuate through identifications. Theologically, Cooper-White's model tends to moralize unhealth as evil, either due to lack or trauma. While she declares that this is, tragically, unavoidable under finite conditions, we are, in view of the Protestant emphasis on free will, nonetheless responsible, and, in this life, rely on God's grace (Cooper-White, 2007, pp. 122–24, 130). As I will argue below, we should avoid the moralization of unhealth to begin with and should find a model that does not postpone a solution into an imaginary future beyond finitude. Rather we should see healthy faith as a function of balancing, without guilt feelings, the finite and the infinite dimension of life.

Research on the Relationship between Religion/ Spirituality and Mental/Health (Koenig, Levin, et al.)

Research on the "relationships between religion/spirituality (R/S)" and health or mental health (mental/health) has rapidly exploded in the first decade of the twenty-first century (Koenig, 2012, p. 460), as documented in a number of handbooks and monographs (Koenig, 1998; Koenig et al., 2001; Koenig, 2008; Koenig et al., 2012). This brief sketch of aspects of the field's assessment of beneficent or toxic faith will rely mainly on these overviews. The research really focuses only on *religion* and mental/health, since researchers typically define "spirituality" not in contrast to institutional religion, as common usage does today, but rather as faith by very devout religious people (Koenig et al., 2012, p. 46). Pargament's broadly encompassing term of "spirituality" differs from this. Koenig et al. recommend excluding from the definition of spirituality everything covered by secular humanism, such as search for meaning, generally profound experiences, or positive character traits. Koenig defines religion basically cognitively and behaviorally by operationalizing it "as a system of beliefs and practices observed by a community, supported by rituals" and focused on the transcendent (Koenig, 2008, p. 11).

R/S and mental/health researchers wonder how correlations between good health outcomes and religion may be explained. Levin and Chatters (1998, p. 34) suggest that religion uses "several salutogenic mechanisms or pathways" to benefit mental/health, which may include "health-related behavior, social support, positive emotions, health beliefs or personality styles, and optimism and hope." Basically these pathways are seen as protective factors mediating health effects. Levin and Chatters propose several models that could help explain how these "mediating factors" might buffer the experience of stress, thereby reducing the mental health effects of stressful situations. A religious coping strategy such as prayer, for instance, can be seen "as a palliative coping strategy" that would alter our threat perceptions and emotions and thus have an epidemiologically protective function against psychiatric disorders (Levin & Chatters, 1998, p. 46). The strength of this approach for assessing faith lies in its research-based evidence that religiousness often functions as a protective factor against behaviors that could put physical or mental health at risk.

When it comes to use of religion for harmful purposes, research suggests that "the content of one's faith" may determine its health or unhealth. For instance, a cross-sectional study showed that benevolent God-images were correlated with better mental health than punitive God-images, and that religious cults tend to have negative mental and physical health effects on members (Koenig et al., 2001, p. 70). While wondering how to account for "the dark side of religion," Koenig et al. entertain two possibilities: either "religious beliefs, attitudes, or practices" impair or worsen health (e.g., "by increasing guilt, causing rigid thinking, suppressing natural desires"). In that case, religion would make people sick. Or mentally or physically ill people gravitate toward religion when they become sick. In that case, sickness would lead to more religiousness (Koenig et al., 2012, p. 58). Koenig et al., however, tend to question findings that suggest that religion itself may have harmful impact, by suggesting, for instance, that a study's subjects were young and had not yet "developed a mature religious faith" (2012, p. 73), or by attributing unhealth to other factors than religion. The third possibility, which I present below, is that the human spirit's existential trust or fear determines whether expressions of religion promote harm or health.

Koenig cites studies that provide "evidence that mortality increases" if people hold certain religious beliefs. However, instead of stating outright that here religion may do harm, which would be equivalent to his clear statements on other occasions claiming that religion promotes health, Koenig (2012) says that in these cases people experience "religious or spiritual struggles," among which he includes, for example, "feeling punished by God or abandoned by their faith community" (p. 462). But these are not just subjective feelings. These struggles are inspired by religious traditions that present ideas of a punishing God, or a faith community that ostracizes. In instances like these, Koenig and others show bias and minimize the negative effects of religious ideas that God, the "Almighty," might punish one or that a faith community might abandon one.

A key argument of the R/S and mental/health research is that religion may have beneficial effect by helping believers turn negative experiences into positive ones by interpreting them as "directed by the divine." Religion

"imbues negative experiences with meaning and purpose and provides ex-
planations for these experiences" (Koenig et al., 2012, p. 92). Koenig speaks
personally about how this belief helps him cope with debilitating progressive arthritis that has bound him to a wheelchair for years. "I generally believe that God can and might someday heal my arthritis; but if he doesn't
do so here on earth, I believe that good can and will continue to result from
it. In addition to providing me understanding and empathy for others, that
purpose may include further building of my character or purifying of my
spirit" (Koenig & Lewis, 2004, p. 125).

The argument that something negative could be turned through religion into something positive lies also at the heart of Freud's classic notion
that religion is a "universal obsessional neurosis of humanity": religion turns
the negative experience of unpleasure from the renunciation of impulses
into religious obsessive ideas and symbols that alleviate the anxiety-driven
guilt feelings associated with the forbidden impulses (Freud, 1924/2001a,
pp. 43–44). Since religion is universal, Freud thought it actually contributed
in religious societies to mental health because the culturally "normal" neurosis of religion spared believers from developing their personal neuroses.
Furthermore, Freud thought that interpretations of events as the result of
divine action or of Destiny were similarly the result of unconscious sado-
masochistic maneuvers of a punitive superego (Freud, 2001, pp. 169–70).
R/S and mental/health research, however, does not consider these or more
current psychoanalytic notions of unconscious sado-masochistic dynamics
at play. In contrast, a nonsadomasochistic appraisal of negative experiences
through religion is found in the experience of oppressed people whose
belief lies not in God using negative experiences to create purpose in life
but rather in seeing God as stronger than death or oppression, which God
disempowers by the positive affirmation of the ultimate value of peoples'
lives (Cone, 2011).

If we apply R/S and mental/health research to the experience of Anne,
the primary question is how her religion as defined by Koenig and associates
influences her experience of her father, herself, and her physical and mental
health. Anne states that she has been angry at God. Koenig and associates
would consider this to be a "spiritual struggle" and would be concerned that
this could increase her risk of mortality. In line with the mostly individualistic perspective on the nature of such spiritual struggles, Koenig's approach
would suggest helping Anne to overcome the grudge she has with God and
find ways to make meaning even out of negative experiences she has had
growing up. Anne could use her realization that she has been shaped by an
oppressive God-image just as much as her father as an opportunity to feel
closer to her father. She could nurture her faith in a God who is "proud in

her" and who would help her see her suffering under colonialism as part of
God's purpose to provide her with an opportunity to build character. For instance, she could overcome her resistance to helping her father take care of
things that he wanted her to take care of by developing "positive emotions"
of gratefulness and generosity toward him for all the things he actually did
do for her, rather than dwell on things he did not do for her.

While R/S and mental/health research finds that religious beliefs and
practices have a largely positive influence on mental/health, the question
whether this is due to the mediating, nonreligious factors listed above or
due to something in faith itself remains open. I agree with Levin (2010) that
as long as research focuses mainly on "discrete religious behaviors" (p. 106),
such as participation in religious events, it is difficult to make sense either of
the "salutary influence of spirituality," (p. 104) or, I would add, of the toxic
effects of certain forms of spirituality. While Levin thinks that focus on subjective perceptions of union with the transcendent might be a fruitful venue
of study, my alternative approach below will argue that this focus remains
external to the human spirit in its outward focus (on the perceived outside
transcendent) rather than looking for something in the structure of the human spirit. To that end, we need to look at the self-reflective nature of our
consciousness, our spirit, to assess the beneficence or toxicity of spirituality.

An Alternative Approach Focused on Fear vs. Trust in Self-Reflective Human Consciousness (Kierkegaard, Drewermann, Beier)

The alternative approach developed here to distinguish between beneficent
and toxic faith finds the criterion not in how well spiritual pathways and
destinations fit pragmatically and ideationally together, as Pargament suggests; nor does it moralize the criterion by couching it in terms of good and
evil, with an undertone of tragically unreachable perfectionism, as Cooper-
White argues; nor, finally, can the criterion be found by measuring objective
behaviors and cognitive beliefs without regard to the self-reflective, highly
subjective aspect of human consciousness that determines what these mean
to each person, as the religion/spirituality and mental/health research of
Koenig and associates suggest.

Faith assessment should not begin with practical, moral, or cognitive-
behavioral dimensions that, in a way, view faith through an external lens,
but rather with a close look at the structure of the human psyche in view
of ultimate questions of meaning—that is, at the human spirit as a relational subject. Particular forms of faith or spirituality are then assessed as

expressions of particular forms of human subjectivity. Faith is then not something that comes from without (from traditions, rituals, beliefs) but something that springs from the human spirit. External artifacts of faiths (traditions, rituals, beliefs) are seen as collectively gathered and individually adapted expressions of the faith of the human spirit. I do not distinguish between *faith* and *spirituality* but use these terms interchangeably. Faith is spirituality because it expresses the human spirit's ultimate longings and the symbols responding to these longings, which are also born from the spirit, albeit on the basis of our common evolutionary psychological history and in specific cultural variations (Beier, 2004/2006, pp. 47–51). As a function of the human spirit, faith is open to effect either harm or healing depending on *the way* the spirit relates to itself and the transcendent in the face of existential fears due to death awareness.

Spirit as defined here is not something that falls from the sky (Beier, 2010). It is self-reflective consciousness and as such constitutes the capacity to infinitize (Kierkegaard, 1983, p. 30). In being aware of ourselves we are aware of our inevitable death, of our ultimate nothingness, which includes the death of our consciousness. At the same time, we are also aware of an infinite dimension of our self-consciousness that colors our deepest longings. Our self-awareness can be compared to two mirrors facing each other reflecting everything between them to infinite proportions, a notion neurologist and Nobel laureate Gerald Edelman conceptualizes as maps of neurons mirroring each other through interacting reentrant loops that create consciousness of consciousness in humans (Drewermann, 2007, pp. 532–35; Edelman & Tononi, 2000). It is this capacity that characterizes our spirit and opens up the dimension of the infinite and the ultimate to us. It is this capacity that lets us attach to the evolutionarily determined symbols of our psyche the infinite meanings of faith, making them archetypal religious symbols in C. G. Jung's sense. Hence a symbol such as a tree or the moon can be more than just a psychological symbol. We are able to "infinitize" anything inside or outside and in relation to us. This infinitizing quality is at the heart of religion and, philosophically speaking, is the condition for the possibility that we as humans are even able to conceive of God or the ultimate. Our self-reflective infinitizing function is neither good nor bad, neither healthy nor unhealthy. It can be used for health or unhealth depending on whether our spirit is caught up in existential fear where life is seen through the lens of nothingness or whether it feels held in existential trust where life is seen through the lens of somethingness and somebodiness and loses the fear of nothingness (Beier, 2014). God-images, whether explicit or implicit, can promote either such fear or trust and, correspondingly, can harm or heal.

To better understand how the human spirit may infinitize either for harm or health, we will take a closer look at the four dimensions classically described by Søren Kierkegaard (Kierkegaard, 1983) that constitute our spirit: infinitude, finitude, possibility, and necessity. Then we will discuss the forms of despair that can emerge around any of these dimensions if we live in existential fear. Next we'll indicate the correlations that theologian and psychotherapist Eugen Drewermann has identified between the forms of suffering that *can* develop in depressive, schizoid, obsessive, and histrionic character structures as described by psychoanalysis and the four forms of despair (Beier, 2004/2006) (see. Fig. 7.1).

Figure 7.1: Spiritual Despair & Psychodynamics

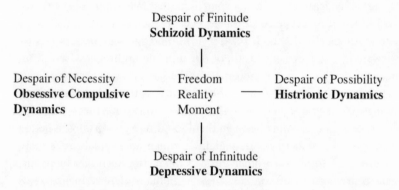

Fig. 7.1 Spiritual Despair & Psychodynamics. Based on Drewermann (1991, pp. 128–162) and Beier (2004, pp. 108–119)

Kierkegaard defines the self or the human spirit as a synthesis between finitude and infinitude, and, related but different, between necessity and possibility. These four polar opposite elements constitute the structure of our self-consciousness, our spirit. The health or unhealth of our spirituality depends on whether we live in the balance of these four poles or whether, in existential fear, we hang ourselves on one of the poles to the exclusion of the others. When we balance these poles, we become and are ourselves, live in the moment, and are free and are real in relation to others. When, out of existential fear, we hang ourselves on one pole as if it was our existence and ultimate ground, we misrelate to ourselves and others, do not live in the moment, are not free, and have a false self. Kierkegaard called this misrelation despair and described four forms of despair depending on the pole we flee to in our effort to counter our fear of nothingness and nobodiness. This can happen whether we are aware of it or not (Kierkeg-aard, 1983). We may despair of infinitude and denigrate or deny finitude, for instance, by feeling guilty even for things not under our control, or by denying certain limitations of nature and our body. This can correspond, according to Drewermann, to the infinite feelings of responsibility and guilt, and to the tendency to minimize the value of finite aspects in life in a de-pressive worldview, where the self may feel required to be as omnipresent, omniresponsible, or omniscient as the classic definitions of God, and the finite is in a way dissolved into the infinite. We may despair of finitude and deny infinitude but inadvertently seek ultimate meaning in the finite, which cannot yield it, such as by achievement or by belonging to a group. This can correspond to a schizoid worldview in which only what is rational or thinkable is real, where things outside one's control may be thought away through withdrawal into fantasy, and where the transcendent may be col-lapsed into the finite. We may despair of necessities and fear possibilities by trying to make ourselves "necessary" through obsessive adherence to rules or through doing the "right" thing. In an obsessive-compulsive worldview, we may, for instance, have a form of religion which rewards us for doing the right rituals or the right actions. Or we may despair of possibility and try to avoid the reality of necessities required to actually realize possibilities. For instance, in a histrionic worldview we may have big, exciting dreams of success but also contempt for the "mundane" steps it takes to realize them. Kierkegaard thought that "despair," not being oneself, is initially inevitable. However, once we are aware of it, we can become a self and live a free and real life in the moment, if we reestablish the synthesis between the four di-mensions, which, he believed, is possible only through trust in an ultimate relational ground, which he called God, who wants us to exist as absolutely valuable persons.

An approach using the criterion of existential fear or trust as the decid-ing factor for what makes faith either toxic or beneficent will begin by asking whether faith is used in desperate fashion as a way to tie a person to one pole of existence to the exclusion of the other poles. Anne presented with feel-ings of depression. While her dream does not explicitly mention God, her associations establish a subjective connection between her father, a colonial white patriarchal God-image, and a wish to push them down from their top position. As we explore the dream, however, we find that Anne's most pro-found affects emerge when she talks about no longer wanting to feel that she has to take care of what her father should take care of himself and, similarly, of what white people should take care of themselves: their white God and the guilt feelings they may have about the oppressive impact of the colonial God on her and others. Mindful of the traumatic, oppressive dimension of colonial God imagery, an approach focused on existential fear vs. trust looks at how Anne's image of God expresses her particular form of despair in this situation. We find then that the dream presents Anne's psychospiritual work of undoing a depressive God-image with which Anne has identified. She realizes that she has taken care of what she feels her father should have taken care of himself. She also realizes in the transference to me as the therapist that she has taken care of white people's guilt and is no longer willing to do so. Taking care of others in that way has starved her own soul of a God who would nurture her, as the reference to "roasting" the God-image and to getting her own roast indicates. The (re)discovery of a God who wants her as a unique person to exist as herself is central to the transformation of a toxic faith into a beneficent faith. In the dream, she is becoming aware of what she really needs and wants. The God-image she dismantles in the dream is the oppressive white God of colonialism and patriarchy which she internalized through her father. But it is also more. It is a God-image that makes her feel omniresponsible for others, especially for her father. This can happen in any context where a depressive God-image is at work, whether it is a politically colonial situation or not. Anne can never feel good enough about herself because she could never meet the omnipotent self-demands she takes on for others. She is learning to trust that she is good enough without having to be "God," without having, in a sacrificial-masochistic-savior fashion, to redeem her own father or others, including the therapist. Nor does she need to fear that those feelings will kill the people she loves. Instead, finding trust by imagining God to be truly nurturing of her allows her to be real and connected with others. There is, in a way, an unacknowledged side to the colonial God-image: it is a manic defense against depression. Structurally, a colonial God-image treats the other as not good enough, as incapable and impotent, as nothing, as in need of being taken care of. The self is seen as both omnipotent and infinite, albeit at the price of omniresponsibility, which then may find expression politically in "manifest destiny" fantasies. Anne's existential fear takes the shape that she would not be enough as her own person, that only if she takes care of others will she in a way earn her right to exist. Psychoanalytically, Anne has been using the defense of turning aggressive feelings toward others against herself. But when this happens in the area of spirituality, the turning against the self is not just about a particular thought, behavior, or feeling, but rather about one's existence as such. In our work, Anne is working through a depressive and oppressive God-image that made her feel omniresponsible for others so that she can instead now find and love herself while also giving others the space to be themselves and let them be and do for themselves what only they can be and do for themselves. This also liberates her as a self in the struggle for justice for herself and for others similarly oppressed, by helping her reclaim her existence apart from the omnipotent fantasies of colonial rulers and religions.

The strength of this alternative approach lies in the fact that it assesses the spiritual dimension not through some impersonal factor defined externally such as balanced thinking, good moral wanting, or right behavior, but rather by paying close attention to the subjective experience of the human spirit itself. Whether or not a person's spirituality heals or harms is determined by whether it promotes existential trust or fear within a person *and* within relationships: that is, whether it facilitates experiences of personal *and* interpersonal somebodiness (ultimately mattering) or nobodiness (ultimately not mattering) in view of the universal human awareness of death. As I have shown in *A Violent God-Image* (Beier, 2004/2006), faith that is caught in a spell of existential fear implies a God-image that does violence and harm to the human spirit. A limitation of the alternative approach may lie in the fact that, given much of especially Western culture's subjective denial of death (Becker, 1973/2007), practitioners may be reluctant or ill-equipped to shift away from the dominant cognitive, moral, and behavioral preconceptions that have been applied to the assessment of spirituality and faith. The alternative approach presented here requires that practitioners listen carefully and patiently to the existential symbolic meanings in the narratives patients present of their lives as a whole.

Conclusion

Illustrated by a case example of working with internalized oppression, this chapter has provided an overview of three common approaches to assessing the benefit or toxicity of faith and spirituality. Each approach's definition of faith, assessment of healing or harmful effects of faith, and strengths and weaknesses were discussed. An alternative approach to the assessment of faith is proposed that seeks the criterion for the health or harm of faith not in cognitive, moral, or behavioral factors external to the human spirit, but instead in the experience of existential trust or fear within the human spirit itself.

References

Becker, E. (2007). *The denial of death.* New York: Simon & Schuster. Orig. publ. 1973.

Beier, M. (2006). *A violent God-image: An introduction to the work of Eugen Drewermann.* New York: Continuum. (Orig. publ. 2004).

Beier, M. (2010). *Gott ohne Angst: Einführung in das Denken Eugen Drewermanns.* Düsseldorf: Patmos.

Beier, M. (2014). Spiritually integrated supervision: facilitating supervisees' competence as expressions of somebodiness while avoiding "Extractive Introjection." *Reflective Practice: Formation and Supervision in Ministry, 34*, 252–67.

Cone, J. H. (2011). *The cross and the lynching tree.* Maryknoll: Orbis.

Cooper-White, P. (2004). *Shared wisdom: Use of the self in pastoral care and counseling.* Minneapolis: Fortress.

Cooper-White, P. (2007). *Many voices: Pastoral psychotherapy in relational and theological perspective.* Minneapolis: Fortress.

Cooper-White, P. (2011). *Braided selves: Collected essays on multiplicity, God, and persons.* Eugene, OR: Cascade Books.

Drewermann, E. (2007). *Atem des Lebens: Die Seele - Die moderne Neurologie und die Frage nach Gott. Religion und Naturwissenschaft: Vol. 4.* Düsseldorf: Patmos.

Edelman, G. M., & Tononi, G. (2000). *A universe of consciousness: How matter becomes imagination.* New York: Basic Books.

Fanon, F. (2004). *The wretched of the earth.* (R. Philcox, Trans.). New York: Grove.

Freud, S. (1961). *The economic problem of masochism.* In J. Strachey (Ed. And Trans.), *The standard edition of the complete psychological works of Sigmund Freud* (Vol. 19, pp. 159–172). London: Hogarth Press. (orig. publ. 1923).

Freud, S. (1996). *The future of an illusion.* In J. Strachey (Ed. and Trans.), *The standard edition of the complete psychological works of Sigmund Freud* (Vol. 21, pp. 5–58). London: Hogarth Press. (orig. publ. 1927).

Kierkegaard, S. (1983). *The sickness unto death: A Christian psychological exposition for upbuilding and awakening* (1st Princeton pbk. print, with corrections). Hong, H. V., & Hong, E. H. (Trans.) *Kierkegaard's writings: Vol. 19.* Princeton: Princeton University Press.

Koenig, H. G. (Ed.). (1998). *Handbook of religion and mental health.* San Diego: Academic.

Koenig, H. G. (2008). *Medicine, religion, and health: Where science & spirituality meet. Templeton science and religion series.* West Conshohocken, PA: Templeton Foundation Press.

Koenig, H. G. (2012). Commentary: Why do Research on spirituality and Health, and What do the results mean? *Journal of Religion and Health, 51*, 460–67.

Koenig, H. G., & Lewis, G. (2004). *The healing connection: The story of a physician's search for the link between faith and science.* Philadelphia: Templeton Foundation Press.

Koenig, H. G. et al. (2001). *Handbook of religion and health.* Oxford: Oxford University Press.

Koenig, H. G. et al. (2012). *Handbook of religion and health* (2nd ed). Oxford: Oxford University Press.

Kohut, H. (2011). The two analyses of Mr. Z. In *The search for the self, Vol. 4*, pp. 395–446. London: Karnac. (Orig. publ. 1979).

Levin, J. S. (2010). Religion and mental health: theory and research. *International Journal of Applied Psychoanalytic Studies, 7*, 102–15.

Levin, J. S., & Chatters, L. M. (1998). Research on religion and mental health: An overview of empirical findings and theoretical issues. In H. G. Koenig (Ed.), *Handbook of religion and mental health* (pp. 33–50). San Diego: Academic Press.

Milton, J. (2005). *Paradise lost.* Indianapolis: Hackett.

Pargament, K. I. (1997). *The psychology of religion and coping: Theory, research, practice.* New York: Guilford.

Pargament, K. I. (2007). *Spiritually integrated psychotherapy: Understanding and addressing the sacred.* New York: Guilford.

8

Professionalism and Ethics

Steven S. Ivy

CONSIDER THESE COMMON SITUATIONS:

- The newly graduated counselor is getting acquainted with others in her practice area. She intuitively recognizes that some are "going through the motions" while others are excited and engaged. Is this what a professional life really offers?

- The younger, tech-savvy therapist works for an organization that avoids technology when possible and forbids social networking with clients. Both stances seem really out of touch. Is this an ethical concern?

- One training program emphasizes that certain forms must be completed fully after every visit. Another program makes suggestions but gives freedom to each trainee to complete what seems essential. Can both be right?

These vignettes simply illustrate the challenges that persons practicing the profession of psychotherapy and counseling face today. Challenges that are both professional and ethical demand the ability to discern when a problem has an ethical component and to analyze an ethical problem toward a satisfying solution.

This chapter first provides an overview of professionalism as the base for an ethical professional life. Then it examines perennial ethics concerns in psychotherapy and counseling, which are addressed by the ethics standards promulgated by the various professional organizations. The chapter concludes by examining emerging ethical issues, as well as older ones that have a new twist today.

Professionalism

The core challenge of professionalism is living a life of service to those in need while depending on that service for one's livelihood. William May (2001) contrasts these equally valuable perspectives as "vocation" (calling, profession) and "career" (technique, work). Finding a creative and life-giving balance between these sometimes competing demands requires integrity rooted in one's spiritual center as well as professional development.

Spirituality poses the ancient question, how can I live faithfully in relationship to God, neighbor, and self? A theological or spiritual approach to the ethics of counseling integrates the *empirical* (reason, intellect, science, the contrast between truth and falsehood), the *good* (morals, will, right relationships, the contrast between virtue and vice), and *beauty* (aesthetics, heart, arts, the contrast between attractiveness and repulsiveness) (Wilber, 1998, p. 141). These dimensions of wholeness interpenetrate any particular experience or encounter yet provide separate perspectives on that encounter. A theological worldview always expresses a particular view on how life is organized, of proper living within that life, and of experiences of beauty within that life. Truth, goodness, and beauty provide the integrating center for a theologically informed counseling practice. With Wendell Berry I believe that "it is possible to see one's work as occurring within a larger and ultimately mysterious pattern of causes and influences . . . There [are] responsible connections between science and the knowledge of how to live, and between art and the art of living . . . a complex connection between art and science" (2000, p. 89).

An integrated life is one mark of human flourishing. The tasks of practical theology, including pastoral counseling, attend to helping persons and communities live more fully the abundant life, helping congregations become centers of abundant living, and forming ministers (both clergy and lay) who embody ways of living that mediate life to others (Bass & Dykstra, 2008, pp. 2–3). Psychotherapeutic professions will always be rooted in that which yields to abundant living and human flourishing. Indeed, one way of discerning the purpose of such counseling is that it receives persons whose lives are limited and distorted by sin, accident, and illness and seeks, through conversation and action, lives open to a new and transformed future. This method of theological and spiritual integration is congruent with that proposed by James McClendon in the first volume of his systematic theology. He understands that Christians experience and speak of life in three perspectives: natural organic existence, corporate social existence, and transformed resurrected existence. The moral world is interpenetrated by all three at each turn of experience (McClendon, 1986, pp. 62–67). Thus the work of counseling participates in the realities of our embodied experience, our relational environment, and our openness to a new future. In this environment the concerns of ethics (what is good?) are integrated into our theories of persons and interventions, into our relational beings, and into our hopes for what is yet to be.

Professions require extensive training, which results in specialized knowledge, uncommon skills, and specific virtues. The advanced knowledge earned through graduate study in medicine, ministry, counseling, or other disciplines is not so esoteric that it cannot be understood by other educated persons. But the disciplines required for that learning are difficult to maintain outside of the academic environment. Professional education forms "habits of the mind" that includes core knowledge and analytic thinking appropriate to that profession. I confront these differences daily in my current administrative role within a healthcare system. I was formed as a minister and a counselor and now work with lawyers, physicians, nurses, and managers. Even though we are all concerned for the well-being of the persons we serve, we must carefully attend to our mental models or we misunderstand each other. For example, counselors will include a deep humanism in their mental model, even while committed to the best science; other professions may integrate little of this humanism.

Professions require skills rooted in an educated perspective. Thus internships, residencies, and other forms of supervised learning are found in almost all professions. Habits of the competent practitioner are developed through these supervised and mentored experiences with persons in need. Perhaps most crucial to ethical practice is awareness of one's competence based upon training, experience, and practice. The counselor must know his or her own limits and have a robust referral network so that the client can receive the most appropriate care possible. The therapist will also learn through case conferences and other group work both the skill of enhancing the ability of colleagues to discharge their responsibilities optimally, and habits of self-reflection on the therapist's own work.

Professions require specific expressions of virtue. Committing oneself to an ethics code and being held accountable to that code is characteristic of almost all professions. "Habits of the heart" (Bellah et al. 1986) are those values, attitudes, and wisdom that express therapists' virtues. One essential virtue is an appropriate professional attitude and behavior toward colleagues. Core values include truth, accountability to clients and society, respect for all, altruism, reliability, and compassion.

In return for education, skill, and ethical virtue, the professional is authorized (credentialed, licensed) to serve a societal need. For most professions this authorization gives members of that profession a virtual or real monopoly on that form of service. Persons cannot practice medicine without a license. Most states restrict who can advertise using the terms *marriage and family therapy* or *counseling*. These restrictions usually determine who can receive third-party payments as well.

Since describing an ethical practice is somewhat rooted in context, we need to amplify the professional point of view. All agree that the client's well-being is the professional's focal concern (Sullivan, 2004). The following list describes criteria for a professional counselor's point of view:

- *Demonstrates a commitment to excellence*: This requires a consistent use of current knowledge and practice while understanding the limits of self and clients. This commitment also challenges mediocrity in self and associates. Excellence requires openness to new knowledge and lifelong learning; thus, continuing education is required for ongoing licensure.

- *Expresses integrity*: Personal integrity aligns the inner self and outer behaviors. Professional integrity aligns the self with the practices and commitments of one's professional association. Thus, integrity requires the therapist to discern what is fitting for personal relationships, self, and social connections.

- *Enjoys meaningful engagement through work*: Work and profession cannot be separate passions. Both deeply engage the professional. A therapist has a ready commitment to cure or care for suffering, which yields a consistent answer to the question, what is my just and worthy way of living in the world?

There are some aspects of the therapist's professional life that are relatively unique and thus require deep integrity. Chief among these is that the work itself requires deep intrapersonal and interpersonal engagement. Thus, therapeutic work requires self-care and self-awareness of unusual maturity.[1] Counselors' habits of the mind, practice, and heart result in a life characterized by integrity.

> Integrity is never a given, but always a quest that must be renewed and reshaped over time. It demands considerable individual self-awareness and self-command. Yet, it also depends for its realization upon the availability of actual social possibilities, since some situations clearly make it more likely that an individual can achieve integrity than others . . . In fact, the qualities of integrity and the demands of professional life are in this way remarkably congruent. Integrity of vocation demands the balanced combination of individual autonomy with integration into shared

1. See Ulanov chapter in this volume.

purposes. Individual talent needs to blend with the best common
standards of performance, while the individual must exercise personal judgment as to the proper application of these communal
standards in a responsible way (Sullivan, 2004, p. 220).

Thus, a professional develops both a centered spirituality and a worldview shaped by professional formation. With this picture of the demands of
the professional life comes an obligation to ethical living. Because professional ethics does not always follow common sense or customary ways of
relating, examination of the essentials of ethics as practices within psychotherapy and counseling settings is required.

Trustworthy Guides for Ethical Analysis

Key Ethical Principles as Guides

The language and concepts of ethics are important to the process of ethical
analysis. One resource for ethical analysis is core internalized perspectives on
life. These internalized perspectives are often referred to as "core values" and
include expressions such as loyalty, generosity, trustworthiness, compassion,
restraint, and cooperation. In large measure these can be recognized as pledges
made by Boy Scouts and Girl Scouts. While some have challenged these core
values as culturally overdetermined, significant research has demonstrated
cross-cultural expressions of these values, though the particular expressions
of each value are certainly changed by cultural mores (Kidder, 1994).

Internalized perspectives are more classically expressed as the "core
virtues." At least in Western traditions these have been discussed as the
theological (or Christian) virtues of faith, hope, and charity (loving-
kindness), and the civic (or cardinal) virtues of prudence, justice, restraint,
and courage. The theological virtues have been mediated by scriptures and
many religious and philosophical traditions. But their articulation as virtues
has been particularly nourished by the Roman Catholic tradition. The civic
virtues are rooted in classical Greek (Plato) and Roman (Stoicism) philosophies, and are mediated via the writings of Aquinas to the modern world.
Modern "virtue theory" articulates these seven core moral expressions in
the contemporary context (Corey et al., 2011, pp. 14–22).

Values and virtue paradigms can assist the therapist in recognizing
what may be ethical or unethical conduct. An act that violates justice may
well be unethical. An action that demonstrates loyalty to a patient will
seldom be unethical. However, these perspectives must be tested by other
systematic principles and a code of ethics.

Six widely discussed moral principles can readily be applied to the analysis of ethical dilemmas. These are summarized in Table 8.1:

Table 8.1: Key Moral Principles

Moral Principle	Brief Definition	Counseling Ethics Illustrations
Autonomy	Self-determination or freedom to choose own direction.	1. Cultural values are respected. 2. Goals of therapy are the client's goals.
Beneficence	Do good for others; promote others' well-being.	1. Make accurate diagnosis of need and resources. 2. Use only proven therapeutic techniques.
Nonmalfeasance	Avoid doing harm.	1. Practice within one's competence. 2. Do not engage in behaviors known to be harmful, such as sexual relationships with clients.
Justice	Be fair; focus on rights of the other; ensure equality and equity.	1. Work for public policies that ensure access to care for all who need care. 2. Provide both information and context that empower clients' humanity.
Fidelity	Make realistic commitments and keep promises.	1. Do not abandon a client in need. 2. Keep case load and work schedule within professional standards.
Veracity	Be truthful and deal honestly.	1. Advertise accurately. 2. Ensure billing processes are transparent and accurate.

Professional "Codes" as Guides

All associations of counselors and therapists promulgate "codes of ethics" and monitor the ethical behavior of association members. This monitoring takes several forms, such as requiring new members to pass an exam or sign a statement of agreement in regard to the code, requiring continuing education on ethics issues, and reviewing and sanctioning members' conduct. Thus, alignment with an ethics code is essential for the new counselor to identify with the profession and orient to the essential purposes and commitments of the profession. Since codes are evolving constructs, it is important for each counselor to maintain awareness of changing expectations and requirements (Sanders, 2010).

A code of ethics creates boundaries ("thou shalt not"), stimulates moral imagination ("oh, I never considered that before"), and provides direction ("do this"). These functions are nicely outlined by the American Counseling Association:

1. The *Code* sets forth the ethical obligations of ACA members and provides guidance intended to inform the ethical practice of professional counselors.

2. The *Code* identifies ethical considerations relevant to professional counselors and counselors-in-training.

3. The *Code* enables the association to clarify for current and prospective members, and for those served by members, the nature of the ethical responsibilities held in common by its members.

4. The *Code* serves as an ethical guide designed to assist members in constructing a course of action that best serves those utilizing counseling services and establishes expectations of conduct with a primary emphasis in the role of the professional counselor.

5. The *Code* helps to support the mission of the ACA.

6. The standards contained in this *Code* serve as the basis for processing inquiries and ethics complaints concerning ACA members. (American Counseling Association, 2014, p. 3)

What issues are addressed by a profession's code of ethics? While there is some variation, depending on the focus of that association specialization, codes address very similar themes. Table 8.2 demonstrates the high degree of similarity in the chapter titles of three associations' codes. An in-depth analysis of each code of ethics is beyond the scope of this chapter, but likely would demonstrate that there is high congruence between the specific expectations of therapists. Since there is such deep agreement on core ethical behaviors, the student and the seasoned professional should develop and maintain working awareness of their profession's code.

Table 8.2: Chapter Titles in Codes of Ethics

American Association of Pastoral Counselors (2011)	American Association for Marriage and Family Therapy (2012)	American Counseling Association (2014)
Professional Practices	Professional Competence and Integrity	Professional Responsibility (includes Advertising)
Client Relationships (includes finances)	Responsibility to Clients	The Counseling Relationship (includes finances)
Confidentiality	Confidentiality	Confidentiality and Privacy
Supervisee, Student, Employee Relationships	Responsibility to Students and Supervisees	Supervision, Training, and Teaching
Interprofessional Relationships		Relationships With Other Professionals
Advertising	Advertising	
Research	Responsibility to Research Participants	Research and Publication
	Financial Arrangements	
	Responsibility to the Profession	
		Evaluation, Assessment, and Interpretation
		Distance Counseling, Technology, and Social Media
		Resolving Ethical Issues

In 2009 I conducted an informal telephone survey of the ethics committee chairs of three pastoral professional organizations. The question was, "What ethics issues are arising to your committee's attention on the basis of complaints?" The key issues were boundary violations (especially sexual relationships), practice outside area of competence, and administrative concerns. The 2010 report of the ethics committee of the American Psychological Association listed categories of cases opened in 2010 (American Psychological Association, Ethics Committee, 2011, p. 400). There were a total of twenty cases opened: nine had to do with dual relationships involving sexual misconduct; five had to do with dual nonsexual relationships; two had to do with practice outside of competence; and six had to do with miscellaneous inappropriate professional practice. (Some cases are counted in more than one category.) This information provides guidance as to where counselors are most vulnerable to violate their professional codes. Thus, attention is given to these in the following paragraphs.

Professional Practices

Professional practices focus on business practices as well as on general principles of truthfulness and disclosure. These principles require disclosure of information such as purpose of therapy, typical procedures, risks of negative outcomes, possible benefits of therapy, the fee structure, limits of confidentiality, rights and responsibilities of clients, the option that a client can withdraw at any time, and what can be expected from the therapist. It is a mistake to consider these simply as business requirements to get a counselee in the door; they are ethical foundations to professional practice.

An example of professional practice involves one's stance in relationship to sexual orientation. The American Association of Pastoral Counselors (AAPC), the Association of Professional Chaplains (APC), and American Association for Marriage and Family Therapy (AAMFT) each include statements committing members to nondiscrimination on the basis of sexual orientation. Should a therapist have convictions that run counter to this commitment, then the therapist should seek consultation and supervision as soon as possible. If the therapist does not seek consultation or supervision, the therapist runs the risk of saying or doing something that leads to professional sanctions.

Administrative concerns have to do with intake processes, billing practices, informed-consent discussions, and the overall environment of practice. Appropriate billing practices may be most challenging when a client wishes to have a third-party payer involved. This tests the therapist's truthfulness in disclosing a diagnosis in tension with what the insurance will pay for and sometimes what the client is willing to have included in the health record. Billing practices may also produce conflicts around justice concerns.

There are many details to consider in establishing and maintaining appropriate records. There are clinical, ethical, and legal reasons for accurate record keeping, but they can be summarized as history, quality, and professional standards. From an ethics perspective, some of the more important elements for inclusion in records are fees and billing information, documentation of informed consent, waivers of confidentiality, client reactions to professional interventions, current risk factors pertaining to danger to self or others, plans for future interventions, consultations with or referrals to other professionals, and relevant sociocultural factors.

Client Relationships

On the part of the counselor, safeguards of the client-counselor relationship depend on dynamics such as telling the truth, not abandoning the client, showing sensitivity to difference, not exploiting trust, not fostering a relationship with the client beyond the counseling room, and refraining from sex with a client. Many of these issues arise from cautions about boundary crossing. Boundary crossings may open the therapist to potential opportunities to exploit a client. But boundary crossings may indeed benefit the client-counselor relationship. The counselor might attend a client's music recital. It is possible that a counselor and client may see and speak to each other at a religious congregation or symphony performance. These are not necessarily boundary violations, but a crossing has the potential to become a violation. For example, a chance meeting at the symphony could lead the counselor to make a comment about their next appointment within hearing of the client's employer, who had no idea of the therapy relationship. Confidentiality is thus violated. Any opportunity for boundary crossing must be carefully examined, and most should be avoided altogether.

Some boundary strategies that promote client welfare include setting healthy boundaries from the start of a relationship; securing clients' informed consent; discussing potential risks and benefits of interventions; seeking consultation, supervision, or both, to resolve any dilemmas; consistently documenting all interactions with clients (sessions, phone messages, and so forth) in clinical notes; and referring a client to another professional when necessary. An especially useful strategy for personal responsibility is to be aware of any reluctance to document an event or interaction in the client record. If the counselor would not want other professionals to read about a boundary crossing, then likely the boundary in question should not be crossed.

Another client-relationship issue involves awareness of racial and cultural differences. The American Association of Pastoral Counselors (AAPC) Code states that one core value is "to promote racial justice and develop multicultural competence as part of our practice" (American Association of Pastoral Counselors, 2011, pp. 97–103). Other codes have similar statements. Research has demonstrated the challenge of integrating traditional theories and practices with multi-cultural responsiveness (Gallardo et al., 2009). Since justice is a very deep commitment, and multicultural competence is a matter for lifelong learning, this expectation should be the subject of continuing education, and one's practices should be frequently reassessed. In the United States where mental health and behavioral health resources do not come close to meeting defined needs, a concern for justice leads to both personal examination (how much charity work do I do?) and public action (how do I advocate for different resource allocations by government and insurance payers?).[2]

There is increasing diversity of religious and spiritual commitments within U.S. culture. Therapists are encouraged to change practices and to attend more directly to clients' spiritual views and resources in order to better understand clients (e.g., Pargament, 2011). Autonomy and beneficence must be activated in order to ensure appropriate attention (Rosenfeld, 2011, p. 196). Since religion or spirituality can be a vehicle for expressing one's problems, the root cause of one's problems, or a resource for solving one's problems, the therapist must exercise great skill to accurately and ethically assess and intervene.[3]

Confidentiality

Confidentiality is among the most essential ethical practices; thus, exceptions to confidentiality are very troubling. Opportunities to unintentionally violate confidentiality range from how records of care are secured to inattentive messages left on an answering machine to misunderstanding legal requirements.

Counselors who see couples and families may face particularly challenging confidentiality issues. For example, if individual members are seen, then the counselor must ensure permission to bring those private conversations

2. See Sheppard (Ch. 4) and Marshall (Ch. 5) chapters in this volume for an in-depth discussion of this competency.

3. See Beier chapter in this volume (Ch. 7) for in-depth discussion of this competency.

back to the family session. If one member of the family signs a waiver of confidentiality, perhaps for a report to be filed with an attorney, usually the therapist cannot act unless all members of the family have signed such a waiver.

Another challenging situation arises when a client discloses having a sexually transmitted disease, and informs the therapist of having engaged in sexual relationships with an unknowing partner. State laws and procedures vary on what course the therapist should take. The therapist must be very careful to follow those legally mandated procedures exactly and to inform the client as to what steps the counselor is taking.

Another challenge to confidentiality arises when the client may be a danger to self or others. One's duty to protect the vulnerable and to warn the endangered is established in law and custom yet may well conflict with the privilege of confidentiality. Legal precedents are important to know in this regard. The Tarasoff [4] case established the therapist's duty to protect endangered persons and to warn of substantive risk of harm. The Jablonski case established the duty to commit a dangerous individual to inpatient care. The Hedlund Case extended the duty to warn to anyone who might be near an intended victim and who might also be in danger. Some general guidelines are usually adequate to meet these competing duties:

- Inquire about a client's access to weapons, about homicidal ideation, and about intentions, which would include whether a specific victim is involved.

- Consider all appropriate steps to take and the consequences of each.

- Know and follow the policy of your employer and the laws of your state.

- Document all actions you take and the rationale behind each of your decisions.

- Consult with an attorney if you are not clear about your legal duty.

Most states have laws that apply to therapists in order to protect vulnerable persons from harm. Mandatory-reporting laws are designed to encourage reporting of any suspected cases of child, elder, or dependent adult abuse. If the therapist suspects or has knowledge of these circumstances the therapist is advised to report. Failure to report according to state law may result in financial penalties, loss of license, or imprisonment. The obligation of beneficence means that the professional has an obligation to protect those who cannot advocate for themselves.

4. Summaries of these cases can be found in standard counseling ethics texts, such as Corey et al. (2011).

Supervisee, Student, and Employee Relationships

Ethics codes focus on the integrity and welfare of supervisees, students, and employees. The key theme is that the counselor should avoid dual relationships including sexual relationships, and should follow established standards of supervision of therapy and employment.

These relationships can be highly complicated. For example, in one situation a supervisor selected a graduating student for employment, which angered another graduating student who thought he was better qualified. Later the supervisor learned through a lawsuit that the selected student was engaging in a sexual relationship with another employee, Joy.[5] The theory of the lawsuit was that the supervisor's poor performance evaluations of Joy were due to disapproval of their sexual relationship. The lawsuit did reach a court hearing but the supervisor prevailed in court, probably since there was never any evidence of the supervisor's awareness of the sexual relationship and since the supervisor maintained excellent personnel records. Similar claims were made against the supervisor in professional associations but were not sustained.

Another aspect of ethical supervisee relationships involves the liability of the supervisor for the supervised work of the student. There are two kinds of liability to be considered. Direct liability can be incurred when the actions of the supervisor cause harm to the student or to the student's client. Vicarious liability can be incurred through the supervisor's potentially lax oversight of the student's actions.

Emerging Challenging Concerns

The issues discussed above have been explored and tested so there is a broad consensus on the boundary between ethical and unethical conduct. But the counselor must also contend with emerging issues where there is less consensus, and perhaps even disagreement.

One of the more vexing ethical challenges for professionals today is the challenge of electronic communication and social media. The user of both tools potentially risks confidentiality and boundary violations.

---

5. In this and other case examples, names are fictitious to protect confidentiality.

Electronic Communications

Electronic communications include phone calls, faxes, and e-mail messages. Unless the therapist has knowledge of a secure communication outcome, possible violations abound.

- During phone calls or when leaving phone messages, the therapist may give out information about a client to an unauthorized third party.

- A message left on a client's phone may be listened to by a spouse or child.

- It is difficult to verify that the person who you are speaking to on the phone is indeed your client, or a person authorized to receive or give information about the client.

- There is never an "off-the-record" conversation in your role as therapist.

- The client may be in a public place when speaking with you, and thus confidentiality may not be maintained.

- E-mail messages have a way of finding their way to unintended locations. E-mail messages sent to a client's business address are usually the property of the business, not the client, and thus subject to review by others.

- Text messages sent to cell phones may also become available to others. The same caution that is involved in leaving voice messages should be exercised in sending text messages and e-mails.

Some are exploring the benefits and dangers of distance therapy utilizing, phone, e-mail, and video technologies such as Skype. This emerging area carries the ethical risks cited above about privacy and confidentiality. Caution should be exercised since the efficacy of these tools has not been well described; thus, beneficence and nonmalfeasance issues are yet to be fully addressed. Another ethical challenge of distance therapy is having resources and plans in place to offer emergency interventions, if required. Nevertheless, these tools offer the potential to benefit many who do not otherwise have access to counseling resources. Although caution is in order, benefits may well outweigh the risks in defined circumstances.

Social Media

Social media include tools such as Facebook, Twitter, blogs, and other forms of personal communication directed to a group of people. These have emerged recently enough that patterns of ethical use are still very much in process. The 2014 edition of the American Counseling Association Code of Ethics includes four provisions directly addressing counselors' presence in social media. In summary they run as follows:

1. If the counselor intends to have both a personal and professional presence in social media, these should be separate and clearly distinguishable.

2. The informed-consent process should include a statement about the counselor's practices regarding social media.

3. The counselor should respect the privacy of clients unless informed consent is granted.

4. The counselor should ensure that no boundary violations (of privacy, of the therapeutic relationship, for instance) occur through social media.

If therapists engage in social media, they risk violating confidentiality, or they risk contributing to clients' perception that confidentiality has been violated. For example, a therapist may blog regularly about matters of emotional and relational health as a community education contribution. Even though the therapist carefully conceals the identity of cases in the blog, clients may see themselves revealed. Client privacy must be a primary consideration in any social-media participation. The American Medical Association (2010) approved a professional policy statement in 2010 on the use of social media that highlights patient privacy and confidentiality, and that recommends the physician take steps to separate personal and professional interaction online and carefully monitor online associations and postings that would tarnish the professional standing of the physician. All these concerns are present for the therapist as well. Nevertheless, social media offer unprecedented positive opportunities for public education and engagement that should be explored.

A study by Bosslet (2011) reviewed physicians' attitudes toward social networking with patients. There was a high degree of skepticism that such media could improve patient communication. The study found that most interaction came at the initiative of the patient, who then frequently expected the physician to respond to either social or patient-related invitations. The ethical danger of dual relationships, boundary violations, and privacy violations is clear.

The following guidance outlines how counselors can ethically utilize social media during a time when mores and laws are in flux:

- Distinguish personal and professional space in social media, though you should proceed with the assumption that nothing that is online can be confidential.

- Restrict access to your personal space through your online profile.

- Always remember that what is placed online may well find its way to surprising and unintended places, a risk that cannot be eliminated.

- Consider whether what you are posting does reduce or could be construed as reducing your credibility as a professional; consider whether your posts could undermine or be construed as undermining the public's trust in your profession.

- Any online relationships with clients or former clients should be managed in the same way that you manage face-to-face relationships.

- Do not access clients' or students' online information. (Some would allow for this with informed consent.)

- Include in your informed-consent documents and discussions your practice related to social networking.

(Kaslow et al., 2011, pp. 110–11; Lehavot et al., 2010, p. 165)

As the "MySpace generation" grows into professional life—people for whom social-media interaction is normative rather than novel—standards related to its use will evolve and be formalized (Lehavot et al., 2010). Both younger clients and younger therapists who have always been immersed in this world are not likely to be satisfied by its prohibition. Social media allow counselors to look into the personal worlds of clients in new ways. Does this facilitate or inhibit effective therapy? And even if it is effective, does it violate client autonomy? Social media allow supervisors and teachers to look into their students' personal worlds in unprecedented ways. Does such knowledge facilitate or inhibit well-grounded selection and training? Thus, this is an important arena for professional associations to develop guidance for their members.

Conclusion

Mark came to counseling for assistance in coping with a world shattered by Sharon's request for a divorce. Mary, his assigned therapist, had been formed in a religious tradition in which divorce was considered a sin to be avoided at all costs. While she shared many values with this tradition still, she recognized that human flourishing sometimes depended on maintaining painful relationships and at other times required severing those relationships. Thus, her spiritual perspective was open to explore the various dimensions of Mark's problem without prejudging the best outcome. Her professional stance was integrated and balanced. As they began therapy, Mark indicated that he wanted his medical insurance plan to pay the cost. Under the provisions of his plan, it became clear that unless Mary documented certain DSM codes,[6] his plan would not pay. While Mark was certainly distressed, she could not accurately diagnose the required conditions. She knew that core principles required veracity and her code of ethics required honest documentation and financial arrangements. And she knew that Mark's financial resources were indeed limited. Rather than not be truthful to his insurance company, Mary made alternate financial arrangements administratively approved in her center. Her code of ethics guided her well. After some time, Mark and Mary agreed that he had moved through the most difficult aspects of reorganizing his life, and they prepared to terminate their relationship. Mary recognized that Mark's goal had been met (autonomy), and her professionalism (generating more abundant living) had been furthered. Thus, they parted with appreciation for the past and anticipation for the future.

It is difficult to overstate the joy of a professional life well lived. The professional experiences deep satisfaction and accomplishment in serving those in need. Ethical standards provide both boundaries and possibilities for this well-lived life. Some of these boundaries are intuitively obvious to most, but others are strange, even countercultural, because of the unique vulnerabilities of the therapeutic relationship. Students of counseling and therapy will do well to ensure that their attitudes, knowledge, and skills are centered within the ethical life of their profession. And experienced professionals will stay current with changes in ethical practice to ensure that they practice within the scope of their education, training, and experience.

References

American Association for Marriage and Family Therapy. (2012). *AAMFT code of ethics.* Alexandria, VA, https://aamft.org/imis15/Documents/AAMFT%20 Code_11_2012_Secured.pdf/.

American Association of Pastoral Counselors. (2011). *Membership Manual: Appendix Q, AAPC code of ethics.* Fairfax, VA.

American Counseling Association. (2014). *ACA code of ethics.* Alexandria, VA, http://www.counseling.org/resources/aca-code-of-ethics.pdf/.

6. DSM codes, used for diagnostic and insurance purposes, are found in the *Diagnostic and Statistical Manual of Mental Disorders* (now in its fifth edition) released by the American Psychiatric Association in May 2013. See chapter 9.

American Medical Association. (2011). *Professionalism in the use of social media*, http://www.ama-assn.org/ama/pub/physician-resources/medical-ethics/code-medical-ethics/opinion9124.page/.

American Psychological Associaton, Ethics Committee. (2011). Report of the ethics committee. *American Psychologist, 66,* 393–403.

Berry, W. (2000). *Life is a miracle: An essay against modern superstition.* Washington, DC: Counterpoint.

Bass, D. C., & Dykstra, C., (Eds.). (2008). *For life abundant: Practical theology, theological education, and Christian ministry.* Grand Rapids: Eerdmans.

Bellah, R. M. et al. (1986). *Habits of the heart: Individualism and commitment in American life.* New York: Perennial Library.

Bosslet, G. (2011). The good, the bad, and the ugly of social media. *Academic Emergency Medicine, 18,* 1221–22.

Corey, G. et al. (2011). *Issues and ethics in the helping professions* (8th ed.). Belmont, CA: Brooks/Cole.

Gallardo, M. E. et al. (2009). Ethics and multiculturalism: Advancing cultural and clinical responsiveness. *Professional Psychology: Research and Practice, 40,* 425–35.

Kaslow, F. W. (2011). Ethical dilemmas in psychologists accessing internet data: Is it justified? *Professional Psychology: Research and Practice, 42,* 105–12.

Kidder, R. M. (1994). *Shared values for a troubled world: Conversations with men and women of conscience.* San Francisco: Jossey-Bass.

Lehavot, K. (2010). Psychotherapy, professional relationships, and ethical considerations in the MySpace generation. *Professional Psychology: Research and Practice, 41,* 160–66.

May, W. F. (2001). *Beleaguered rulers: The public obligation of the professional.* Louisville: Westminster John Knox.

McClendon, J. W. Jr. (1986). *Systematic theology, Vol. 1: Ethics.* Nashville: Abingdon.

Pargament, K. I. (2011). *Spiritually integrated psychotherapy: Understanding and addressing the sacred.* New York: Guilford.

Rosenfeld, G. W. (2011). Contributions from ethics and research that guide religion in psychotherapy. *Professional Psychology: Research and Practice, 42,* 192–99.

Sanders, R. K. (2010). Ethics codes: monitoring the major changes. *Journal of Psychology and Christianity, 29,* 263–67.

Sullivan, W. M. (2004). *Work and integrity: The crisis and promise of professionalism in America* (2nd ed.). San Francisco: Jossey-Bass.

Wilber, K. (1998). *The marriage of sense and soul: Integrating science and religion.* New York: Random House.

9

The Art and Discipline of Diagnosis

Ryan LaMothe

Psychotherapists must be knowledgeable . . . but they must be humble in that knowledge. Let's be straight about it: We never know enough. We never can know enough. As fast as we learn, just so fast do we learn there is ever more to learn.

—Bugental, 1987, p. 273

BUGENTAL IS RIGHT WHEN it comes to grasping, intellectually and emotionally, the suffering of those who seek our help. Yet, this is not a counsel for despair but instead a challenge to embrace the creative tension between knowing and not knowing. This is no easy task for new or seasoned pastoral psychotherapists, especially when people arrive at our offices desperate for relief from emotional turmoil and relational conflicts. Their anxious pleas initiate a therapist's quest to arrive at a preliminary, accurate diagnosis of the patient's malady—a diagnosis intended to reduce life-limiting ways of being in the world and to increase the client's flourishing.

Diagnosis is an art and a discipline. To say that diagnosis is an art implies that there is a body of knowledge and tradition—possessing ethical principles and skills—that pastoral psychotherapists draw upon in their work with clients. The notion of discipline connotes careful attention to the practices and knowledge associated with diagnosis. In this chapter, I unpack the various features of diagnosis by first defining the concept of diagnosis. This sets the stage for identifying five central principles in the art and discipline of diagnosis in pastoral psychotherapy. Next, I address four general perspectives that frame one's diagnosis, namely, psychological, physical, social, and religious. Each of these aspects of being human contains diverse interpretive frameworks that pastoral psychotherapists use to develop a comprehensive and dynamic diagnosis. After providing two case illustrations, I address how diagnosis leads to therapeutic frames that benefit the clients.

Meaning and Principles of Diagnosis

Many students are initially uncomfortable with the idea of diagnosing people. They associate diagnosis with psychologists or psychiatrists—the experts. Some are rightly concerned about objectifying people, placing them into restrictive, impersonal categories. More often than not, students do not realize that when an individual seeks their help, they are compelled to use an interpretive framework to organize and make sense of the person's story and communications. There must be, then, some assessment if one is to create helpful interventions. Students' anxieties usually abate when we talk about the meaning of diagnosis and the underlying theological principles in the ethical practice of diagnosing.

The term *diagnosis* comes from the Greek *diagignōskein*: "to distinguish, to know."[1]

To know is to grasp, to comprehend. Pruyser (1976) argued that diagnosis "means to grasp things as they really are, so as to do the right thing" (p. 30). While I would dispute the modernist assumption that we can know things as they really are, Pruyser correctly connects knowing with ethical action. Diagnosis, as knowledge, in pastoral psychotherapy should never be divorced from therapeutic interventions. Diagnosis, then, has a fundamental ethical component; that is, diagnosis involves knowledge for the sake of acting, and the action is for the sake of benefiting the Other, which is the first principle of the pastoral practice of diagnosing. This first principle is rooted in the theological notion of *imago dei*, which means that the individual is created in the image and likeness of God and therefore possesses an inherent dignity and value linked to the flourishing of the individual. This places an ethical demand on treating the client as a person and to intervene to promote the person's flourishing.

It may be obvious that our diagnoses are aimed at helping individuals, yet there are routine situations when this principle is in question. Therapists

1. http://www.merriam-webster.com/dictionary/diagnosis/.

and counselors, for example, may be motivated to diagnose in order to alleviate their own anxiety—an anxiety linked to uncertainty and not knowing. The proclivity to eschew uncertainty, ambiguity, and ignorance is noted in a letter John Keats wrote to George Keats, wherein he said that negative capability "is when a man [sic] is capable of being in uncertainty, mysteries, doubts, without irritable reaching after fact and reason" (in Bion, 1970, p. 125). Keats recognized that anxiety forecloses one's negative capability, or the capacity to tolerate not-knowing. The foreclosure of negative possibility also obstructs openness, creativity, and caring imagination. Keats could have been talking about struggles in pastoral psychotherapy. In a similar way, Phillips (2001) wrote that "diagnosis is the way analysts cure themselves of anxiety, when their anxiety can be the most valuable thing they have" (p. 290). An individual, for instance, arrives with a sense of urgency, and the pastoral psychotherapist is anxious to be of help, which requires obtaining enough knowledge to act rightly, by which I mean therapeutically. If the therapist has difficulty containing anxiety, the therapist may rush the diagnosis to reduce the anxiety of not knowing. In those moments, the therapist has lost negative capability and, as a result, the diagnosis is for the therapist's sake.

Therapists may also diagnose for the sake of the insurance industry. Many therapists are dependent on obtaining remuneration from insurance companies and feel pressure to arrive at a diagnosis that will be accepted by the client's insurance. Anxiety, in brief, can impel a pastoral psychotherapist to make a diagnosis for the therapist's own sake and, secondarily, for the patient. This does not mean the diagnosis is wrong or even unhelpful, but what this does mean is that the ethical, theological aim of diagnosis is distorted. To reemphasize: a foundational principle of diagnosis is the *ethic of knowing for the sake of right action*, which is an action that benefits the Other, which stems from the theological principle of *imago dei*—the centrality of the Other as person—unique, inviolable, valued, agentic.

A second and related principle of diagnosis emerges from the existential realities of the relationship. An individual, having some psychological and spiritual distress, seeks the assistance of someone the individual believes and hopes will provide aid. The client is vulnerable and the therapist is not, which points to the asymmetrical reality of the therapist-patient relationship. The pastoral psychotherapist has more authority and power, which means that the therapist is accountable for what takes place in relation to the client. This does not imply that the patient is powerless, but the therapist possesses primary responsibility to benefit the patient's dignity and human flourishing. The therapist's *accountability* for best practices includes supervision, consultation, certification, licensure, and continuing education (LaMothe, 2001, 2005). Also required is therapeutic and diagnostic attentiveness and sensitivity to power and vulnerability in the interactions (Sussman, 1992). This means attending to the client's conscious and unconscious communications, therapeutic boundaries (see Caruth & Eber, 1996; Gabbard, 1994b), and the power of suggestion (see Imber, 2000)—all of which reveal a person's ways of being in the world.

A third principle is that all diagnoses are partial and flawed. Theologian Edward Farley (1990) noted that human life is fundamentally tragic. To live we must grasp reality, but in the act of grasping it, we distort it. This maxim highlights the incredible complexity of human beings and that no matter how much knowledge we have of the Other, we can never fully comprehend the other (Bugental, 1987). Implied here, as well, is that we can never be absolutely certain of our therapeutic knowledge and interventions. Indeed, diagnostic certainty may be said to be a form of idolatry or sin in that there is a distorted belief that I have *the* truth, which denies the mystery and dignity of the Other as *imago dei*. Accepting this principle should lead to both diagnostic humility and openness to other perspectives, including overt and covert corrections from the client. Diagnostic *humility* means that while I have confidence in my assessment, I do not believe it is *the* answer or that my interventions are the only possible ones or even the best options. Ideally, this fosters creative space for surprise, rectification, and repair that comes from the patient or supervisor (see Casement, 1985). More important, diagnostic humility preserves the dignity of the client by leaving room for the client's freedom, as well as for the lived expression of the client's unique and ineffable personhood.

The limitations of diagnoses naturally lead to a fourth principle, namely, diagnoses are *culturally and historically conditioned* (Doerner, 1981; Gilman, 1985; Porter, 1989; Ramsay, 1998). The interpretive frameworks we use to diagnose people contain biases, assumptions, and premises regarding gender, race, class, intimacy, vulnerability, and so forth, which are often unconscious or unstated features of theory and culture (Frie & Coburn, 2011; Gadamer, 1991/1975). Indeed, our psychological theories are anthropologies, revealing diverse visions about the aims of human life (Marcus & Rosenberg, 1998). These biases and assumptions shape how pastoral therapists "know" the patient, as well as therapeutic interventions and goals. Like the second principle, this principle should increase our humility, as well as our willingness to be conscious of our biases and assumptions and how they influence our work. This can be done through supervision or in consultative relationships with colleagues and a critical, constructive stance toward the various interpretive frameworks we use.

The fifth principle of diagnosis is *compassion*. Theologically, compassion is expressed and founded in God's embodied communication (incarnation) through Jesus Christ whereby Christ recognizes and is moved by the suffering and needs of all human beings and stands in solidarity with us (Farley, 1996). In terms of therapy, compassion includes the capacity for empathy[2] along with the willingness to witness and be moved by the client's suffering. It is compassion that invites the client to feel less alone in suffering. If we find ourselves unable or unwilling to be compassionate, whether it is momentary or characteristic, we know the knowledge obtained is either lacking or too overwhelming, and that some aspect of our subjectivity has impeded our motivation to care for the client. Stated differently, diagnosis without compassion signals the presence of negative countertransference (see Maroda, 2004; Sussman, 1992), which means that the therapist's subjectivity is interfering with therapeutic knowledge, interventions, and aims.

Given these principles, and before addressing specific interpretive frameworks, I take a short detour and briefly address a key feature of pastoral diagnosis that undergirds these principles. The notion of diagnosis refers to knowing, yet diagnostic knowledge depends on the faculty of imagination. *Diagnostic imagination*, if you will, signifies the disciplined and creative use of interpretive frameworks to understand the client and the interaction. Further, diagnostic imagination comprises (a) an embodied knowing that includes using subjectivity to understand the Other, (b) the creative use of multiple interpretive frameworks, (c) empathy, and (d) critical reflection vis-à-vis one's diagnosis and interventions. Diagnostic imagination, then, is not separated from caring imagination (Hammington, 2004), and both are inextricably yoked to knowledge and actions aimed at benefiting the Other.

2. Empathy is the capacity to recognize accurately the emotional experiences of the Other (Cook, 2006). This capacity, which is largely learned, can be used in instrumental or functional ways (e.g., when a salesperson accurately reads the emotional experiences of the eventual buyer) that exclude the intention to care for the Other. Compassion necessarily includes a nonpurposive, noninstrumental form of empathy, as well as a willingness to suffer with the Other.

Figure 9.1 - Psychological, Physical, Social, and Religious/Faith

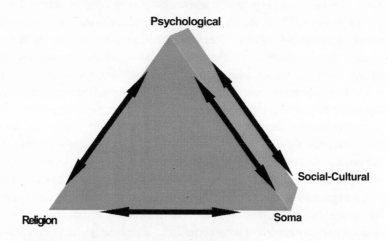

Figure 9.2 - Psychological Frameworks Used in Diagnosis

Psychological Frameworks	Soma	Social-Cultural	Religion/Faith
Psychoanalytic Theories	Western Medical Sciences	Sociological sciences	Christian Theologies
Cognitive	New Age (e.g., aroma therapies, herbal)	Anthropological approaches	Judaism
Attachment	Eastern Medicine (e.g., acupuncture)	Political science	Islam
Family Systems		Linguistics	Buddhism
DSM-5 & PDM			New Age spiritualities
Behavioral			Agnosticism
			Atheism

Interpretive Frameworks in Pastoral Diagnosis

When diagnosing, I typically use four points on a pyramid, with each point representing a feature of human life, namely, psychological, physical, social, and religious/faith[3] (see figure 9.1). Each of these aspects of life mutually influences the others to varying degrees, depending on the context and issue. Moreover, each corner has a number of possible interpretive frameworks used in diagnosis (see figure 9.2). Clearly, it is not possible to

3. Niebuhr (1989) argued correctly that faith is an anthropological category and not simply or solely a religious category. This broadens one's understanding of faith and its dynamics to include people who are atheists or agnostics.

possess expertise about each of the four features, let alone be knowledgeable about the various interpretive frameworks in each column. Pastoral psychotherapists will be proficient in one or two psychological and theological frameworks, but relatively less knowledgeable and proficient in medical or social-cultural frameworks.[4] The relative lack of knowledge and expertise in, say, the medical area does not mean that one should avoid attending to it when attempting to understand the client's dilemma. Instead, the pastoral psychotherapist recognizes his or her own limitations (scope of practice),yet considers whether there is some aspect of the person's dilemma that needs to be attended to or ruled out. For instance, a person who presents with depression clearly has a psychological malady, but it would be essential to attend to the soma, which involves a physical exam by the client's physician and a psychiatric consult. Moreover, it would be important to understand the social-cultural context and resources vis-à-vis the depression. A person suffering from depression may come from a culture where depression is deemed a spiritual malady. Lack of familial or social support can also exacerbate depression.

An important diagnostic framework that pastoral psychotherapists must be familiar with is the Diagnostic Statistical Manual (DSM-5).[5] This manual covers three of the four features above, though there is greater emphasis on the psychological and medical aspects of human suffering. In an attempt to systemize psychiatric maladies, the DSM-5, unlike the DSM-IV's multiaxial format, organizes diagnoses into twenty-two general categories in section 2 of the manual, ranging from neurodevelopmental disorders to personality disorders to "Other Conditions That May Be a Focus of Clinical Attention." Section 3 of the DSM-5 covers assessment measures, cultural formulations, an alternative DSM-5 model for personality disorders, and conditions for further studies, such as persistent complex bereavement disorder and suicidal behavior disorder.

For pastoral psychotherapists familiar with psychodynamic theories, the Psychodynamic Diagnostic Manual (PDM, 2006), which complements the DSM-5, can be another helpful tool in diagnosis. This manual has three axes, namely personality, mental, and subjective. The P axis refers to personality patterns and disorders, emphasizing the distinctions between

4. Those with Clinical Pastoral Education (CPE) may have more knowledge of medical concerns and issues while those with Marriage and Family Therapy (MFT) training may be more familiar with social, cultural, and family-systems perspectives.

5. It is important to recognize that the DSM-5 is a cultural artifact that categorizes and systematizes human suffering. By this, I mean that it is culturally and historically situated and, therefore, not a document that is universal or timeless. It is important for clinicians to be aware of the limitations of the DSM-5 and PDM (see Szasz, 1970).

personality, personality patterns, and personality disorder. The M axis addresses such areas as capacity for affect regulation, capacity for relationships, quality of internal experience (self-confidence, esteem), psychological mindedness, defensive patterns and capacities, self-observing capacity (self-reflection), and basic mental functioning. The S axis comprises symptom patterns, which are yoked to subjective experience. The authors write, "We depict individual subjectivity in terms of affective patterns, mental content, accompanying somatic states, and associated relationship patterns" (p. 93). Examples would be adjustment disorders, anxiety disorders, dissociative disorders, mood disorders, to name a few. Three advantages of this manual are (a) the inclusion of the therapist's subjective experience (countertransference) given the various disorders, (b) the client's experiences (thoughts, feelings, fantasies), and (c) criteria for suitability for psychodynamic therapy. Unlike the DSM-5, the PDM embraces, with caveats, the use of the therapist's subjectivity as *an* interpretive framework in diagnosing clients.

I offer two brief vignettes to illustrate the four features of diagnosis and the use of each manual in diagnosis. Karen[6] (a pseudonym), a thirty-six-year-old divorced women with two adolescent children, sought counseling three weeks after being released from a psychiatric hospital. Several months prior to hospitalization, Karen began having vivid, intrusive images of childhood experiences of rape by her brother and brother-in-law. These flashbacks accompanied intense vaginal pain and an overall muscle ache, which were later deemed to be body memories. Understandably, these intense experiences came with waves of anxiety and, at times, panic. Throughout the first eighteen months of therapy, Karen kept mostly to her house, venturing out to go to therapy and to get necessities from the store. During her second year, Karen went back to work.

Occasionally, Karen would cut herself off from people when the emotional intensity became unbearable. She would get close to people in her church and then simply cut them off, because of a real or imagined offense. During the six years we worked together (three to five times a week), Karen changed jobs at least seven times, usually because she felt mistreated and distrustful of her coworkers and management. Self-mutilation helped her deflect her focus from painful emotions and memories to physical pain, which was more manageable for her. Low self-esteem and a fragile self were part of her emotional suffering. Karen, for instance, said she felt "dirty, damaged, and different." I understood her flight from relationships and her self-mutilation as ways to protect a very fragile sense of self and ward off intense emotional pain. The first two years of therapy were tumultuous.

6. Both case examples have been disguised.

Karen, at times, would tell me that I was the only one she trusted, while at other times (frequently in the same session) she said I was stupid, uncaring, and insensitive. Threats of suicide, aimed at her tormentors, and threats of not returning to therapy were frequent, especially at the beginning of our work together.

In terms of the DSM-5 and PDM, Karen's symptoms fell primarily into three categories, namely, borderline personality disorder (DSM-5 301.83; PDM, pp. 582–92), anxiety disorder (DSM-5 300), and posttraumatic stress disorder (DSM-5 309.81; PDM, pp. 100–104). Prior to hospitalization, Karen's PTSD symptoms emerged when her daughter was the same age that Karen had been when the abuse started. It is important to point out here that Karen was seen by a physician who ruled out physical problems that may have fostered and maintained her distress. Also, Karen's psychiatric hospitalization and the fact that she did not have family and community support were clear psychosocial and environmental factors contributing to her distress. At the beginning of therapy, Karen's overall psychosocial functioning was fairly low, because of suicidal ideation and threats, as well as self-mutilation. Moving to the PDM, Karen manifested most of the eighteen features of borderline personality disorder—features having to do with affect regulation, object relations, and cognitions (pp. 584–85). In addition, the PDM identifies psychological defenses associated with PTSD and borderline disorders, such as projective identification, dissociation, and splitting—all of which were evident in Karen's ways of relating.

Since Karen had already had physical and psychiatric exams, I asked and received permission from her to view these reports. In terms of a diagnosis, three of the four features of the pyramid (psychological, physical, and social) were addressed in the diagnosis above and in these reports. It was especially helpful to understand the specific medications prescribed during and after Karen's stay at the psychiatric facility. In terms of diagnosis, what remained was Karen's religious/faith perspective and its relation to the social reality of her life. Not surprisingly, Karen had stormy relationships with people in her church, whom she would disparage as having "bumper-sticker theologies." At the same time, several church members reached out to her and helped Karen, though she would run hot or cold about these relationships. Her view of God was strongly idealized, yet, on occasion, she would rage against a God who had not answered her prayers to stop the abuse. Often, Karen viewed God as just, bringing divine retribution on those who had harmed her in the past and who were harming her in the present. "They may get away with it here," she said, "but they will have to answer to God when they die." This view of God, which parallels aspects of our relationship and work, changed slowly during the six years of therapy. Toward the end of therapy, Karen was able to talk about a more loving and merciful God. That said, whenever she became anxious or stressed, previous modes of thinking and organizing experience (i.e., borderline) were present.

A crucial piece of a psychodynamic diagnosis is the subjectivity of the pastoral psychotherapist. The therapist's emotions, thoughts, and fantasies, which are evoked in the context of the client's communications, serve as another interpretive framework in making a diagnosis (McWilliams, 1994). In psychoanalytic parlance, this is called countertransference (Cooper-White, 2004; Epstein & Feiner, 1993). Naturally, making use of one's subjectivity in diagnosis is only one interpretive framework and must be carefully monitored, because of our own projections and biases (Giovacchini, 1993; Maroda, 2004). Nevertheless, it can be a useful tool in empathic diagnosis, highlighting the art and discipline of diagnosis. For instance, when initially working with Karen, I would have rescue fantasies, including feelings of helplessness, powerlessness, and hatred (see Chessick, 1997). These emotions occurred in relation to Karen's suicidal and self-mutilating behaviors. In addition, my strong emotions vied with genuine concern and a sense that our relationship was fragile. I recall one early session when I was working hard to be helpful. At one point, I said, "Karen, I feel like my hands are tied." With a slight grin, Karen replied, "Good. Now you know how it feels." These intense experiences helped confirm the diagnoses (PTSD and borderline personality disorder) yet at the same time provided me with some hypotheses about Karen's internal world and suffering. That is, I had a greater sense of her fear, powerlessness, alienation, loneliness, and fragile vulnerability, which she fought hard to protect.

Another client, David, sought help after being passed over for promotion. A forty-year-old father of three, David was well educated and exceedingly intelligent. When he was denied the promotion, his boss told David that he was a valuable member of the company, but that people found it difficult to work with him because of his arrogance and seeming insensitivity to the needs and feelings of those around him. David accepted this with apparent calm, though he was deeply hurt and angry. As the day wore on, he felt increasingly defeated and empty. David had expected to be much further along in his career. Anna, his wife of fifteen years, listened with patience and, later, when David felt understood, Anna told him that she hoped he would talk to someone. Heeding his wife's advice, David sought help, reluctantly.

David grew up in Manhattan and attended the best possible schools. His father was a successful banker, spending most of his time away from home. David never felt he knew his father but recalls that he always admired him. His mother was a Southern belle who met David's father when she was in college. Disappointed and lonely in her marriage, David's mother turned her attention to David, praising him for his precocious intelligence and confiding in him about her marital struggles. While initially gratifying, this became onerous when David was in high school and college. As David withdrew, his mother turned to alcohol.

David's lack of empathy toward his fellow workers; his grandiose fantasies of success, his arrogance and contempt for people whom he judged intellectually inferior; his experiences of shame, inadequacy, and emptiness; and his emotional distance from his children pointed to narcissistic personality disorder (DSM-5 301.81; PDM P104.1). To protect his fragile sense of self-worth, David relied on a combination of defenses, namely, idealization, de-idealization, and rationalization. In terms of his social relationships, David had no close friends, though he expressed strong affection for his wife. David remarked that Anna had always been someone who respected and admired his intelligence and gifts. Moreover, she would comfort him whenever he felt empty and defeated. While David professed no religious faith, he was an ardent patriot, which represents a secular faith. Intense idealization of the U.S. enabled David to bask in the rays of power and grandiosity, shoring up a fragile and dependent sense of self. David's ability to function at work and with others was high. Put another way, unlike some people diagnosed with narcissistic personality disorders, David did not somatize his fears and anxieties, which can contribute to a diminished ability to function in social situations.

A colleague referred David to me, and part of this referral involved lauding my work. As a result, David arrived with an idealized view of me, which evoked some anxiety in me because I recognized that disillusionment, disappointment, and rage would inevitably follow. While I was initially attracted to David's quick wit and intelligence, I found myself, at times, bored and impatient. I also had a sense that David was keeping me at arm's length, which evoked my impatience. That is, I was impatient at his remarkable ability to avoid vulnerability. These subjective responses helped confirm the diagnosis, while at the same time providing some clues to David's suffering (see Gabbard, 1994a, pp. 501–6; McWilliams, 1994, p. 178; PDM, p. 39). I took my anxiety vis-à-vis disappointment as a clue to David's painful disappointment, hurt, and anger with regard to his parents, who had let him down. Boredom and impatience led me to wonder about David's profound sense of loneliness and his fear that people might see how bad he really felt about himself. I understood my boredom to be related to David's lack of spontaneity and aliveness, which was screened by his false self (Winnicott, 1971). My subjective experiences, then, were one part of the interpretive frameworks vis-à-vis diagnosis and empathy.

What I hope is clear in these all too brief formulations, is the presence of various interpretive frameworks that address the psychological, physical, social, and religious elements of Karen's and David's lives. Less clear is the shifting nature of diagnosis in therapy, as well as how these diagnoses can be used to benefit Karen and David. In the initial weeks of working with individuals and couples, we are beginning to learn about their way of being in the world. Early diagnoses should be held lightly, because other information may alter how we understand the client's suffering. Moreover, as therapy progresses, the client hopefully changes, which should lead to alterations in our assessments.

Diagnosis and Therapeutic Interventions

The art and discipline of diagnosis lies not simply in one's ability to use the PDM or DSM-5, but rather in collaboratively crafting therapeutic interventions, frames, and processes. A comprehensive, empathic diagnosis, then, should lead one to consider how to establish a therapeutic frame and consider therapeutic interventions aimed at facilitating the client's healing and flourishing. In Karen's situation, I quickly moved to recommending that we meet three times a week. Her low Global Assessment of Functioning (GAF) scores and recent psychiatric hospitalization suggested to me that therapy needed to be structured to contain her intense feelings and fear of falling apart. At times, we would increase our meetings to five times a week, whenever she began to feel out of control, which usually accompanied a return to deeply painful and disturbing memories. Because of her fragile state and PTSD, at the beginning of therapy, I kept my interpretations and questions on the immediate or present circumstances. That is, I did not initially seek to delve into Karen's past or to pursue unconscious fantasies and memories, because I wanted to ensure that we had established a relationship of relative trust and stability. When memories came up, I listened empathically, while inviting her to say what she was able. Karen tested the boundaries of therapy. For instance, during the first year, she repeatedly called wanting more time. I agreed to take her calls between sessions but limited them, both in terms of frequency and length. Understandably, Karen felt hurt and angry by these boundaries, and we found ways to address these feelings in therapy. In time, Karen's trust in me deepened when she saw that I was not going to leave, abandon, or attack her. This trust did not mean, however, that there were not ongoing relational disruptions or threats to leave, though these gradually decreased.

One difficulty that emerged early on in our work together was Karen's refusal to take medication for anxiety. Her resistance emerged from her experiences of being bound as a child and later in her experiences of being bound in the psychiatric facility. Karen believed that taking medication meant being subjugated by powerful people (including me) who wanted her to keep quiet. I believed that any motion on my part to demand this would only heighten Karen's resistance and contribute to her experiences of feeling misunderstood. We talked about this on a number of occasions, but Karen was adamant. We then shifted the focus, working on various techniques or practices (emotional self-regulation). For instance, when Karen began to feel the first waves of anxiety, she would light candles and turn on soothing music. On other occasions, she would call and listen to my answering machine, because my voice (a connection to her experiences of my caring about her) provided some measure of security.

In David's case, given his high GAF scores, the therapeutic frame involved weekly therapy. David was highly functional and therefore did not require a therapeutic frame that would contain troubling affect or memories. He was quite adept at this himself. I also turned to Kohut's (Kohut, 1968; Kohut & Wolf, 1978; Lee & Martin, 1991) perspective on working with narcissistically wounded people. That is, I remained consistently empathic vis-à-vis David's past and present experiences. We also explored his relationships with both parents and the concomitant losses associated with both. At the same time, I sought to attend to moments in David's life when he felt alive, when he was spontaneous, whether that was in session or with others. These moments gave glimpses of what Winnicott (1971) called a true self. In my assessment, I considered these moments to be worth highlighting and nurturing. By contrast, I made empathic interpretations around David's leading with his false self. For instance, David, at times, would come across as demeaning in therapy, or would try to engage me in argument about this or that psychological theory. Many of his critiques were accurate, but I viewed them as moments of defending against vulnerability vis-à-vis his low self-worth and my importance to him. After one of these interactions, David remarked, "I know that when I get on my high horse, I am afraid of what you think of me or if you will think of *me*." In terms of his parents, David was "thought of" vis-à-vis meeting their needs. It was important that my therapeutic interventions consistently involved keeping David in mind rather than a projection of him.

A diagnosis represents a tentative attempt to understand empathically a person's suffering. In understanding the person's struggle, I am then in a position to consider the joint construction of a therapeutic frame that aims to facilitate the process toward healing and self-flourishing. In addition, diagnoses ideally help pastoral psychotherapists consider the kinds of therapeutic interventions aimed at attending to the particular client's emotional experiences and psychological maladies. The brief case discussions above do not do justice to the shifting nature of diagnosis. By this, I mean two things. First, while there may be a number of clients diagnosed as borderline, each person is unique (*imago dei*), and this means that we must consider shaping our interventions in terms of the client's unique personality and experiences, instead of simply placing the client under an impersonal category. In my view, no matter how accurate the diagnosis, we will fail to be of help if we do not tailor our stance and interventions in ways that take into account the uniqueness of the person-client. Second, diagnosis shifts as we get to know the person and as the person begins to change. It is helpful to reconsider one's diagnosis every few months, testing to see if and how the client has changed and how we have changed together.

Conclusion

Diagnosis in pastoral psychotherapy is an art and discipline. If one accepts this formulation, then the implication is that we can never know or be skilled enough in working with suffering souls. This reality reveals the complexity and mystery of human beings, suffering, and moments and processes of healing. Put another way, human beings are wonderfully unique and endlessly fascinating, implying that our work will rarely be boring and that we will always be learning about diagnosis and its relation to therapeutic action.

References

American Psychiatric Association. (2013). *Diagnostic statistical manual* (5th ed.). Washington DC: American Psychiatric Association.
Bion, W. R. (1970). *Attention and interpretation*. London: Tavistock.
Bugental, J. F. T. (1987). *The art of the psychotherapist: How to develop the skills that take psychotherapy beyond science*. A Norton Professional Book. New York: Norton.
Caruth, E., & Eber, M. (1996). Blurred boundaries in the therapeutic encounter. *Annual of Psychoanalysis, 24*, 175–85.
Casement, P. (1985). *On learning from the patient*. New York: Guilford.
Chessick, R. (1997). Psychoanalytic treatment of the borderline patient. *Journal of the American Academy of Psychoanalysis, 25*, 91–109.
Cook, C. (2006). Empathy: A bridge between worlds: A landscape of care. *Family Ministry, 20*, 29–38.
Cooper-White, P. (2004). *Shared wisdom: Use of the self in pastoral care and counseling*. Minneapolis: Fortress.

Doerner, K. (1981). *Madmen and the bourgeoisie: A social history of insanity and psychiatry*. (J. Neugroschel & J. Steinberg, Trans.). Oxford: Blackwell.

Epstein, L., & Feiner, A. H. (Eds). (1993). *Countertransference: The therapist's contribution to the therapeutic situation*. Northvale, NJ: Aronson.

Farley, E. (1990). *Good and evil: Interpreting a human condition*. Minneapolis: Fortress.

Farley, E. (1996). *Divine empathy: A theology of God*. Minneapolis: Fortress.

Frie, R., & Coburn, W. J. (2011). *Persons in context: The challenge of individuality in theory and practice*. New York: Routledge.

Gabbard, G. (1994a). *Psychodynamic psychiatry in clinical practice* (2nd ed.) Washington, DC: American Psychiatric Press.

Gabbard, G. (1994b). On love and lust in erotic transference. *Journal of the American Psychoanalytic Association, 42*, 385–403.

Gadamer, H. (1991/1975). *Truth and method*, (J. Weisheimer & D. Marshall, Trans.). (2nd ed.). New York: Crossroads.

Gilman, S. L. (1985). *Difference and pathology: Stereotypes of sexuality, race and madness*. Ithaca: Cornell University Press.

Giovacchini, P. L. (1993). *Countertransference: Triumphs and catastrophes*. Northvale, NJ: Aronson.

Hammington, M. (2004). *Embodied care: Jane Addams, Maurice Merleau-Ponty, and feminist ethics*. Urbana: University of Illinois Press.

Imber, R. (2000). The dilemma of relational authority. *Contemporary Psychoanalysis, 36*, 619–38.

Kohut, H. (1968). The psychoanalytic treatment of narcissistic personality disorders. *Psychoanalytic Study of the Child, 23*, 86–113.

Kohut, H., & Wolf, E. (1978). The disorders of the self and their treatment: An outline. *International Journal of Psychoanalysis, 59*, 413–425.

LaMothe, R. (2002). Rethinking supervision of ministry. *Journal of Pastoral Care & Counseling, 56*, 145–56.

LaMothe, R. (2005). A challenge to church leaders: The necessity of supervision for ordained ministers. *Journal of Pastoral Care & Counseling, 59*, 3–16.

Lee, R. R., & Martin, J. C. (1991). *Psychotherapy after Kohut: A textbook of self psychology*. Hillsdale, NJ: Analytic.

Marcus, P. and Rosenberg, A. (1998). *Psychoanalytic version of the human condition: Philosophies of life and their impact on practice*. New York: New York University Press.

Maroda, K. (2004). *The power of countertransference: Innovations in analytic technique*. Hillsdale, NJ: Analytic.

McWilliams, N. (1994). *Psychoanalytic diagnosis: Understanding personality structure in the clinical process*. New York: Guilford.

Niebuhr, H. R. (1989). *Faith on earth: An inquiry into the structure of human faith*. R. Niebuhr (Ed.). New Haven: Yale University Press.

Phillips, A. (2001). *Promises, promises: Essays on psychoanalysis and literature*. New York: Basic Books.

Porter, R. (1989). *A social history of madness: The world through the eyes of the insane*. New York: Dutton.

Pruyser, P. W. (1976). *The minister as diagnostician: Personal problems in pastoral perspective*. Philadelphia: Westminster.

PDM Task Force. (2006). *Psychodynamic diagnostic manual.* Silver Springs, MD: Alliance of Psychoanalytic Organizations.

Ramsay, N. J. (1998). *Pastoral diagnosis: A resource for ministries of care and counseling.* Minneapolis: Fortress.

Sussman, M. B. (1992). *A curious calling: Unconscious motivations for practicing psychotherapy.* Northvale, NJ: Aronson.

Szasz, T. (1970). *The manufacture of madness: A comparative study of the Inquisition and the mental health movement.* New York: Harper & Row.

Winnicott, D. (1971). *Playing and reality.* London: Tavistock/Routledge.

10

Posttraumatic Stress Disorder:
Coping and Meaning Making

Carrie Doehring

SOPHIA IS A THIRTY-EIGHT-YEAR-OLD *divorced computer programmer living in San Francisco. Her life changed after a business trip to a nonprofit organization. She felt a spiritual connection with the CEO, whose vision for founding the nonprofit resonated with her deepest values. When she went with him to his condo after they had eaten out together, he sexually assaulted her and then threatened to discredit her if she told anyone what had happened. She blamed herself for drinking too much and using poor judgment. She thought that she could put this horrible experience behind her after a negative test for pregnancy and STDs. However, she has had difficulty sleeping and feels anxious when she is alone with male colleagues. She had a panic attack when she was offered another work-related travel opportunity. She used her employee-assistance program to request a female therapist who would respect her Germanic American Roman Catholic faith.*

Sam is a twenty-year-old African American Army reservist from Atlanta. During a deployment in Afghanistan, his unit came under attack. Sam provided immediate emergency medical care to his buddy because they were cut off from ordinary medical supplies. While the makeshift tourniquet he used on his buddy's leg saved his life by stopping blood loss, improvising with a bootlace caused secondary damage, requiring amputation below the knee. Sam was tormented by guilt that he didn't provide the best emergency care under fire that he could have and regretted not thinking of using his uniform web belt as a tourniquet. When he returned home with his unit, Sam met with his Baptist minister to talk about struggles with guilt that surface when he talks to his

buddy and encounters him and his family at the church they all attend. After
several conversations, his minister suggested that Sam meet with a colleague, a
pastoral counselor who could help with his trauma-related symptoms.

The clients in these fictional scenarios are seeking help from counselors who will respect their religious beliefs and spiritual practices. Pastoral counselors bring expertise in psychology and theology that helps clients discern whether particular beliefs, values, and spiritual practices alleviate or exacerbate posttraumatic stress. The purpose of this chapter is to introduce key theories and concepts from psychological, theological, and religious studies related to posttraumatic stress disorder (PTSD), religious coping, meaning making, and spiritual struggles. I will use the following step-by-step guidelines to describe how an interdisciplinary approach can be implemented in pastoral counseling with trauma survivors.

1. **Building a relationship of trust** through intercultural compassion and respect for the individual nature of religious beliefs and spiritual practices, and how they shape and are shaped by trauma and trauma-related moral distress and spiritual struggles (Drescher et al., 2011; Kinghorn, 2012; Litz et al., 2009; Murray-Swank & Waelde, 2013; Pargament, 2007).

2. **Enhancing life-giving coping** with trauma-related symptoms by exploring and intentionally using religious and spiritual practices that help clients experience safety and self-compassion when traumatic memories are triggered so that they can stay relationally engaged with goodness—their own goodness and the goodness of others and life in general. Using these coping strategies consistently will enable clients to explore traumatic memories in terms of values and beliefs called into question by the threat and violation of trauma.

3. **Assessing trauma-related symptoms** in terms of intensity, duration, and impact on the client's physical, emotional, relational, spiritual, and behavioral well-being.

4. **Fostering spiritual integration by identifying life-giving beliefs and values about suffering associated with spiritual practices of compassion,** which can be used to counteract the automatic beliefs and values generated by trauma-related emotions like fear and shame (Doehring, 2014, 2015).

A Compassionate Reminder about Self Care

Readers can reflect upon their own process of spiritual integration by paying attention to any traumatic memories evoked by this chapter. Use religious and spiritual practices that help you feel safe and connected with the
goodness of your lives. Remember the values and beliefs that anchor you.
Use spiritual practices that help you integrate your core values and beliefs
into coping with trauma-related emotions and memories, so that they become an invaluable resource and not a roadblock in working with trauma
survivors. By using spiritual practices that enhance compassion, you will be
more likely to experience compassion rather than distress when listening to
trauma stories (Klimecki et al., 2013).

Building Trust

When clients bring the most sacred aspects of their lives into counseling—their religious and spiritual beliefs, values, and practices—they need
pastoral counselors skilled in intercultural care, who use a *hermeneutic of
searching for differences* in order to appreciate the alterity, or otherness, of
their clients' religious and spiritual beliefs and practices (Doehring, 2015;
Lartey, 2006). A hermeneutic of searching counteracts the tendency to universalize and look for one God (Moyaert, 2012; Prothero, 2010), a tendency
that makes counselors more likely to impose their religious beliefs onto the
client. Without formal religious and theological education, counselors risk
being theologically naïve, of being unable to distinguish their embedded
religious beliefs and values from those of their clients (Doehring, 2009).

A counselor might assume, for example, that Sophia, as a Roman Catholic, associates sin with sexual contact, which exacerbates her guilt about
being sexually assaulted; further, the remedy is belief in the compassionate
God at the core of all theistic religions of the world. This counselor's tendency
to universalize and make theological assumptions about Sophia's religious
upbringing will make her less attuned to Sophia's Germanic-American Roman Catholic upbringing and her college education at a liberal arts Roman
Catholic college. Sophia's Germanic-American self-reliance and formation
as a Roman Catholic feminist shape her guilt that she should have known
about the risks of date rape. A counselor attuned to the unique features of
Sophia's religious formation will gain Sophia's trust. Within this relationship
of trust, clients like Sophia will become more able to articulate and elaborate
deeply personal and intrinsically meaningful religious and spiritual beliefs
and practices, especially those related to trauma experiences. These clients

will, in turn, be more likely to share this spiritual dimension of themselves with trusted others, enhancing posttraumatic growth by deepening their capacity for spiritual self-reflection and spiritual intimacy within their relational network.

Coping that Enhances a Sense of Safety and Goodness

Using an intercultural approach that attends to the client's unique ways of coping, pastoral counselors will not assume that religious and spiritual practices always help clients experience a sense of safety and goodness. Indeed, psychological research on religious coping has found that religion and spirituality are multidimensional, "made up of a myriad of thoughts, feelings, actions, experiences, relationships, and physiological responses" and, hence, related to acute stress and trauma in a variety of life-enhancing, life-limiting, and destructive ways. "The critical question isn't *whether* religion and spirituality are good or bad, but *when, how,* and *why* they take constructive or destructive forms [in the aftermath of trauma]" (Pargament et al., 2013, p. 7). Psychological studies on religious coping and trauma have demonstrated that many victims experience *transitory religious and spiritual struggles* that often involve questioning and searching for spiritual and religious practices and meanings. They may conserve practices and beliefs that have helped them in the past and also discover new beliefs and practices that become integrated into their lives. Many clients will experience psychospiritual growth when they use *positive religious coping* that includes (for those in theistic religious traditions) (1) believing in and experiencing God as benevolent, (2) collaborating with God in problem solving rather than deferring to God or being self-directing, and (3) seeking spiritual support in their communities of faith. Extensive research demonstrates that positive religious coping decreases psychological and spiritual distress (e.g., anxiety, depression) and increases posttraumatic psychological and spiritual growth. Those who end up experiencing *chronic religious struggle often use negative religious coping*, which, for those in theistic traditions, involves (1) believing in and experiencing God as punitive and abandoning, (2) questioning God's love, and (3) being discontented with their religious communities (Pargament et al., 2005). Ongoing struggles and negative coping are associated with increased psychological and spiritual distress. Some clients will experience a transitory or chronic sense of *spiritual violation* and *desecration* of that which is sacred (e.g., one's body), which can threaten clients' spiritual well-being (Murray-Swank & Pargament, 2005; Pargament, 2007; Pargament et al., 2005). Without any explicitly religious education about sexual violence, someone like Sophia might assume that her community of faith would shun her if she were to disclose what happened (Leslie, 2002). This life-limiting theology contains many spiritual "sticking points"—conflicts between pre-trauma beliefs and values and trauma-related doubts and questions, like, how could a loving God allow this to happen to me? (Murray-Swank & Waelde, 2013, pp. 344–47).

When clients intentionally engage in religious and spiritual practices in order to help themselves feel safe when they reexperience traumatic memories, they will be more able to stay relationally engaged with goodness: their own goodness, and the goodness of others and life in general. Identifying which ways of coping with traumatic memories are life-giving or life-limiting will enhance a client's sense of safety and well-being. After initially exploring and keeping track of their habitual coping strategies, clients can become more intentional about using specific spiritual coping strategies in response to trauma-related symptoms and related automatic negative thoughts about self, others, God, and life in general. They can keep notes on how effective these strategies are in helping them experience safety and goodness (inner, relational, and cosmic). Psychospiritual approaches to fear- and shame-based trauma focus on helping survivors use spiritual practices to experience the goodness of life (Harris et al., 2011; Whitehead, 2010). Spiritual practices that foster self-compassion can uncover and alleviate the shame that often is part of privatized religious meaning making (Doehring, 2015; Herman, 2011). Such practices help survivors compassionately counteract hyperarousal, intrusive memories, and avoidant coping when they begin to explore traumatic memories. Emerging research on trauma and moral distress suggests that in addition to issues of fear, shame and guilt also need to be considered at the outset of psychospiritual care (Herman, 2011). Spiritual caregivers are uniquely equipped to help morally distressed trauma survivors find spiritual practices that help them experience a sense of self-compassion or a transcendent experience of the compassion of God or the goodness of creation (Doehring, 2015; Kinghorn, 2012). When shame is compassionately addressed at the outset of spiritual-care relationships, thus allowing morally distressed trauma survivors to experience compassion through spiritual practices, they will be able to compassionately explore intrusive memories involving moral distress.

Empathically Assessing
Trauma-Related Symptoms

Sophia experienced the violation of a sexual assault with someone she admired who seemed to share many of her values. Sam faced death when his patrol came under attack. He witnessed his buddy being seriously injured and tried to keep him alive until medics arrived. These clients experienced existential and physical danger. In the weeks following these life-threatening events, they reacted with symptoms of acute stress: reexperiencing the horror of what happened in flashbacks and dreams, being on alert for danger, having sleep problems, feeling numb, and avoiding trauma-related cues and reminders.

These reactions to intensely fearful events, while upsetting and disruptive, are the way people grapple with and adjust to life-threatening experiences. Fear is an evolved and adaptive response to threats that helps people like Sophia and Sam survive the initial trauma and cope in its aftermath. Their fear-based neurophysiological alarm system alerts them to danger and triggers cognitive, emotional, and motor responses designed to help them survive during the traumatic event and as they adjust to having survived. Pastoral theologian Jason Whitehead (2010) argues that the hope of survival is part of how fear works as a neurophysiological survival mechanism. Hope of survival is the undercurrent of fear that pulls Sophia and Sam out of danger. Trauma-related symptoms (reexperiencing fear in flashbacks and dreams, hypervigilance, and avoidance) are all ways that human beings automatically try to protect themselves from further life-threatening stressors. For example, when Sophia is alone with male colleagues, her fear-related shortness of breath and racing heart function like an alarm system warning of danger, as Figure 10.1 illustrates.

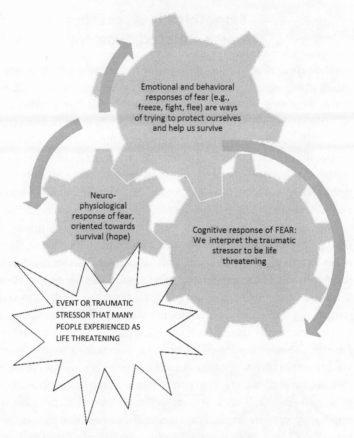

Figure 10.1 – Trauma Related Symptoms:. A life-threatening stressor triggers an immediate cognitive assessment that we are in danger, which almost instantaneously sets off a neurophysiological fear response (fright) followed by emotional and behavior responses (i.e., flight/freeze)

Usually trauma-related symptoms subside in three to six months, as survivors cognitively process these fear-based responses to threat, experience social support, and gradually learn to manage the lingering effects of their traumatic experiences. At least half of all trauma survivors are resilient.[1] When symptoms remain intense and persist past a month, people may develop acute PTSD; symptoms that persist beyond three months may indicate chronic PTSD. Chronic trauma-related symptoms often negatively affect the survivor's moods and thoughts about themselves and others, sometimes resulting in shame, guilt, blaming, and unhappiness with life in general. Sophia, for example, used to enjoy work relationships and felt

1. "Resilience is a multidimensional construct that includes genetic, neurohormonal, cognitive, personality, and social factors" (Friedman et al., 2007, p. 11).

confident exploring interests with men to whom she was attracted. Now she questions and blames herself, is fearful around male colleagues, and takes no pleasure in work or work-related travel. These trauma-related emotions are linked with values and beliefs based on rape myths that support the "cultural scaffolding of rape" (Gavey, 2005)—"an underlay of contradictory values, norms, ideas and practices [forming] a matrix of rape-supportive discourses" (Gavey & Senn, 2014, p. 347). Social systems like sexism, heterosexism, racism, and classism intersect to form specific rape myths that Sophia has internalized (Ramsay, 2013). She would benefit from a safe and trusting counseling relationship that helps her compassionately understand persistent trauma-related symptoms, find ways to experience safety and goodness, identify life-limiting beliefs and practices that exacerbate PTSD, and claim life-giving beliefs and practices that connect her with goodness.

PTSD is more likely when the threat of death or violation is severe (like combat and sexual assault) and especially when there are injuries and powerlessness. PTSD is also more common among people without support systems and relationships where they can process what has happened. Sophia's shame and fears about retaliation from her assailant prevented her from telling anyone what had happened. She tried to cope on her own. Without being able to rely on a compassionate and affirming circle of supporters, she was more vulnerable to negative moods, shame, and self-blaming. Another contributor to PTSD is a history of trauma or psychological vulnerabilities (i.e., anxiety, depression, addictions).

In summary, PTSD will be more likely when there is

- A severe sense of threat and injury
- A lack of social support—the most important posttraumatic factor in whether people recover (Brewin et al., 2000)

Pretraumatic risk factors include

- A history of trauma
- A history of mental illness
- Being girls and women, and thus more likely to experience sexual abuse, sexual assault, and intimate-partner violence—particularly toxic kinds of trauma
- Being young
- Being in a minority race
- Being in a lower socioeconomic status and educational level (Brewin, et al., 2000)

Pastoral counselors can help clients track trauma-related symptoms and whether they continue to be intense and disruptive a month or more after a traumatic event. They can also assess risk factors that make PTSD more likely (listed above).

Emerging research on trauma and moral distress suggests that, in addition to issues of fear, shame and guilt also need to be considered at the outset of psychospiritual care (Herman, 2011). Spiritual caregivers are uniquely equipped to help morally distressed trauma survivors find spiritual practices that help them experience a sense of self-compassion and/ or a transcendent experience of the compassion of God or the goodness of creation. Many military service members and veterans deployed to Iraq or Afghanistan faced morally questionable or ethically ambiguous situations that are typical of counterinsurgency, guerilla warfare (Litz, et al., 2009, p. 696). Sam's experience illustrates a combat-related event in which he tried to do his best but still felt like he had failed. His moral distress arises from the interacting values and beliefs of his religious and military cultures.

In the spiritual domain, clients experiencing spiritual and moral struggles may feel disillusioned and hopeless. They may have difficulties feeling thankful and not be able to access practices or routines that foster self-compassion, or to connect with God or a sense of the sacred. These *spiritual* struggles have a ripple effect in the following domains. In the *physical domain*, clients may experience trauma-related startle responses, hypervigilance, headaches, stress-related health problems, stress-related pain, and sleep problems. In the *emotional domain*, they may experience numbness, emotional shutdown, worry, anxiety, depression, anger, distraction, difficulties calming down, being on an emotional rollercoaster, and craving an adrenaline rush. In the *cognitive domain*, they may experience trauma-related automatic thoughts that reinforce negative beliefs about self and others. In the *behavioral domain*, they may struggle with impulsive behavioral ways of coping like using addictive substances, overeating, using the Internet excessively (in, say, social networking or cybersex), and gambling. In the *relational domain* they may end up withdrawing from or avoiding others, experiencing social anxiety and isolation, and feeling impatience or displeasure with more superficial socializing. They may also have difficulties with intimacy and may use coercive and violent ways of handling relational stress.

Twenty-year-old Sam, for example, has a recurrent nightmare of not being able to find his emergency medical supplies while his buddy bleeds and cries for help. He wakes up shaking and then is tormented by guilt that makes it hard for him to fall asleep again (a physiological effect of PTSD). He is tempted to use a prescription painkiller to dull his psychological torment. He knows that getting up and starting his morning routine of exercise would help (a life-giving behavioral and physiological way of coping), but instead he lies in bed, ruminating about how tired he's going to be all day, generating more negative thoughts. He feels totally alone and misses the physical comfort and release of tension he experienced in a previous partnership that ended when he was deployed. He's tempted to go online to a pornographic website (another life-limiting behavioral way of coping). He tries to use a meditative prayer that he practiced with the chaplain. As he focuses on the prayer, he can hear his minister's voice coaching him. He is finally able to physically relax and starts to have more positive thoughts about himself and his life. The more he can intentionally use this kind of spiritual practice that evokes positive thoughts and memories, the more he will experience beneficial ripple effects.

When clients access spiritual ways of fostering self-compassion, these spiritual practices can lead to posttraumatic and spiritual growth and resilience to traumatic stressors. Signs of posttraumatic and spiritual growth include feeling increased self-compassion; feeling connected with God, with a sense of the sacred, or with the beauty of life; finding supportive spiritual communities; and experiencing a sense of purpose. Spiritual integration will in turn have ripple effects in the following domains: In the *physical domain*, signs of posttraumatic and spiritual growth and resilience include better health overall, the ability to relax and cope with startle responses and hypervigilance, and healthy and efficient sleep patterns. In the *emotional domain* signs of post-traumatic/spiritual growth include calmness, peacefulness, feeling confident, being fully present in the here and now, and growing emotionally through adaptive responses to stress. In the *cognitive domain*, clients will be able to draw upon life-enhancing religious and spiritual beliefs and values that can counteract automatic negative thoughts. In the *behavioral domain*, signs of posttraumatic and spiritual growth will manifest in a healthy lifestyle, and habits like exercise, nutritious eating, moderate use of pleasure-inducing substances, and routines. In the *relational domain*, clients will find relational ways of coping with stress that deepen intimacy, including increased enjoyment of quality time with partners, family, and friends.

Psychospiritual education about trauma, along with journaling that tracks various aspects of trauma-related symptoms, are strategies used in cognitive behavioral therapy (CBT), one of the best evidence-based treatments (Resick et al., 2008). Spiritually integrated approaches to PTSD are showing promise (Murray-Swank & Pargament, 2005, 2008; Murray-Swank & Waelde, 2013). Throughout my description of intercultural pastoral counseling I incorporate (1) spiritual practices that foster compassion, and (2) cognitive behavioral treatment strategies that focus on the client's trauma-related emotions and thoughts.[2]

Specific features of CBT incorporated into this chapter's description of pastoral counseling for PTSD are the use of journaling and psychospiritual education about trauma, trauma-related symptoms, and their impact on all aspects of well-being, especially spiritual well-being. Clients use journaling in order to track trauma-related symptoms and their associated thoughts, feelings, and behaviors, along with coping strategies (what works and what doesn't). Journaling helps clients identify and break the associations between trauma-related automatic thoughts and their effects on emotions and physical sensations, behaviors, and all aspects of well-being—spiritual, physical, emotional, cognitive, behavioral, and relational.

Clients, for example, can keep a daily record of when they experience trauma-related symptoms, how disruptive they are (on a ten-point scale), what seems to have triggered symptoms, and how they coped. These journal entries help counselors and clients track type, frequency, and severity of trauma-related symptoms and the initial ways clients cope. As pastoral counseling moves from the assessment and psychoeducational phase into a psychospiritual focus on coping, clients can use journaling to track whether the spiritual and religious ways they cope enhance or undermine a sense of safety.

Identify, Evaluate and Integrate
the Client's Lived Theology

Once clients have identified and evaluated habitual coping strategies and tested life-giving spiritual practices, they will be ready for the final phase of counseling: exploring their lived theology. Lived theologies and spiritual orienting systems consist of the emotionally-charged constellations of beliefs and values that clients put into practice in coping behaviors. Journal entries about trauma-related emotions and automatic thoughts provide clients with data for exploring the underlying beliefs and values of their lived theologies and spiritual-orienting systems. Clients will have the opportunity to assess whether these orienting systems are congruent with their espoused or intentional theology (what they say they believe in).

---

2. Pastoral counselors will need specialized training and supervision in order to use CBT treatment strategies like exposure treatment (graduated levels of prolonged exposure to imaginal and *in vivo* trauma-related stimuli using the client's hierarchy of anxiety-provoking situations/memories), Eye Movement Desensitization and Reprocessing (EMDR) and Dialectical Behavioral Therapy (DBT).

Many trauma survivors find that traumatic events and memories tap into lived theologies formed in childhood. Clients can be invited to think about their lived theology as multilayered (Doehring, 2015):

- Precritical childhood beliefs and values shaped by family and experienced as literally and absolutely true, one could say in a premodern sense.

- Values and beliefs formed in adolescence and young adulthood, using critical perspectives gained developmentally and through mentoring and higher education. Often these values and beliefs draw upon more modern ways of thinking.

- Maturing values and beliefs shaped through ongoing formative experiences and relationships. These beliefs and values are usually intrinsically meaningful in terms of more contextual, postmodern approaches to knowledge.

Metaphorically speaking, trauma is like an earthquake that exposes beliefs and values formed in childhood that may be buried but still exerting an influence in the form of emotionally charged automatic thoughts. Pastoral counselors can help clients assess this embedded childhood theology in terms of whether it is still relevant and life-giving to them in adulthood, especially as they cope with trauma-related symptoms. As clients keep track in their journals of trauma-related emotions and automatic thoughts, they can note whether such thoughts are rooted in life-giving or life-limiting embedded values and beliefs from various phases in their lives. They can also test whether trauma-related symptoms are alleviated by intentional use of spiritual practices that reflect enduring life-giving core values and beliefs.

Over time, this journaling and use of intentional practices will help clients identify and set aside life-limiting values and beliefs triggered by automatic thoughts, countering them with life-giving values and beliefs that anchor their sense of who they are. The more these anchoring values and beliefs are claimed and intentionally put into practice, the more clients will experience trauma-related spiritual and psychological growth and the integration of traumatic memories into life-giving self-narratives. Clients will then be able to remember without being overwhelmed and will slowly be able to digest the horror of what happened and incorporate traumatic experiences in life-giving ways into their life narratives.

Theologically Reflecting on the Benefits and Liabilities of Lived Theologies of Trauma

Counselors trained in pastoral theological studies[3] can draw upon their theological expertise in helping clients assess the consequences of the theologies of trauma inherent in their values and beliefs, especially embedded theologies from childhood. Religious and theological education gives counselors a historical and comparative understanding of various religious and theological ways that people have tried to make sense of and live with suffering. There are, of course, innumerable philosophical and theological treatises on evil and the problem of suffering. Theologian Susan Nelson (2003) provides a helpful introductory typology of five ways of understanding suffering within Christian traditions.[4] In reviewing various ways that religious traditions have struggled to make sense of suffering, pastoral counselors can consider how such understandings may be life-giving or life-limiting in the process of coping with trauma-related symptoms, and also in the long-range meaning-making process.

The most common Christian ways of understanding suffering described by Nelson are moral and redemptive theologies. Some traditional moral theologies function in life-limiting ways when people inappropriately blame themselves, believing that trauma and suffering is a consequence of their personal sin and a punishment from God. More complex moral theologies function in life-giving ways when people need to hold themselves accountable. Sam held himself accountable when he didn't provide the best emergency care he could have. He felt as though he had compromised moral ideals instilled during his military training. Sam realized that his guilt was exaggerated when he and his counselor talked about Sam's commander's assessment that everyone had done the best job they could. Sam also realized that his all-or-nothing thinking and sense of overresponsibility contributed to his automatic thoughts of guilt and his moral approach to suffering.

Sam also found that some of his childhood beliefs in redemption became life limiting when he automatically thought that his anguished ruminations on his buddy's amputation were his cross to bear. Sam recalled

3. Pastoral theological studies are a form of practical theology in which pastoral praxis is brought into dialogue with relevant theoretical perspectives, including religious, psychological, and theological studies.

4. Interculturally, counselors need to refrain from "translating" beliefs about suffering from other religions of the world into this Christian typology. They need to receptively explore what and how each client describes and assesses his or her lived theologies. Nonetheless, summaries about theologies of suffering can orient counselors to some of the benefits and liabilities of these theologies.

his minister's counsel: tormenting himself with blame was not a cross to bear that would somehow redeem his buddy's suffering.[5] Sam found that redemptive theology was life-giving when he experienced God's compassion with him in his suffering, and later, when he looked back and saw that this compassion, especially embodied in his minister, brought forth new life (Jones, 2009; Rambo, 2010; Swain, 2011).

A third historically significant Christian theology of suffering is eschatological, focused on moments of hope that point to a future when suffering will be alleviated. Nelson makes this theology especially relevant for trauma survivors by describing the moments of hope that pierce unrelenting fear or horror and help survivor see a light beyond the darkness. Sophia remembered such a moment when she experienced the kindness of the woman at her employee-assistance program who helped her find a pastoral counselor. After speaking with her, Sophia felt a sense of hope amid her lonely struggles to cope and stay engaged at work. She later wondered whether her determined self-reliance was a reaction to the way her mother endured suffering in the hope of future justice. Her Catholic feminism made her question this kind of hope. Her self-directing way of coping was a lived theology in which her only hope was herself. When she realized she could trust her pastoral counselor, a more life-giving sense of hope emerged, that she would eventually regain her self-confidence and begin to enjoy work again.

Nelson also describes theologies of lament or radical suffering, and theologies of ambiguous creation. Lament theologies help many trauma survivors interrogate and lament terrible suffering (Graham, 2006). Sophia lamented how much her assailant had violated her sense of trust by seeming to share her deepest values. She later sought out a spiritual director who could help her engage deeply with God, especially when she was angry.

Theologies of ambiguous creation use twentieth-century worldviews of creation as systemic, finite, and diverse, with human beings embedded in relational webs that inevitably result in limits and conflicted choices. Relational theistic theologies like process theology describe God's power "as persuasive and relational rather than unilateral, ordered by love and compassionate judgment" (Graham, 2006, pp. 11–12). Feminist theologian Wendy Farley (1990, p. 133) highlights the role of compassion in a process theological understanding of tragedy: "The radical love of God . . . is not overcome by evil . . . In seeing and tasting this love, human beings . . . come

---

5. Marie Fortune rightly argues against this kind of life-limiting redemptive theology: "Rather than *sanctification of suffering*, Jesus' crucifixion remains a witness to the horror of violence. It is not a model of how *suffering should be borne*, but a witness to God's desire that no one should suffer such violence again" (Fortune, 2005, p. 140).

to burn with the incandescent compassion for the world, to feel the grief of the world without being destroyed by it."

Theologically oriented approaches to trauma and moral distress have been proposed by Jones (2009), Kinghorn (2012), Rambo (2010), and Whitehead (2010). Kinghorn (2009, p. 2) argues for the "irreducibly moral context of the combat situation." Spiritual care is not simply a supplement to mental health care but has its own unique expertise and purpose, says Kinghorn (2009, p. 11): "Christians (and religious communities in general) must provide for combat veterans what Shelly Rambo, following Serene Jones, refers to as 'morphological spaces' which provide form and structure to experiences which, due to linguistic and conceptual impoverishment, would otherwise remain unnarratable."

Rambo's, Jones's and Swain's theologies of suffering are primarily oriented to Christian traditions, and specifically theologies of lament and redemption. Such theologies often shape how healing is understood. In an exploratory study interviewing Vietnam veterans who use Buddhist practices to cope with trauma, Doehring and Arora (2013) found that these veterans qualified the idea of healing from trauma by describing how Buddhist practices have enabled them to respond compassionately to posttraumatic stress and moral distress without the resurrectionist overtones of redemptive theologies of suffering. Such practices help them, first, recognize triggers and how they automatically respond to them; and second, help them contemplate their reactions through the lenses of self-compassion and complex understandings of suffering. Each of the veterans came to Buddhist practices after searching for ways to reconnect with some sense of goodness, especially when they reexperienced the horrors of their Vietnam experiences and tried to avoid morally distressing memories. Buddhist practices dramatically changed their experience of posttraumatic suffering and, indeed, their lives.

In reflecting on these veterans' experiences, Doehring and Arora (2013) explore how Buddhist approaches provide an alternative to commonly used redemptive theologies of suffering. These approaches offer (1) meaning-making frameworks for understanding morally distressing memories, (2) practices for emotionally and spiritually processing disturbing memories related to moral distress, and (3) value-based commitments to helping other veterans. The role of self-compassion was central in helping the veterans no longer avoid the moral distress of their traumatic experiences. Buddhist beliefs about suffering helped them develop more complex ways of understanding their experiences, such that they could begin to comprehend the ambiguous and interconnected relational and cultural webs in which they were caught as young soldiers. Understanding the tragic interrelated dimensions of their suffering and the suffering they may have caused helped them give voice to lament and also assume appropriate responsibility for their actions. Buddhist worldviews helped them accept their moral agency in complex ways that allowed them to incorporate distressing memories into an integrated self-narrative.

The experiences of these veterans highlight the need to monitor how embedded theologies of redemptive suffering are often used to understand trauma but are sometimes unable to hold the lament associated with moral distress within the ambiguity of such suffering. Spiritual caregivers and pastoral counselors need to draw upon their theological expertise to appreciate the radical ways some survivors live out an ambiguous theology of suffering at odds with commonly used redemptive theologies. While Rambo (2010), Jones (2009), and Swain (2011) offer a much more sophisticated theology of suffering that makes room for lament, embedded theologies of redemption often push people beyond lament to accept resurrection as the ultimate sign of healing. In exploring the intricacies of lived theologies of healing, spiritual caregivers and counselors need theological expertise, even within the context of intercultural care that values the uniqueness of survivors' existential worlds.

In the process of exploring the benefits and liabilities of clients' lived and espoused theologies, clients and their counselors will coconstruct and elaborate life-giving theologies of suffering that are deeply anchored in the client's values and beliefs. These theologies can be practiced in several ways. They can be used to counter automatic trauma-related thoughts based on embedded theologies no longer relevant and meaningful. They can also be tested in the client's spiritual and religious practices. Posttraumatic growth will increase as clients develop a well-integrated spirituality that is "broad and deep, responsive to life's situations, nurtured by the larger social context, capable of flexibility and continuity [and] large enough to encompass the full range of human potential and luminous enough to provide the individual with a powerful guiding vision" (Pargament, 2007, p. 136).

References

Brewin, C. R. et al. (2000). Meta-analysis of risk factors for posttraumatic stress disorder in trauma-exposed adults. *Journal of Consulting and Clinical Psychology, 68*, 748–66.

Doehring, C. (2009). Theological accountability: The hallmark of pastoral counseling. *Sacred Spaces, 1*(1), http://www.aapc.org/media/75733/theologicalaccountability3.pdf/.

Doehring, C. (2014). Emotions and change in intercultural spiritual care. *Pastoral Psychology*. doi: 10.1007/s11089-014-0607-3

Doehring, C. (2015). *The practice of pastoral care: A postmodern approach* (Revised and expanded ed.). Louisville: Westminster John Knox.

Doehring, C., & Arora, K. (2013). Putting into practice an intercultural approach to spiritual care with veterans. *Theological Education, 47*(2), 39–47, http://www.ats. edu/uploads/resources/publications-presentations/chapp-reports/iliff-school-of-theology.pdf/.

Drescher, K. D. et al. (2011). An exploration of the usefulness of the construct of moral injury in war veterans. *Traumatology, 17*(8), 8–13. doi: 10.117/1534765610395615

Farley, W. (1990). *Tragic vision and divine compassion: A contemporary theodicy.* Louisville: Westminster John Knox.

Fortune, M. M. (2005). *Sexual violence: The sin revisited.* Cleveland: Pilgrim.

Friedman, M. J. et al. (2007). PTSD: Twenty-five years of progress and challenge. In M. J. Friedman et al. (Eds.). *Handbook of PTSD: Science and practice* (pp. 3–18). New York: Guilford.

Gavey, N. (2005). *Just sex? The cultural scaffolding of rape.* London: Routledge.

Gavey, N., & Senn, C. Y. (2014). Sexuality and sexual violence. In D. L. Tolman et al., (Eds.), *APA handbook of sexuality and psychology, Vol. 1: Person-based approaches.* (pp. 339–82). Washington DC: American Psychological Association.

Graham, L. K. (2006). Pastoral theology and catastrophic disaster. *Journal of Pastoral Theology, 16*(2), 1–17.

Harris, J. I., Erbes et al. (2011). The effectiveness of a trauma-focused spiritually integrated intervention for veterans exposed to trauma. *Journal of Clinical Psychology, 67*, 425–38. doi: 10.1002/jclp.20777

Herman, J. L. (2011). Posttraumatic stress disorder as a shame disorder. In R. L. Dearing & J. P. Tangney (Eds.), *Shame in the therapy hour* (pp. 261–75). Washington DC: American Psychological Association.

Jones, S. (2009). *Trauma and grace: Theology in a ruptured world.* Louisville: Westminster John Knox.

Kinghorn, W. (2009). *Religious communities and the moral context of combat-related post-traumatic stress disorder among American military veterans.* Paper presented at the AAR Annual Meeting, Montreal, QC, Canada.

Kinghorn, W. (2012). Combat trauma and moral fragmentation: A theological account of moral injury. *Journal of the Society of Christian Ethics, 32*(2), 57–74.

Klimecki, O. M. et al. (2013). Functional neural plasticity and associated changes in positive affect after compassion training. *Cerebral Cortex, 23* 1552–61. doi: 10.1093/cercor/bhs142

Lartey, E. Y. (2006). *Pastoral theology in an intercultural world.* Cleveland: Pilgrim.

Leslie, K. J. (2002). *When violence is no stranger: Pastoral counseling with survivors of acquaintance rape.* Minneapolis: Fortress.

Litz, B. et al. (2009). Moral injury and moral repair in war veterans: A preliminary model and intervention strategy. *Clinical Psychological Review, 29*, 695–706. doi: 10.1016/j.cpr.2009.07.003/.

Moyaert, M. (2012). Recent developments in the theology of interreligious dialogue: From soteriological openness to hermeneutical openness. *Modern Theology, 28*, 25–52.

Murray-Swank, N. A., & Pargament, K. (2005). God, where are you?: Evaluating a spiritually-integrated intervention for sexual abuse. *Mental Health, Religion & Culture, 8*, 191–203.

Murray-Swank, N. A., & Pargament, K. (2008). Solace for the soul: Evaluating a spiritually-integrated counselling intervention for sexual abuse. *Counselling and Spirituality / Counseling et spiritualité, 27*(2), 157–74.

Murray-Swank, N. A., & Waelde, L. C. (2013). Spirituality, religion, and sexual trauma: Integrating research, theory, and clinical practice. In K. Pargament et al. (Eds.), *APA handbook of psychology, religion, and spirituality: An applied psychology of religion, and spirituality.* (Vol. 2, pp. 335–54). Washington DC: American Psychological Association.

Nelson, S. (2003). Facing evil: Evil's many faces; Five paradigms for understanding evil. *Interpretation, 57,* 398–413.

Pargament, K. (2007). *Spiritually integrated psychotherapy: Understanding and addressing the sacred.* New York: Guilford.

Pargament, K. et al. (2005). Sacrilege: A study of sacred loss and desecration and their implications for health and well-being in a community sample. *Journal for the Scientific Study of Religion, 44,* 59–78. doi: 10.1111/j.1468–5906.2005.00265.x

Pargament, K. et al. (2005). Spiritual struggle: A phenomenon of interest to psychology and religion. In W. R. Miller & H. Delaney (Eds.), *Judeo-Christian perspectives in psychology: Human nature, motivation, and change* (pp. 245–68). Washington DC: American Psychological Association.

Pargament, K. et al. (2013). Envisioning an integrative paradigm for the psychology of religion, and spirituality: An introduction to the APA handbook of psychology, religion and spirituality In K. Pargament et al. (Eds.), *APA handbook of psychology, religion, and spirituality* (Vol. 1, pp. 3–19). Washington DC: American Psychological Association.

Prothero, S. (2010). *God is not one: The eight rival religions that run the world and why their differences matter.* New York: HarperOne.

Rambo, S. (2010). *Spirit and trauma: A theology of remaining.* Louisville: Westminster John Knox.

Ramsay, N. J. (2013). Intersectionality: A model for addressing the complexity of oppression and privilege. *Pastoral Psychology 63,* 453–69, doi: 10.1007/s11089–013–0570–4

Resick, P. A., Monson, C. M., & Rizvi, S. L. (2008). Posttraumatic stress disorder. In D. H. Barlow (Ed.), *Clinical handbook of psychological disorders: A step-by-step treatment manual* (4th ed., pp. 65–121). New York: Guilford.

Swain, S. (2011). *Trauma and transformation at ground zero: A pastoral theology.* Minneapolis: Fortress.

Whitehead, J. C. (2010). *Constructing a neuroscientific pastoral theology of fear and hope.* (Unpublished doctoral dissertation). Iliff School of Theology and University of Denver, Denver, CO.

11

Initial Interviews

Insook Lee

INITIAL INTERVIEWS SET THE overall tone of the psychotherapeutic process.[1] First impressions really matter. Subsequent intersubjective developments may alter the relationship, but it takes time to erase, correct, or modify the impressions formed in the first meetings. Pastoral psychotherapists learn to take advantage of these critical moments to build an initial foundation on which a meaningful, therapeutic relationship with the client can be established.

The pastoral psychotherapist must engage in this critical process as a person, as a clinician, and as a pastoral theologian. As a person, the psychotherapist presents herself as a genuine, honest, and relationally capable human being; as a clinician, she shows professionally competent knowledge and skills; and as a pastoral theologian, she collaborates with the client to explore, deconstruct, and reconstruct theological and spiritual meanings regarding clients' concerns. Balancing these three dimensions helps establish "a controlled, but warm and human, situation" (Chessick, 1991, p. 93), which leads to a successful encounter with the client in the initial interview or interviews.

In this chapter, I consider ways to structure and conduct the first interview or interviews, and what specific knowledge, skills, and competencies are required of the pastoral psychotherapist.[2] As a way to understand what

1. Richard Chessick, psychoanalyst, discusses the importance of initial interviews in his book, *The Technique and Practice of Intensive Psychotherapy* (1991).

2. Some of these topics overlap with the content of other chapters, such as "Diagnostic Consideration" (chapter 9) and "Individuals: The Therapeutic Relationship" (chapter 12). I attempt to focus on the areas not covered by those chapters.

a successful initial contact with the client may look like, I begin by defining the concept of initial interviews. Then I proceed to discuss the topics of holding environment, working alliance, and the therapeutic subjectivity of the psychotherapist for the client. Theological reflection is also presented as a dimension of the therapeutic process. After having discussed those basics of successful pastoral psychotherapy, I explore practical and clinical concerns and details, such as intake process, information gathering, initial assessment, treatability, therapeutic contract and goals, referrals, and transference and countertransference.[3]

What is an Initial Interview?

An initial interview or interviews refers to the first session or sessions (and any initial phone call) in which the psychotherapist and the client meet with each other to determine the client's need for treatment and to decide whether or not to begin psychotherapy. This definition highlights two points: (1) the decisions are reciprocal and must occur in the *relationship* between the client and the psychotherapist; and (2) to serve the client's need is the priority. Even the phone call setting up the first session is influenced by the subtle relational dynamics between the client and the psychotherapist, including transference-countertransference. In other words, establishing a relationship is a critical component in determining the success of the ensuing psychotherapy. The three relational components to which the psychotherapist should pay careful attention in the initial interviews are the holding environment, the therapeutic alliance, and the therapeutic subjectivity of the psychotherapist.

Holding Environment

Donald Winnicott (1960), a psychoanalytically trained pediatrician, argued that a child needs a holding environment in which a caretaker both protects the child and gives the child appropriate freedom to explore the wider world. This holding environment is both a physical and psychical space within which the child experiences himself or herself in the process of strengthening his or her ego to grow and mature.

Wilfred Bion (1970), a British psychoanalyst, discusses the similar concepts of the "container" and the "contained" in parenting. Infants often

3. For definitions of transference and countertransference, see the section headed Initial Therapeutic Assessment, below.

become overwhelmed by affect and communicate that affect through cries, coos, or facial expressions. A good caretaker pays attention to, listens to, and takes in those communicated affects, and tries to make sense of them. The processed affect or distress is introjected by the baby, who is now contained by the caretaker's empathic soothing.

Most psychotherapy depends on a unique therapeutic relationship characterized by such "holding" and "containing" to build a trusting, nurturing, and therapeutic relationship with the client. A good holding environment makes the client feel taken care of, understood, protected, and held in a way that provides a sense of safety and security. In this protected space, the client is encouraged to explore his or her own inner feelings and thoughts, impulsive fantasies and instincts, without feeling threatened or retaliated against. This holding and containing environment must be dependable, consistent, and attuned to the client's needs.

How can we create a holding and containing environment in pastoral psychotherapy? Just as there is no such thing as a perfect mother but instead a good enough mother (Winnicott, 1960), the psychotherapist cannot create a perfect—only a good enough—holding environment. The holding environment is often subtle but can be described in two ways. One is the therapist's internal capacity of empathic attunement to the client, and the other is the therapist's ability to maintain the therapeutic frame and boundaries. The first—empathic attunement—includes the therapist's ability to receive the client's unprocessed, chaotic, and inchoate psychic materials and respond to them without acting out the therapist's own wishes and fantasies. In particular, the therapist is expected to hold the client's difficult emotions such as rage, hatred, and ruthlessness as well as eroticized transference toward the therapist. To develop this nonreactive holding capacity, the therapist must continuously work on his or her own hidden issues and impulsive desires through supervision, consultation, or personal psychotherapy as necessary. The psychotherapist needs to know how to pay attention to and work on his or her countertransference that may interfere with creating a holding environment for the client.

Establishing a therapeutic frame and boundaries includes a wide range of elements, starting with how to arrange office furniture, since the therapist's office itself is a holding environment. A good arrangement of the office space maximizes the holding effect of the physical space and its accompanying effect on the psychological dimension.[4] The therapeutic frame is also maintained by the way the therapist structures the treatment,

---

4. The psychotherapist pays attention to the positions of chairs, clock, lighting, and soundproofing of the room. Distracting items, such as stimulating pictures or photos, must be avoided.

including providing a therapeutic contract, determining the frequency of sessions, setting basic ground rules (both implicit and explicit), defining the length of each session, setting fees, and arranging many more details. In this carefully structured setting, the client feels *held* and knows what to expect, and the therapist is experienced as reliable and consistent. When the client experiences the holding environment as *good enough*, he or she is ready to build a relationship with the psychotherapist. This relationship between the client and the psychotherapist is unique in its ultimate purpose, which is to benefit the client and to serve his or her needs. We name this relationship a therapeutic alliance or working alliance.

Therapeutic Alliance

For decades, there have been debates about the most important components of successful psychotherapies. Research shows that the therapeutic alliance is the strongest predictor of success.[5] The therapeutic alliance refers to the positive and collaborative working relationship between the psychotherapist and the client. It includes the general feeling of being together as a team and working together toward common goals for the benefit of the client. Psychologically defined, the clients' reasonable and conscious ego, often weakened, joins the working or analyzing ego function of the therapist to serve the positive outcomes of the desired changes. A good working alliance requires a degree of ego strength on the part of the client. She or he has to be able to look at herself or himself objectively together with the therapist. A successful psychotherapy thus depends upon this relatively intact part of the client's ego that can work in a therapeutic alliance with the psychotherapist.

The task of creating a therapeutic alliance also requires special capabilities of the psychotherapist. Richard Chessick (1991) calls these capabilities broadly the "maturity of the psychotherapist" (p. 82), and more specifically enumerates eleven factors that show the psychotherapist's maturity (p. 88), mostly focusing on the psychotherapist's integrity and health. For example, the psychotherapist must deal first with his or her own needs and must achieve a certain level of self-critical understanding through an intensive psychotherapy for himself or herself. These personal qualities of the psychotherapist are also similar to those required to establish a good holding environment. Holding environment and therapeutic alliance go hand in hand, mutually enhancing the effect of successful psychotherapy. For this task, the

5. Horvath and Symonds (1991) in *Journal of Consulting Psychology* (38), 139–49 and Martin, Garske, and Davis (2000) in *Journal of Consulting and Clinical Psychology* (68), 438–50.

psychotherapist must develop a unique subjectivity of his or her own, called a therapeutic subjectivity, in order to cultivate a therapeutic alliance in a reliable holding environment.

Therapeutic Subjectivity of the Pastoral Psychotherapist

Pastoral psychotherapists need to be trained to develop and cultivate a unique subjectivity that is attuned to the otherness of the Other.[6] Emmanuel Levinas's concept of subjectivity as "the Other in the Same" (1981, p. 112) is helpful to understand this critical subjectivity required for all competent pastoral psychotherapists. Levinas is a Jewish philosopher born in Lithuania in 1906. Throughout his scholarly career, he pursued the problem of otherness or alterity.[7] Based on this lifelong exploration, he eventually theorized and defined human subjectivity as "the Other in the Same." It means that one's subjectivity cannot be formed by itself but is supported and created by the existence of the Other. Such subjectivity transcends the "egocentric"[8] approach to the Other in order to take in, embrace, and hold the psychic and mental materials of the Other without assimilating them into one's existing systems of knowing.

Levinasian subjectivity emphasizes the transcendent aspect of the Other that "I"[9] cannot completely understand through a cognitive process of analysis and interpretation. Psychology is a discipline that attempts to un-

6. The Other opposes the Same. The Other often refers to a person other than one's self and therefore is identified as "different." The Same refers to the subjective self.

7. Alterity is a philosophical term meaning "otherness." Its meaning is well described in the following excerpts from http://ordinary-gentleman.com/kylecupp/2012/01/what-is-alterity/, written by Kyle Cupp, a freelance writer. "I remember well my first real experience of alterity. I was standing in line with my younger brother, looking at his face, when it suddenly dawned on me that I both knew and didn't know who he was. I realized in that moment that no matter how well I would or could come to know him, there would always be a mysterious remainder to my knowledge. I knew then that I could never know him or anyone else completely. I understood that there would always be something *other* about every other. Levinas, I imagine, would be pleased to know that my experience of alterity literally came from looking into another's face."

8. According to Levinas, ego refers to subjective consciousness of perceiving and assimilating the objective world into its system. The Same in the ego often exercises mastery upon what is thought. In this way, the Other becomes interior to thought and falls under the power of the Same, losing the otherness of the Other. Levinas calls this subjective, interior process *solipsistic* and *egocentric* approach to the Other.

9. Levinas argues that the "I" is the subject that functions mostly based on ego activities and therefore tends to reduce the Other to the Same. The "I" in the ego understands the Other through "representation" and "projection," and thus the distinction between the "I" and "non-I" disappears.

derstand people's subjective experiences from within. In this process, therefore, clients inherently may become "objects" of our cognitive process which
would alter their unique otherness and experiences to become immanent
to our therapeutic analysis. In this sense, psychology, though a powerful
tool to understand human experience from within, has the potential to be
a reductionistic approach to the Other. To overcome this potential short-
coming, psychology needs dialogue partners from other disciplines, such as
theology, anthropology, philosophy, and sociology. These disciplines would
help balance pastoral psychotherapists' perception by focusing on the wider
contexts of cultural, social, political and spiritual dimensions. These dimensions are critical to and essential in caring for human beings as "living
documents within the web" (Miller-McLemore, 2012, p. 63).[10] Subjectivity
as "the Other in the Same" is thus vital for the pastoral psychotherapist.

Miroslav Volf (1996), a Christian systematic theologian, also argues
for the radical otherness of the Other in relationships. He models his argument on the self-giving love of Jesus Christ of the cross and resurrection.
For Volf, self-giving means to "distance ourselves from ourselves and our
cultures in order to create a space for the other" (p. 30). This psychological
distancing requires the development of "double vision" (p. 253). Wolf argues
that God views things from everywhere and thus God's vision is perfectly
balanced without being tainted by self-interest, biases, or presumptions.
Human beings are limited in their visions and can never duplicate God's
vision in a perfect sense. However, we are created in God's image and can
imitate God's vision in a limited way. If not divine multiple visions, we can
develop at least a "double" vision by which to see things from both *here* (the
perspective of *I* or the Same) and from *there* (the perspective of the Other).

Volf's double vision and Levinas's concept of subjectivity are the essentials for creating a therapeutic holding environment. Such a holding
environment is both a psychological and theological space in which a trusting, nurturing, and therapeutic relationship is born and nurtured. Based on
these psychological and theological meanings of a holding environment, I
next discuss practical details of structuring the first interviews, such as information gathering, initial assessments, and therapeutic contract. All these
performances continue to strengthen the emerging therapeutic alliance in
the holding environment.

---

10. Bonnie Miller-McLemore is a pastoral theologian. She initially proposed the
metaphor of "the living web" in contrast to Anton Boisen's "living human document."
Later, she changed the term to "living human document within the web" to emphasize
the interconnection between person and web. This new term implies more active interplay among psychology, other human sciences, religion, and spirituality.

Information Gathering

In the first interview or interviews, the psychotherapist gathers information with which to make a first therapeutic assessment and diagnosis. This is an effort to build an informed, intimate, and therapeutic relationship in the concrete context where the client is situated. Information gathering is not just about collecting factual data. It is about an interpersonal exchange and requires clinical, relational and pastoral competencies on the part of the psychotherapist.

Information gathering can take place both by using a formal intake form, usually before the first face-to-face session, and through observation and conversation during a face-to-face session. A formal intake form generally includes basic personal information, such as the client's name; gender; address; educational level; and ethnic, racial, and cultural background, religious affiliation, marital status, family background, medical and psychological history, and presenting problem or problems. This basic information helps the psychotherapist see the big picture and decide where and how to begin the first interviews. The face-to-face interview provides a more intimate level of information conveyed through the client's tone of voice, gestures, mood, eye contact, verbal choices, and proficiency of expression.

The first face-to-face interview usually begins with a discussion of the client's presenting problem or problems. It is important for the psychotherapist to hear the client's complaints in his or her own words and try to discern whether there are any repeated words, themes, or patterns in the client's narratives. For this task, the pastoral psychotherapist needs disciplined multifocal listening skills. For example, one psychotherapist listens not only for factual data but also for empathetic connection with the client. Another psychotherapist might listen to every detail of the client's stories, but without losing sight of the bigger picture of the hidden but potential causes and problems. John Patton (2005), a pastoral theologian, uses bifocal listening to hear the client's conflicting experiences of God. A client experiencing difficulties in his or her life often uses the two contrasting voices of testimony and countertestimony to describe what is going on. Testimony includes the words of faith, hope, and trust, and countertestimony refers to the client's voice expressing doubts, mistrust, despair, fear, and anger towards God. Here the psychotherapist must know how to listen and respond to both kinds of narrative, but particularly to countertestimony because this is the more painful narrative with which the client is struggling to make sense of his or her experience.

There are different opinions regarding history taking. I agree with Chessick that, as far as the practice of intensive psychotherapy is concerned, it is "mandatory for the psychotherapist to take a careful history in the first few interviews" (1991, p. 107). Such history taking includes the details of familial and marital history, sexual history, social and work history, educational history, religious history, mental- and physical-health history, relational history, and so forth. I often use a genogram[11] as a tool to collect this data in a systematic, relatively nonintrusive, and collaborative way with the client. Through conducting and interpreting the genogram, I can often create an ethos of working together as a team to examine the information presented and revealed through the genogram. It also presents a good opportunity to test how much the client can follow and endure the self-reflective psychotherapeutic work that will follow. I usually schedule this formal history taking only after we have already completed one or two sessions and the client feels relieved of anxiety about the psychotherapy itself and as heard about the current pain with which he or she is struggling. Too early a formal history taking can be counterproductive, inducing the sense of alienation for the client who may not understand its immediate relevance. It may interfere with the formation of a good working alliance and holding environment. To avoid this situation, the psychotherapist must tell the client why genogram information and history taking are necessary and how they will contribute to the understanding of the client's current problems.

Information gathering is not about an open-ended, free-association type of conversation but about the ultimate assessment outcomes of the client's problems and situations. The pastoral psychotherapist should collect data to assess the nature of the client's presenting problems, their treatability, and to design treatment plans informed and supported by this data. Information gathering is a process. It continues with the ongoing, updated assessments which will, in turn, continue to evolve and be modified as new data is available and collected. Such information gathering is also about an interpersonal exchange in which both the pastoral psychotherapist's relational and clinical skills are required.

11. A genogram is a graphic representation of a family tree that displays detailed data on relationships among individuals. It goes beyond a traditional family tree by allowing the user to analyze hereditary, psychological, and relational patterns in the family. Genograms allow a psychotherapist and his or her client to quickly identify various patterns in the client's family history which may have had an influence on the client's current state of mind. Genograms are presented by Monica McGoldrick and Randy Gerson in their book, *Genograms in Family Assessment* (1985).

Therapeutic Contract

Establishing a therapeutic contract provides a "holding" and "containing" environment in which the client feels cared for and protected. Long-term intensive psychotherapy is a very intimate and personal experience.[12] The client invites the psychotherapist to hear the most private thoughts and feelings of his or her inner life. Facing a journey into the unknown territory of pastoral psychotherapy, the client may feel anxious and uncertain. It is the pastoral psychotherapist's responsibility to create a safe and secure environment by implicitly and explicitly setting caring boundaries for the client. A therapeutic contract informs the client of what to expect from the psychotherapy, including what is expected from the client. The contract must be made at the very beginning, though it may be changed and negotiated in its details over the course of psychotherapy. It is crucial, however, for the pastoral psychotherapist to consistently and persistently keep the therapeutic contract in effect. Consistency is important particularly in working with severely psychotic clients who have not yet formed object constancy.

The therapeutic contract refers to any implicit and explicit structures, rules, and policies in the pastoral therapeutic relationship. It includes payment of fees, meeting times, frequency of sessions, length of treatment, confidentiality, therapeutic goals and methods, how to deal with missed sessions and holidays, phone calls between the sessions, emergency contact, and interaction outside the sessions (e.g., contact at conferences, seminars, restaurants, or in the street). Some of these details are discussed in a straightforward manner in the very beginning, while others evolve and wait until the need shows up.

Establishing the contract is a collaborative process shared between the client and the pastoral psychotherapist. For the client who does not know much about therapy, therefore, contracting is a good moment to educate the client about how to work collaboratively in therapy sessions. For example, the pastoral psychotherapist may say, "These sessions are yours. You can talk about anything on your mind. Sometimes, you may have topics of pressing importance and sometimes not. In either case, I encourage you to talk freely about anything that comes to mind, including thoughts and feelings that are difficult to talk about, such as anxiety, anger, fear, shame, and embarrassment. I am here to listen to anything you want to say and to work with you to explore your feelings and thoughts." In this way, the pastoral

12. Psychotherapists must assess if the client is ready for this intensive psychotherapy. Some clients are not qualified for this treatment and may rather benefit from short-term ego-supportive psychotherapy. The criteria for this assessment will be discussed later in this chapter under the heading Initial Therapeutic Assessment.

psychotherapist informs the client that each of them has a specific role in this therapeutic relationship.

One of the sensitive issues in the contract is how to deal with missed sessions. The general rule is that the client is financially responsible for the missed sessions, and the pastoral psychotherapist must clearly communicate this rule in the first sessions. However, this general rule must not be too rigid, considering our human situations where many unexpected emergencies can occur. The pastoral psychotherapist needs to be flexible to embrace exceptions to this rule. Each pastoral psychotherapist defines the exceptions in a different way. Some therapists do not charge if the client gives sufficient notice (e.g., twenty-four hours) or if the client's situation is an emergency. This policy, however, is often difficult to enforce equitably because it is up to the psychotherapist to determine whether a situation is an emergency or not. This dynamic may induce the subtlety of power struggle, against which the client may show resistance and produce a specific transference. Therapeutically, this is a good chance to observe the client's relational dynamic with others, particularly authority figures, in a real-life situation. The pastoral psychotherapist must know how to grasp this opportunity to carefully guide the client to observe and explore what is going on in both the inner and external worlds of the client and to gain insight.

Phone calls between sessions are another area about which each psychotherapist has a different policy, often with good reason, particularly when working with a client with borderline personality. A borderline client comes to the therapist with a strong need for dependency and intimacy, which will be dramatically manifested in a mixture of love and hatred. Until the client begins to gain some level of object constancy, the pastoral psychotherapist must provide the client with a sense of security through consistent and persistent availability and presence, but balanced by clear boundaries. One way to deal with the immense need of the borderline client is to set a more frequent number of sessions per week. Other suggestions are to allow the client to call whenever the client has a need for the psychotherapist's presence, but either limit those phone calls to five minutes or invite the client to leave messages without expecting the psychotherapist's return call. The contents and motivations of those calls will become part of the next session's discussion. In some instances, simply listening to the therapist's voice on the answering machine may soothe the client's crisis emotions.

To establish and maintain the therapeutic contract is both an art and a discipline in the sense that the pastoral psychotherapist needs to balance flexibility and consistency. How he or she deals with the details of the therapeutic contract manifests the psychotherapist's personality and maturity.

Initial Therapeutic Assessment

The initial therapeutic assessment refers to a dynamic process of gathering information, diagnosing, and determining the overall course of the psychotherapy. It carries a broader meaning than the narrow, more clinically oriented diagnosis of the client's problems and situations. Initial therapeutic assessment typically includes but is not limited to the following: determining the client's needs and their treatability; determining the types of psychotherapy appropriate for the client; assessing a match or mismatch between the client and the psychotherapist; in the case of a mismatch, determining what referral should be made; establishing the psychotherapist's limitations; assessing the client's ego strength and psychological mindedness; making a spiritual assessment; and making an initial assessment of transference and countertransference. Anything that can enhance the effect of the psychotherapy needs to be assessed to make the most informed decisions to serve the needs of the client.

Those who potentially benefit most from and are best qualified for long-term, intensive psychotherapy are regarded as the most treatable. Treatability is determined by assessing the client's readiness for this specific type of psychotherapy. The client's readiness can be measured in part by assessing his or her psychological mindedness and ego strength. The Psychodynamic Diagnostic Manual (PDM)[13] describes psychological mindedness as an individual's ability to observe his or her own internal life and lists four criteria to define the ability on a sliding scale. Those four criteria measure the client's capacity for (1) self-examination, (2) self-observation, (3) introspection, (4) personal insight to see the connections between the current problems and the past, and their impact on present functioning and attitudes. Without this capacity, the work of intensive, long-term psychotherapy is meaningless for the client.

The level of the client's ego strength is another indicator for successful psychotherapy. Ego strength refers to the client's ability to tolerate psychological and relational conflict and stress without using extremely regressive means of destructive conflict and acting out. Paul DeWald (1964), a psychodynamically oriented therapist, suggests that to assess this capacity the

13. The PDM is a diagnostic handbook similar to the *Diagnostic and Statistical Manual of Mental Disorders* (DSM) published by the American Psychiatric Association to provide a common language and standard criteria for the classification of mental disorders. The difference between the DSM and the PDM is that the PDM uses a new perspective on the existing diagnostic system as it enables practitioners to describe and categorize personality patterns, related social and emotional capacities, unique mental profiles, and personal experiences of the patient. The PDM was published on May 28, 2006.

psychotherapist explore the client's relationships with others in their real lives. If the client has never related to others in a meaningful way, he or she may not be able to tolerate and survive intense emotions such as frustration, anger, and anxiety which are inevitably triggered in long-term, intensive psychotherapy. In this case, it is better for the psychotherapist to provide supportive psychotherapy to help the client develop some level of object constancy and the corresponding ego strength. Supportive psychotherapy uses an empathic approach to validate and affirm the client's feelings and thoughts, rather than interpreting, analyzing, or confronting the client. Assessment of the client's defense mechanisms is yet another way to measure ego strength (Chessick, p. 111).

Chessick states that intense reliance on projection, massive denial, or major withdrawal precludes a good prognosis. Such a client is at risk for psychotic breakdowns, addiction, or acting out due to insufficient ego strength. The psychotherapist can briefly test the client's ego strength and psychological mindedness in the initial interviews. For example, the psychotherapist may try a "minor trial interpretation to see how the client reacts to it or to see if he can grasp it and deal with it" (Chessick, p. 108). Based on how well the client receives the interpretation, the psychotherapist determines which type of therapy will work best for the client at the moment.

In determining what type of care is suitable for the client, the pastoral psychotherapist first has to assess whether the client is in crisis or not. Crisis situations need different approaches from chronic, personality disorders. David Switzer (1986), pastoral theologian and crisis counselor, suggests that three basic questions be asked to determine if the situation is crisis or not: (1) Has there been a recent (within a few weeks) onset of the troublesome feelings and behaviors? (2) Have those troublesome feelings and behaviors grown worse? (3) Can the time of onset be linked with some external event, some change in the client's life situation? The major task of crisis counseling is to identify the immediate, precipitating event or events and to intervene to relieve the client from the stresses caused by the immediate, precipitating event or events. If the client is in crisis, the pastoral psychotherapist must take immediate action using crisis intervention strategies. Suicidal ideation or attempts, domestic violence, and drug abuse require specific strategies of crisis intervention.[14]

Match or mismatch of the client and the psychotherapist is another area that should be assessed in the initial interviews. The first component to be considered is the psychotherapist's limitation in expertise and skills to effectively respond to the client's specific needs. The psychotherapist should

14. For more information about pastoral crisis counseling, refer to Stone (1993).

be realistic and honest in this self-assessment for the benefit of the client. Other components include a personality match, racial and cultural compatibility, social backgrounds, and therapeutic approaches. Transference and countertransference, in general, play an important role in decision making regarding these components.

Transference refers to "the unconscious transferring of expectations from the important figures in one's early childhood, particularly the parents/ primary caretakers, onto other people in current-day life" (Cooper-White, 2007, p. 190). Transference that has evolved from unresolved childhood experiences is often projected onto the psychotherapist, a figure of primary caregiving. Countertransference operates with the same principles but refers to the psychotherapist's reactions, behaviors, thoughts, and feelings toward the clients and their transferences. The psychotherapist must be skillful in observing, processing, and interpreting this intersubjective dynamic with the client and must decide if they can potentially develop a fruitful working alliance. For example, if the psychotherapist is in the middle of a divorce, he or she may carry strong, mixed feelings of loss, conflict, anger, abandonment, and grief. These feelings can be easily projected onto a therapeutic situation in which the client is dealing with a similar, difficult process. Without a thorough and careful self-critical awareness supported by consistent consultation and supervision, the psychotherapist may end up dealing with his or her own agenda and problems, not the client's. To avoid this potentially disastrous situation, the psychotherapist needs to consider referring the client to another psychotherapist.

If the pastoral psychotherapist decides referral is the best course of action for any of the above reasons, the psychotherapist must first summarize and assess the interview conversations that have occurred so far and then give clear reasons why he or she is not the best resource to help with the specific problems and situations. Sometimes the pastoral psychotherapist decides to work with the client but requires additional tests, assessments, or therapy for which he or she needs to refer the client. For example, the psychotherapist may refer a husband to an anger-management class before or while dealing with his relational problems in marriage when any type of violence is detected.[15]

Assessing theological/spiritual mindedness of the client is as important as assessing the client's psychological mindedness for successful pastoral psychotherapy. People with theological/spiritual mindedness are capable of recognizing a reality greater than themselves to reflect 'theo-logically' and spiritually. This ability opens them to the possibility of being related with

---

15. Note that couples work is contraindicated if domestic violence is found to occur.

the 'Holy Other' and is the potential power to alter and transform the explicit and implicit meanings of a reality given. Paul Pruyser (1976), clinical
psychologist, developed the assessment model of seven theological themes,
which is the best-known and most used classical model for spiritual assessment. Pruyser's seven theological themes include awareness of the Holy,
providence, faith, grace or gratefulness, repenting, communion, and vocation.[16] For example, many of my clients who were theologically minded had
rich resources of creating and re-creating the meanings of their suffering
and thus could integrate their pains and brokenness into their overall lives
and personalities. They, with some significant struggles however, eventually
realized that they were "bigger" than the traumatic experience in the larger
plan of God's providence, and could regain the sense of control from mere
victims to agents. This kind of spiritual and theological integration and reconciliation often lead to the path of a healing process

Conclusion

The initial interviews set the overall tone of the psychotherapy. They must
be carefully structured around the specific goals of providing a holding
environment, beginning to establish a therapeutic alliance, making a therapeutic contract, gathering information, conducting assessments, and making appropriate treatment plans. The pastoral psychotherapist must engage
in this critical process as a person, as a clinician, and as a pastoral theologian, demonstrating multilayered relational, clinical, and spiritual/theologi-
cal/pastoral competences. Relational competence helps develop a genuine,
honest, and empathetic relationship with the client. Clinically informed
knowledge and accuracy promotes the quality of the therapeutic service to
meet the client's need. Spiritual/theological/pastoral competence helps the
pastoral psychotherapist engage with the client as the Other who cannot be
completely assimilated and analyzed into a diagnostic paradigm of clinical treatment. All of these competences mutually reinforce one another to
create a holding environment and therapeutic working alliance early in the
process of an initial interview or initial interviews. Balancing the three competences is a way to establish a controlled but warm and human situation
within the circumference of a divine space radically open to the possibility
of exploring the otherness of the Other. Successful initial interviews prepare
the psychotherapist and the client to become a team for the collaborative

16. See Pruyser (1976). For another model of spiritual assessment, see Fitchett
(1993). See also Matthias Beier's chapter on faith assessment in this volume (Ch. 7).

and "redemptive work of pastoral psychotherapy" (Kelcourse, Introduction Ch. 2, p. 22).

References

Bion, W. R. (1970). *Attention and interpretation*. London: Tavistock.

Chessick, R. D. (1991). *The technique and practice of intensive psychotherapy*. Northvale, NJ: Aronson.

Cooper-White, P. (2007). *Many voices: Pastoral psychotherapy in relational and theological perspective*. Minneapolis: Fortress.

Dewald, P. A. (1964). *Psychotherapy: A dynamic approach*. New York: Basic Books

Fitchett, G. (1993). *Assessing spiritual needs: A guide for caregivers*. Guides to Pastoral Care. Minneapolis: Augsburg Fortress.

Horvath, A. O., & Symonds, B. D. (1991). Relation between alliance and outcome in psychotherapy: A meta-analysis. *Journal of Consulting Psychology, 38*, 139–49.

Levinas, E. (1981). *Otherwise than being: Or beyond essence* (A. Lingis, Trans.). Martinus Nijhoff Philosophy Texts 3. Pittsburgh: Duquesne University Press.

Martin, D. et al.(2000). Relation of the therapeutic alliance with outcome and other variables: A meta-analytic review. *Journal of Consulting and Clinical Psychology, 68*, 438–50.

McGoldrick, M., & Gerson. R. (1985). *Genograms in family assessment*. New York: Norton.

Miller-McLemore, B. J. (2012). *Christian theology in practice: Discovering a discipline*. Grand Rapids: Eerdmans.

Patton, J. (2005). *Pastoral care: An essential guide*. Abingdon Essential Guides. Nashville: Abingdon.

Pruyser, P. (1976). *The minister as diagnostician: Personal problems in pastoral perspective*. Philadelphia: Westminster.

PDM Task Force. (2006). *Psychodynamic diagnostic manual*. Silver Springs, MD: Alliance of Psychoanalytic Organizations.

Stone, H. W. (1993). *Crisis Counseling*. (Rev. ed.). Creative Pastoral Care and Counseling Series. Minneapolis: Fortress.

Switzer, D. K. (1986). *The minister as crisis counselor*. (Rev. and enl. ed.). Nashville: Abingdon.

Volf, M. (1996). *Exclusion and embrace: A theological exploration of identity, otherness, and reconciliation*. Nashville: Abingdon.

Winnicott, D. W. (1960). The theory of the parent-child relationship. *International Journal of Psychoanalysis, 41*, 585–95.

———————— 12 ————————

Individuals: The Therapeutic Relationship

Chris R. Schlauch

Varieties of Unique Experience

RECALL, FOR A MOMENT, the last time someone turned to you for help. Try and remember some of the details about the person, what was wrong, how things unfolded, and what the relationship felt like. Whether or not you had any formal education and training in care and counseling, you probably did not respond, "I'm sorry. I can't talk to you. I don't have a clue about what to do." More than likely you listened, thought, and spoke, as you were guided by (tacit) theories formed over your lifetime and bearing the imprint of specific experiences with certain people in particular situations. These comments point toward a crucial observation: every person, problem, clinical process, and relationship are in some measure *unique*. In the face of such diversity, how should we develop concepts relevant to care?

In the Midst of Varieties, a Conceptual Fulcrum: The Therapeutic Relationship

Research has concluded, repeatedly, that regardless of approach, something pivotal is characteristic of all successful care: the quality of the relationship established between the person seeking and the person providing care (see, for example, Bachelor & Horvath, 1999; Beutler, 2010; Bozarth & Motoma-sa, 2008; Carlson, et al., 2006; Comas-Diaz, 1994; Fraser & Solovey, 2006; Gelso & Carter, 1994; Haugh & Paul, 2008; Joiner et al., 2009; Paolino, 1981; Paul & Haugh, 2008a; Paul & Haugh, 2008b; Priebe & McCabe, 2008; Safran & Muran, 2006). Gelso and Carter (1994) write:

> Some psychotherapy practitioners and theoreticians believe that the relationship that develops between therapist and client is the essence of effective treatment. Others believe that although the relationship is not the *sine qua non* of therapy, it provides significant leverage for the implementation of therapy techniques. Regardless of one's position on whether the relationship is the essential ingredient of therapy or a means to an end, there is striking agreement that the client-therapist relationship plays an important role in treatment. (p. 296)

Determining *that* "the therapeutic relationship" is deeply significant has required considerable research; explaining *what* it means necessitates further study. As Fraser and Solovey (2006) remark, "The definition of a therapeutic relationship is anything but simple and clear. Historically, . . . it has traveled many paths" (p. 67). Many concepts in various clinical approaches have been developed to illumine its nature. Our task, accordingly, will not be to "name" the "essence" of the therapeutic relationship but to introduce relevant ideas in elaborating on the contours of one approach.[1]

Therapeutic Relating: Constituted of Varieties[2]

Pause, again, and think about the relationship you had with the person who sought your help. You likely experienced a variety of competing if not conflicting feelings: sadness about the person's pain, curiosity about what was left unspoken, anxiety about not truly knowing what was wrong, frustration about not finding the "right words," hope about your finding a way to relate that was helpful. Even more, you probably became aware of many

---

1. Elucidating the therapeutic relationship in *pastoral psychotherapy* is complicated by the fact that the literature on this concept has been written by researchers who examine (secular) counseling and psychotherapy without reference to, and likely with little awareness of, pastoral counseling and psychotherapy. Any theorizing about this concept will require, at some level, addressing a more general question about how to understand the relationships between the concepts, methods, norms, assumptions, and sensibilities of secular and "religious" communities and traditions (see Poling and Miller, 1985).

2. There is some merit to thinking about "the therapeutic relationship" as an *activity*: "therapeutic relating" (see Schafer, 1976).

sensations, ideas, memories, and questions—some of which made more sense than others; others of which were surprising, unexpected, as if "out of the blue":

- "I feel unusually 'at home' with this person, as if we already know one another."

- "As we continue to talk I'm not only surprised but also discomfited by the kind of intimacy the person seems to presume."

- "I don't know why I don't believe some of what this person is saying. No, that's not it. I believe *this person* does not believe some of what she or he is saying."

All these musings are relevant to an understanding of the concept of therapeutic relationship.

The concept of therapeutic relationship arose within the context of psychoanalytic theorizing (see Bachelor & Horvath, 1999, p. 134) and *originally encompassed several forms of engagement* (see Paolino, 1981). The first is called *transference* (an unconscious reenactment of a "pattern of expectation" or "anticipatory configuration" [Basch, 1980, p. 35] formed in childhood). For example, one relates to someone providing care in a manner that resembles how, as a child, one related to one's parent. A second form of engagement is called *the working alliance* or *the therapeutic alliance* (an in-part conscious collaboration of a sector of the client's psyche that is not engaged in transference with a sector of the clinician's psyche). For example, while the client relates to the therapist as a child relates to a parent (transference), the client also relates to the therapist as one partner relates to another, because the partners are solving a problem together. A third form of engagement is *the real relationship* (those actual, nonconflictual, nontransferential connections between the two human beings who are working clinically together). For example, even as the client relates to the therapist as a child relates to a parent, and as a partner relates to a partner, the client and therapist are also engaged simply as one human being with another. [3] These forms of engagement are themselves dynamically related. For example, forming a good-enough alliance provides the occasion (or "permission") for the emerging expression of *deepening* transference; and working through

3. Safran and Muran (2006) note, "Traditional conceptualizations of the alliance . . . assume that a distinction can be made between the distorted or transferential aspects of the therapeutic relationship and the more rational or mature dimension of the collaboration between therapist and patient, even though there has been some acknowledgement that this distinction is a heuristic one and that transference and alliance always overlap in reality . . . Critics, however, argue that all aspects of the therapeutic relationship are transferential, insofar as the perception of the present is always shaped by one's past" (p. 287).

that expression of transference *strengthens the alliance*, which itself allows for further expression of a deepening transference, and so on.

Therapeutic relating is constituted of interacting dimensions.[4] Information is exchanged through *a variety of media*: in words, in registered affect (that is, feelings), in behavioral signals sent and received (e.g., posture, eye contact), and in the pace and process of the interaction. Information is communicated at *several levels of awareness*: in what is spoken and heard consciously, directly, and explicitly, and in what is implied by a speaker, and inferred by a listener. For example, what is intimated may be conscious to a speaker and conveyed, intentionally, through indirect communication, or it may be less conscious to both speaker and listener, present at the horizon of awareness. Finally, some information is communicated outside of the awareness of both parties, as if by contagion. (One or another person may experience something coming to mind that on the one hand does not seem to have been exchanged but on the other hand does, in fact, seem to have been sent and received without conscious knowledge of either party.) Exchanged information expresses different *kinds of judgments* (for example, about consciousness and conduct; right and wrong, good and evil, virtue and vice; what is "ultimate," what one "holds dear")—judgments that are the express purview of particular *fields of inquiry* (e.g., psychology; ethics; religious and theological studies, respectively).

Relating may take different forms. Martin Buber (1958) speaks of I-it (impersonal, objective, and objectifying) and I-Thou (personal and mutual). Thomas Ogden (see, for example, 1986, 1989, 1994), in the object-relations tradition of Melanie Klein and Donald Winnicott, outlines three "positions": making contact with features of the environment; interacting, impersonally, with other objects; and forming a relationship, consciously and deliberately, with another subject or agent (see Schlauch, 2007a). Recent discussions of gender, race, and ethnicity have identified features of therapeutic relating that should be addressed: the use, abuse, and imbalance of power; the explicit recognition of race and racism, prejudice and privilege; the consideration of social location, opportunity, and marginalization (see, for example, Comas-Diaz, 1994).

---

4. That the relationship is constituted of multiple ways of relating presupposes that the human self or subject is "multiple" (cf. Schlauch, 2003; Cooper-White, 2007).

Basic Interpretive Distinctions: One-person, Two-person; Hierarchical, Collaborative

It had become commonplace in the West to think about a person as a free-standing, isolated entity, and about a relationship as the interplay of two autonomous agents. Over the past several decades researchers and scholars in many fields—including in philosophy and philosophy of science; in studies of gender, race, ethnicity, and culture—have appropriately challenged this "one-person" psychology and have formulated versions of a "two-person" psychology (see Fosshage, 1992; Mitchell, 1988; Rickman, 1957): persons are social beings; relationship is the most basic subject matter of analysis. As theories of person and of clinical care have moved from assumptions expressing one-person psychologies toward relational and systemic approaches, they have also moved away from models of hierarchy employing vertical images—where an "expert" (the clinician) cures the "object" (the patient)—toward models of collaboration employing horizontal images.[5]

The Contours of a Clinical Attitude

Every approach to clinical care expresses a theory of change, and every theory of change reflects ideas about the nature and roles of participants. Furthermore, the process of teaching and learning any approach to clinical care should, ideally, parallel or mirror the process of clinical care itself. Thus, for example, if one views change as a matter of providing knowledge, solving problems, and guiding behavior, then the clinical instructor or supervisor will carry out these activities with a clinician, much like a clinician will carry out, in an analogous way, these activities with a client.

This section outlines the contours of a theory of change that differs from what was just illustrated. It focuses less on teaching, solving, or guiding through the provision of a set of knowledge and skills than it does on forming and lending an "attitude" (see, for example, Schafer, 1983; Kohut, 1987; Loewald, 1988; Schlauch, 1995). Everything one does or says issues from an attitude. Even more, the people to whom a clinician provides care will, at some level, learn or "internalize" features of the clinician's attitude.

5. In pastoral theology and care, Hunter (2007) reflects on the movement from the "classical-clerical paradigm" (Laertey, 2006) that focused on "communicating the message" to the "clinical pastoral paradigm" that focused on "assisting persons who receive the message," and more recently to the "communal contextual model" in which "its domain of pastoral concern widened from individuals to whole communities and classes of persons in need" (pp. 68–69). These authors are indebted to John Patton (1993).

One's attitude can be thought of as expressing a canon, a set of ideas we "hold dear," ideas that are, functionally, sacred. Even more, our attitude expresses a canon-within-a-canon (Grant, 2001): an "inner circle" of core beliefs; root metaphors (Pepper, 1942) from which we move and to which we are elementally tethered; our basic truths, our "givens." Typically, knowledge of one's canon tends to be more tacit (Polanyi, 1962) than conscious, more enacted (Toulmin, 2001) than verbalized. There are, however, benefits to discerning and articulating these givens, though the process of doing so often contributes to their revision if not reconstruction. Consider one set of ideas, one canon.[6]

Ideas from Christian Scripture

Pastoral therapeutic relating incarnates the good news that is of "first importance" that we have received and pass on: through service, we love (as we have been loved), we accept (as we have been accepted).[7]

1. Saint Paul writes:

   For I handed on to you as of first importance what I in turn had received. (1 Corinthians 15:3, NRSV)

   In care, I am participating within a community and tradition, transmitting some version of "the good news."

2. St. Paul writes:

   So if there is any encouragement in Christ, any incentive of love, any participation of the Spirit, any affection and sympathy, complete my joy by *being of the same mind, having the same love*, being in full accord and of one mind. Do nothing from selfishness and conceit, but in humility count others better than yourselves. Let each of you look *not only to his own interests, but also the interests of others*. Have this mind among yourselves, which you have in Christ Jesus, who, though he was in the form of God, did not count equality with God a thing to be grasped,

---

6. Compare these ideas with those of other contributions to the literature in pastoral counseling and psychotherapy, including but not limited to, for example, De Marinis (1994); Lapsley (1972); Stone (1993).

7. There are many ways in which receiving and passing on have been construed. Jennings (1985) differentiates three forms that may be understood in dialectical relation with one another: "[simply] transmitting," "interpreting or adjusting," and "reconstruct[ing] and reinvent[ing]" (p. 76).

but *emptied himself, taking the form of a servant*. (Philippians 2:
1–7a, italics added)

I transmit and model a way of being and being-with, taking the form
of a servant, looking after not only my own interests (and beliefs and
needs) but also the interests (and beliefs and needs) of the person for
whom I care.

3. The Gospel of Mark (Mark 12:28–31 [NRSV]) records these words:

> One of the scribes came near and heard them disputing with
> one another, and seeing that he answered them well, he asked
> him, "Which commandment is the first of all?" Jesus answered,
> "The first is, 'Hear, O Israel: the Lord our God, the Lord is one;
> you shall love the Lord your God with all your heart, and with
> all your soul, and with all your mind, and with all your strength.'
> The second is this, 'You shall love your neighbor as yourself.'
> There is no other commandment greater than these."

The person receiving care experiences that she or he matters—that she
or he is worthy of abiding care and, in fact, *cherished* (Young-Bruehl
& Bethelard, 2000).

4. Paul Tillich (1948), in a sermon titled, "You Are Accepted," writes:

> Do we know what it means to be struck by grace? . . . Sometimes
> at that moment a wave of light breaks into our darkness, and
> it is as though a voice were saying: "You are accepted. *You are
> accepted,* accepted by that which is greater than you, and the
> name of which you do not know. Do not ask for the name now;
> perhaps you will find it later. Do not try to do anything now;
> perhaps later you will do much. Do not seek for anything; do
> not perform anything; do not intend anything. *Simply accept the
> fact that you are accepted!*" If that happens to us, we experience
> grace. After such an experience we may not be better than be-
> fore, and we may not believe more than before. But everything
> is transformed. (pp. 162–64)

The service to the well-being of the person for whom care is provided takes
the form, also, of basic acceptance.

Being and Being-With-and-For

Pastoral therapeutic relating presupposes and enacts certain qualities and capacities within and between persons.

Being real

Pastoral therapeutic relating involves being real.

At a time when there are so many theories and practices, so many technologies, of care, it is not difficult to be cultivated in sensibilities in which the best care has evolved in research on evidence-based practice (see, for example, Mullen & Streiner, 2004; Nolan & Brady, 2008; Satterfield et al., 2009). Ironically, the quest for optimal care at times lends researchers and practitioners to objectify not only processes but also people in a manner in which the participants in a relationship are significant to the degree to which they carry out standardized, manualized procedures. Though such research is unquestionably valuable, the tendency to objectify and even dehumanize care is not uncommon. To temper that tendency, consider a Sufi saying: "If a word comes from the heart, it will enter the heart; but if it comes only from the tongue, it will not get past the ear" (quoted by Toulmin, 2001, p. 127). What we say and do will "hit home" only if it has arisen *from* "home." Being real engenders being real.

Being real refers to a number of things. First, be *here* in the moment and not somewhere else. Be authentic (Mitchell, 1993), true to yourself or to your "true self" (Winnicott, 1960/1965a, 1960/1965b). Don't be someone who you are not, or put on a false front.

Being real, here, authentically, as true self, is a dynamic process, actualized in matters of degree. The degree of realness may shift *from one moment to the next*; *within a relationship* (for example, in certain moments I am more real), as well as *from one relationship to another* (for example, with some people I tend to be more real); *within a context or situation* (for example, I tend to be more real at home during the weekends) as well as *from one context or situation to the next* (for example, I tend to be more real at home than at work).

Being empathic

Pastoral therapeutic relating involves practicing a way of observing, engaging, and providing life-giving sustenance via introspection and empathy.[8]

---

8. Fraser & Solovey (2006) report, "With respect to individual therapy, the APA Task Force's final element that has been shown to be demonstrably effective is empathy.

Consider these ideas, elaborating upon the contributions of Heinz Kohut (see, for example, 1959/1978b; 1966/1978a; 1971; 1973/1978d; 1973/1978e; 1975; 1975/1978c; 1977; 1979/1991; 1984; 1985). In an empathic relationship, the clinician carries out two interrelated processes: First, she *introspects* (attends to and reflects upon her unfolding experiencing). Second, she *introspects vicariously* (attends to and reflects upon experiencing from the other's point of view, *as if she were the client*).

Empathy (vicarious introspection) is "a tool of observation" (Kohut, 1973/1978d). The clinician works, moment to moment, to understand the client from the inside, as if she were the client. Empathy is "a psychological bond" (Kohut, 1973/1978d). While persistently seeking, in part, to experience what unfolds from the client's point of view, the clinician is enlisted to execute psychic functions on behalf of the client's self, as part of the client's self (Kohut 1979/1991, 1984).[9] Empathy provides "psychological nutriment" (Kohut, 1973/1978d). Empathy provides a kind of reassuring *immediate presence*, of the other "being-with"; the experience of *being understandable* and *being known* that are conducive to a sense of *safety*. Though perhaps not consciously, one may register the other's *intention*: the persistent effort to understand, in the face of regular "failure."[10] *Empathy is an expression of*

Bohart, Elliot, Greenberg, and Watson (2002) concluded in the task force review that there is no consensual definition of empathy" (p. 70). Fraser & Solovey continue: "Bohart and his colleagues (2002) cited Orlinsky et al. (1994) and suggested that client active involvement is the most important factor in making therapy work. They concluded by suggesting that 'First, empathy promotes involvement. Second, empathy provides support for clients' active information-processing efforts . . . Third, empathy helps the therapist choose interventions compatible with the clients' frame of reference' (Bohart et al., 2002, p. 101)" (Fraser & Solovey, 2006, p. 71).

9. Kohut developed the concept of "selfobject" to refer to this phenomenon. Interestingly, this phenomenon has been explored in cognitive neuroscience in terms of the concept of "social prosthetic system" (Kosslyn, 2006). Social prosthetic systems are "human relationships that extend one's emotional or cognitive capacities. In such systems, other people serve as prosthetic devices, filling in for lacks in an individual's cognitive or emotional abilities . . . According to this theory, humans are motivated to behave in ways that create, extend, and support social prosthetic systems, in part because the self becomes distributed over other people who function as long-term social prosthetic systems. Moreover, some human behavior may be directed toward establishing conditions that will induce others to serve as one's social prosthetic systems" (Kosslyn, 2006, p. 541). Human beings are hardwired to understand others in this way. However, in many instances we develop habits of mind that restrict and distort this natural ability.

10. Mishne (2002) speaks of the client experiencing the clinician's "desire to be educated," a view consonant with but distinct from what I am describing. She writes, "An initial major goal in culturally sensitive, optimally responsive treatment is engaging a client and beginning a meaningful collaborative interaction—one in which the client experiences attunement, attentive listening, spontaneity, empathy, and evidence of the therapist's emotional availability. In order to engage and connect, the client needs to

grace: not earned or perhaps deserved but freely given. Experiencing empathy naturally engenders a need to (continue to) experience empathy.[11]

What is Unique to Therapeutic Relating in Pastoral Psychotherapy?

Whereas everyday instances of care and formal theories of care involve what is religious (matters of life and death, what one "holds dear"), and what is moral (matters of good/bad, right/wrong, virtue/vice), pastoral psychotherapists intentionally, explicitly, and systematically formulate approaches that critically coordinate religious and secular resources to address these concerns. There are, similarly, some features of therapeutic relating that are more explicitly formulated and thus more directly characteristic of pastoral psychotherapy:

The pastoral psychotherapist, whether or not ordained clergy, "represents" a community and tradition. As she speaks for herself, for a community and tradition, and for that community's tradition regarding what is "God" or "divine," she is accountable to that community and tradition, and to that divine (see Browning, 1991; Purves, 2004).

The pastoral psychotherapist, as a member of a religious community and tradition, participates in relationships in which "God" is present and active, whether God is symbolized, variously, as "a something more" (James, 1902/1982), "God" (Grant, 2001), "the Eternal Thou behind every I-Thou relationship" (Buber, 1958), or in other symbols of another narrative tradition (see Gerkin, 1984).

The pastoral psychotherapist maintains a "critical" stance. Using Paul Ricoeur's (1970) idea of a "hermeneutics of suspicion," our approach to every report is twofold: on the one hand, accepting what is presented, in plain sight, as valuable; on the other hand, assuming that other valuable information is hidden, present initially in disguised form in hints and clues, and is to be sought and found through a deliberate exploratory process. This critical

---

experience the therapist's desire to be educated about the client's values, preferences, world view, and belief system" (p. 35).

11. In a related vein, Stern (1985) writes, "Once intersubjectivity has been tasted, so to speak, does it just remain a capacity to be used or not, or as a perspective on self and other to be adopted or not? Or does it become a new psychological need, the need to share subjective experience?" (p. 135). Consider, by implication, that once *empathy* has been tasted, it becomes a new psychological need. The recurrent or periodic experience of empathy that generates a need for further experiences of empathy may naturally unfold in terms of the most powerful of all schedules of reinforcement: random reinforcement.

stance is, in addition, taken toward one's own approach: "'Critical' implies awareness of one's method and suppositions, and the definition includes the willingness to revise one's perspective under certain conditions" (Poling & Miller, 1985, p. 32).[12]

The pastoral psychotherapist participates in a dynamic clinical process in which therapeutic relating is continually changing. As she empties herself, "taking the form of a servant," she must remain open to forming and reforming relating with a unique person whom she does not know. Further, she must in her critical stance be receptive to altering, flexibly, some of the way she practices care.[13]

The pastoral psychotherapist facilitates formation in faith. Someone seeking care may be an *agnostic* for whom religious sensibilities are *absent*. He may have little recognition of "something (that is, faith) lacking or missing," or may feel this absence acutely, as if aware of an unactualized potentiality. Someone may be like on-again, off-again *searchers* for whom a faith life is more or less present but comparatively *muted and neglected*. Having "the religion of the masses" (Weber, 1922/1991; Berger, 1967/1969a, p. 75), he experiences periodic "signals of transcendence" (Berger, 1969b, p. 52). Someone may be a devout *believer* for whom faith *is prominent*, that is, *primary but not exclusive*. Many so-called religious leaders manifest this level of awareness and commitment. Finally, someone may be like what Max Weber called "*religious virtuosi*," "great figures of religious history" (Berger, 1992, p. 132), for whom faith is *dominant*, more or less *constant, and enduring*.

A Particular Version, in Sum

In therapeutic relating in pastoral psychotherapy, the clinician facilitates an unfolding process in which clinician and client collaboratively practice, moment to moment, ways of relating with one another and with themselves. The clinician facilitates by embodying an attitude that the client, over time, in part internalizes (see Schlauch, 1995). Initially the participants practice more or less unconsciously; increasingly they consciously practice together and with others. Though their work focuses, at the outset, on chief

12. This critical stance towards oneself is expressed in attention to ever-present countertransference.

13. Comas-Diaz (1994) considers the "assertion that individuals of one cultural group may require a form of psychotherapy different from that required by members of another cultural group. It is clear that more studies are needed comparing diverse treatment orientations, including culturally sensitive psychotherapy" (p. 86). Further, "The ideal psychotherapist-client relationship varies from culture to culture (Portela, 1971)" (p. 90).

complaints—the forms of illness and suffering that precipitated the seeking of care—the target of their efforts widens to take into account patterns of experiencing and relating. Thus, pastoral psychotherapy potentially and optimally enhances different kinds of change—in symptomatology, personality/character, patterns of relationship, the world or "reality," and in one's path and place in the world. Of course, the kinds and degrees of work and change differ person to person, and relationship to relationship.[14]

Therapeutic relating involves practicing being-there-with-and-for

First, therapeutic relating is, in its very nature, *constituted of multiple forms of engagement*. Whereas the psychoanalytic literature differentiates between transference, working alliance, and real relationship, one may distinguish between psychological, religious, and moral reflection and action. Second, therapeutic relating is *the medium through which change, healing, and development unfold*; more specifically, where patterns of relating are enacted, identified, and revised. Whereas the literature speaks of repetition, recollection, and working through, one may cast the clinical process as a matter of practicing and altering habits of engagement. Third, among the ways in which change, healing, and development unfold is through *the internalization of an attitude* (see, for example, Kohut, 1987; Loewald, 1988; Schafer, 1983; Schlauch, 1995). Fourth, therapeutic relating *as* practicing being-there-with-and-for joins the primary commitments of two pivotal psychoanalytic theorists, *being real* (Winnicott) and *being empathic* (Kohut) (see Schlauch, 2007b). Finally, being-there-with-and-for, *as* at once psychological, religious, and moral engagement, re-presents *the interdisciplinary project* at the heart of pastoral psychotherapy.[15]

14. Each participant in a therapeutic relationship has different contributions, limitations, and judgments about what is efficacious (Bachelor & Horvath, 1999, esp. pp. 139–40).

15. Being-there-with-and-for calls for psychological analysis to explain personality style, signs of health and symptoms of illness, basic wants and needs, general and specific motivations, and so forth. It calls also, for ethical analysis of issues having to do with good and bad, right and wrong, virtue and evil. To "be there with and for another" is akin to the Golden Rule, the Categorical Imperative, the claim upon us to provide a nonmoral good for the current and future well-being of another. Finally, being-there-with-and-for also expresses religious features to consider how we provide occasion for identifying some of what is not yet known—"a something more" (James, 1982) that lies at the horizon of our awareness and at the edge of our being (Schlauch, 2006).

References

Bachelor, A., & Horvath, A. (1999). The therapeutic relationship. In M. A. Hubble et al. (Eds.), *The heart and soul of change: What works in therapy* (pp. 133–78). Washington DC: American Psychological Association.

Basch, M. F. (1980). *Doing psychotherapy*. New York: Basic Books.

Berger, P. L. (1969a). *The sacred canopy: Elements of a sociological theory of religion*. Garden City, NY: Doubleday. (Orig. publ. 1967)

Berger, P. L. (1969b). *A rumor of angels: Modern society and the rediscovery of the supernatural*. Garden City, NY: Doubleday.

Berger, P. L. (1992). *A far glory: The quest for faith in an age of credulity*. Garden City, NY: Doubleday.

Beutler, L. E. (2010). Predictors of sustained therapeutic change: some thoughts about conceptualizations. *Psychotherapy Research, 20*(1) 55–59.

Bozarth, J. D., & Motomasa, N. (2008). The therapeutic relationship: A research inquiry. In S. Paul & S. Haugh (Eds.), *The therapeutic relationship: Perspectives and themes* (pp. 132–44). Ross-on-Wye, UK: PCCS Books.

Browning, D. S. (1991). *A fundamental practical theology: Descriptive and strategic proposals*. Minneapolis: Fortress.

Buber, M. (1987). *I and thou*. (Ronald Smith, Trans.). New York: Collier Books.

Carlson, J. et al. (2006). Establishing the therapeutic relationship. In *Adlerian therapy: Theory and practice* (pp. 65–81). Washington DC: American Psychological Association.

Comas-Diaz, L. (1994). Cultural variation in the therapeutic relationship. In C. Goodheart et al. (Eds.), *Evidence-based psychotherapy: Where practice and research meet* (pp. 81–105). Washington DC: American Psychological Association.

Cooper-White, P. (2007). *Many voices: Pastoral psychotherapy in relational and theological perspective*. Minneapolis: Fortress.

DeMarinis, V. M. (1994). *Critical caring: A feminist model for pastoral psychology*. Louisville: Westminster John Knox.

Fosshage, J. L. (1992). Self psychology: The self and its vicissitudes within a relational matrix. In N. J. Skolnick & S. C. Warshaw (Eds.), *Relational perspectives in psychoanalysis* (pp. 21–42). Hillsdale, NJ: Analytic.

Fraser, J. S., & Solovey, A. D. (2006). The therapeutic relationship. In *Second-order change in psychotherapy: The golden thread that unifies effective treatments* (pp. 65–86). Washington DC: American Psychological Association.

Gelso, G. S, & Carter J. A. (1994). Components of the psychotherapy relationship: Their interaction and unfolding during treatment. *Journal of Counseling Psychology, 41*, 296–306.

Gerkin, C. V. (1984). *The living human document: Re-Visioning pastoral counseling in a hermeneutical mode*. Nashville: Abingdon.

Grant, B. W. (2001). *A theology for pastoral psychotherapy: God's play in sacred spaces*. New York: Haworth.

Haugh, S. & Paul, S. (2008). *The therapeutic relationship: Perspectives and themes*. Ross-on-Wye, UK: PCCS Books.

Hunter, R. (2007). Book reviews. *Journal of Pastoral Theology, 17*(1), 68–79.

James, W. (1982). *The varieties of religious experience: A study in human nature*. Penguin Classics. New York: Penguin. (Orig. publ. 1902).

Jennings, T. W. (1985). Theology as the construction of doctrine. In *The vocation of the theologian*, T. W. Jennings (Ed.). (pp. 67–86). Minneapolis: Fortress.

Joiner, T. E. Jr. et al. (2009). The therapeutic relationship. In *The interpersonal theory of suicide: Guidance for working with suicidal clients* (pp. 145–66). Washington DC: American Psychological Association.

Kohut, H. (1971). *The analysis of the self: A systematic approach to the psychoanalytic treatment of narcissistic personality disorders*. The Psychoanalytic Study of the Child Monograph 4. Madison, CT: International Universities Press.

Kohut, H. (1977). *The restoration of the self*. New York: International Universities Press.

Kohut, H. (1978a). Forms and transformations of narcissism. In P. H. Ornstein (Ed.). *The search for the self: Selected writings of Heinz Kohut: 1950–1978*, Vol. 1 (pp. 427–60). New York: International Universities Press. (Orig. publ. 1966).

Kohut, H. (1978b). Introspection, empathy, and psychoanalysis: An examination of the relationship between mode of observation and theory. In P. H. Ornstein (Ed.). *The search for the self: Selected writings of Heinz Kohut: 1950–1978*, Vol. 1 (pp. 205–32). New York: International Universities Press. (Orig. publ. 1959).

Kohut, H. (1978c). The future of psychoanalysis. In P. H. Ornstein (Ed.). *The search for the self: Selected writings of Heinz Kohut: 1950–1978*, Vol. 2 (pp. 663–84). New York: International Universities Press. (Orig. publ. 1975).

Kohut, H. (1978d). The psychoanalyst in the community of scholars. In P. H. Ornstein (Ed.), *The search for the self: Selected writings of Heinz Kohut: 1950–1978*, Vol. 2 (pp. 685–724). New York: International Universities Press. (Orig. publ. 1973).

Kohut, H. (1978e). Conclusion: The search for the analyst's self. In P. H. Ornstein (Ed.), *The search for the self: Selected writings of Heinz Kohut: 1950–1978*, Vol. 2, (pp. 931–38). New York: International Universities Press. (Orig. publ. 1973).

Kohut, H. (1984). *How does analysis cure?* A. Goldberg (Ed.), with the collaboration of P. E. Stepansky. Chicago: The University of Chicago Press.

Kohut, H. (1985). *Self psychology and the humanities: Reflections on a new psychoanalytic approach*. C. B. Strozier (Ed.). New York: Norton.

Kohut, H. (1987). Extending empathic understanding, sharing an attitude. In M. Elson (Ed.), *The Kohut seminars on self psychology and psychotherapy with adolescents and young adults* (pp. 188–202). New York: Norton.

Kohut, H. (1991). Four basic concepts in self psychology. In P. H. Ornstein (Ed.), *The search for the self: Selected writings of Heinz Kohut: 1978–1981*, Vol. 4 (pp. 447–70). Madison, CT: International Universities Press. (Orig. publ. 1979).

Kohut, H., & Seitz, P. (1978). Concepts and theories of psychoanalysis. In P. H. Ornstein (Ed.), *The search for the self: Selected writings of Heinz Kohut: 1978–1981*, Vol. 1 (pp. 337–74). Madison, CT: International Universities Press. (Orig. publ. 1963).

Kosslyn, S. M. (2006). On the evolution of human motivation: The role of social prosthetic systems. In S. M. Platek et al. (Eds.), *Evolutionary cognitive neuroscience* (pp 541–54). Cognitive Neuroscience. Cambridge: MIT Press.

Lapsley, J. N. (1972). *Salvation and health; the interlocking process of life*. Philadelphia: Westminster.

Lartey, E. Y. (2006). *Pastoral theology in an intercultural world*. Peterborough, UK: Epworth.

Loewald, H. W. (1988). On the mode of therapeutic action of psychoanalytic psychotherapy. In A. Rothstein (Ed.), *How does treatment help? On the modes of therapeutic action of psychoanalytic psychotherapy* (pp. 51–59). Madison, CT: International Universities Press.

Mishne, J. (2002). *Multiculturalism and the therapeutic process*. New York: Guilford.

Mitchell, S. A. (1988). *Relational concepts in psychoanalysis: An integration.* Cambridge: Harvard University Press.

Mitchell, S. A. (1993). *Hope and dread in psychoanalysis.* New York: Basic Books.

Mullen, E. J., & Streiner, D. L. (2004). The evidence for and against evidence-based practice. *Brief Treatment and Crisis Intervention, 4*, 111–21.

Nolan, P., & Bradley, E. (2008). Evidence-based practice: Implications and concerns. *Journal of Nursing Management, 16*, 388–93.

Ogden, T. H. (1986). *The matrix of the mind: Object relations and the psychoanalytic dialogue.* Northvale, NJ: Aronson.

Ogden, T. H. (1989). *The primitive edge of experience.* Northvale, NJ: Aronson.

Ogden, T. H. (1994). *Subjects of analysis.* Northvale, NJ: Aronson.

Paolino, T. J. (1981). *Psychoanalytic psychotherapy: Theory, technique, therapeutic relationship, and treatability.* New York: Brunner-Routledge

Patton, J. (1993). *Pastoral care in context: An introduction to pastoral care.* Louisville: Westminster John Knox.

Paul, S., & Haugh, S. (2008a). The therapeutic relationship: Background and context. In S. Paul & S. Haugh (Eds.), *The therapeutic relationship: Perspectives and themes* (pp. 1–8). Ross-on-Wye, UK: PCCS Books.

Paul, S., & Haugh, S. (2008b). The relationship, not the therapy? What the research tells us. In S. Paul & S. Haugh (Eds.), *The therapeutic relationship: Perspectives and themes* (pp. 9–22). Ross-on-Wye, UK: PCCS Books.

Pepper, S. C. (1942). *World hypotheses: A study in evidence.* Berkeley: University of California Press.

Polanyi, M. (1962). *Personal knowledge: Towards a post-critical philosophy.* New York: Harper & Row. (Orig. publ. 1958).

Poling, J. N., & Miller, D. E. (1985). *Foundations for a practical theology of ministry.* Nashville: Abingdon Press.

Priebe, S., & McCabe, R. (2008). Therapeutic relationships in psychiatry: The basis of therapy or therapy in itself? *International Review of Psychiatry, 20*(6), 521–26.

Purves, A. (2004). *Reconstructing pastoral theology: A christological foundation.* Louisville: Westminster John Knox.

Rickman, J. (1957). *Selected contributions to psycho-analysis.* New York: Basic Books.

Ricoeur, P. (1970). *Freud and philosophy: An essay on interpretation.* (D. Savage, Trans.). The Terry Lectures. New Haven: Yale University Press.

Safran, J. D., & Muran, J. C. (2006). Has the concept of the therapeutic alliance outlived its usefulness? *Psychotherapy: Theory, Research, Practice, Training, 43*, 286–91.

Schafer, R. (1976). *A new language for psychoanalysis.* New Haven: Yale University Press.

Schafer, R. (1983). *The analytic attitude.* New York: Basic Books.

Schlauch, C. R. (1985). Defining pastoral psychotherapy. *39*, 219–28.

Schlauch, C. R. (1987). Defining pastoral psychotherapy. *Journal of Pastoral Care 41*, 319–27.

Schlauch, C. R. (1990). Empathy as the essence of pastoral psychotherapy. *Journal of Pastoral Care 44*, 3–17.

Schlauch, C. R. (1995). *Faithful companioning: How pastoral counseling heals.* Minneapolis: Fortress.

Schlauch, C. R. (2003). Varieties of selves: A Study in religious matters. In W. W. Meissner & C. R. Schlauch (Eds.), *Psyche and spirit: Dialectics of transformation* (pp. 43–73). Lanham, MD: University Press of America.

Schlauch, C. R. (2006). Deeper affinities: Fundamental resonances between psychoanalysis and religion. *Pastoral Psychology, 55*, 61–80.

Schlauch, C. R. (2007a). Introducing the concepts of "positions," "space," and "worlds": Seeing human being and becoming—and religion—in new ways. *Pastoral Psychology 55*, 367–90.

Schlauch, C. R. (2007b). Being-there-with-and-for: Contemporary psychoanalysis characterizes notions of being religious. *Pastoral Psychology 56*, 199–221.

Schlauch, C. R. (2009). Do I hear what you hear? Thinking about psychotherapy and spirituality from a self psychological approach. *Journal of Spirituality in Mental Health, 11*, 26–50.

Stern, D. N. (1985). *The interpersonal world of the infant: A view from psychoanalysis and developmental psychology.* New York: Basic Books.

Stone, H. W. (1994). *Brief pastoral counseling: Short-term approaches and strategies.* Minneapolis: Fortress.

Satterfield, J. M. et al. (2009). Toward a transdisciplinary model of evidence-based practice. *Milbank Quarterly, 87*, 368–90.

Tillich, P. (1948). *The shaking of the foundations.* New York: Scribner.

Toulmin, S. (2001). *Return to reason.* Cambridge: Harvard University Press.

Weber, M. (1991). *The sociology of religion.* (Ephraim Fischoff, Trans.). Boston: Beacon. (Orig. publ. 1922).

Winnicott, D. W. (1965a). The theory of the parent-infant relationship. In *The maturational process and the facilitating environment* (pp. 37–55). London: Hogarth. (Orig. publ. 1960).

Winnicott, D. W. (1965b). Ego distortions in terms of true and false self. In *The maturational process and the facilitating environment* (pp. 140–52). London: Hogarth. (Orig. publ. 1960).

Winnicott, D. W. (1971a). Playing: A theoretical statement. In *Playing and reality* (pp. 38–52). New York: Basic Books.

Winnicott, D. W. (1971b). The place where we live. In *Playing and reality* (pp. 104–10). New York: Basic Books. (Orig. publ. 1970).

Young-Bruehl, E., & Bethelard, F. (2000). *Cherishment: A psychology of the heart.* New York: Free Press.

13

Sacred Ties: Helping Couples Find Faith in Love

James L. Furrow

ALL COUPLES FACE A common question of commitment. Whether cohabitating, married, or in a civil union, the definition of being in a relationship is distinguished by some expression of commitment. Therefore couples must make meaning of what defines their particular relationship apart from others and consider the purpose of this exclusive relationship. Religious traditions often provide a context and rituals for symbolizing the commitment of marriage. For many married couples pastoral counseling provides a unique context where the experience and meaning of a relationship can be explored, enhanced, or at times relinquished in conversation with one's faith. This chapter offers resources for pastoral counselors who work with couples facing the inevitable uncertainties experienced in a distressed relationship, often most profoundly expressed at an emotional level. Emotionally Focused Couple Therapy (EFT) is introduced as a powerful empirically supported therapeutic approach that a pastoral counselor may engage when confronting the emotional realities that organize a couple's everyday experience and future hopes. The practice of EFT is illustrated with a case example where the role of emotion and commitment are explored within a theological context where fidelity is not reduced to a simple constraint but is seen as a virtue of love.

The Personal Pursuit of Love

Popular notions of love and marriage often assume an ethic rooted in expressive individualism. Following three decades of research on marriage in America, sociologist Andrew Cherlin (2004) contends that pervasive shifts in cultural values have resulted in a new orientation toward marriage. Cultural changes have placed increasing pressure on the institution of marriage to meet the psychological needs of each partner, and as a result it is reasonable to presume that a marriage may be terminated based on one partner's failure to live up to the expectations of the other. Increases in rates of divorce and cohabitation are seen as both evidence of these shifts and influential in sustaining these changes.

Barbara Dafoe Whitehead (1996) concluded that shifts in psychological justifications for divorce reinforce a divorce culture that shifts the balance of interests in marriage to the individual. In contrast, sociologist Bradford Wilcox (2002) notes that many religious institutions uniquely represent an interest in and commitment to the human virtues necessary to sustain a lifelong commitment of marriage. Theologians have observed that pastoral practices in premarital preparation might serve a necessary function in preparing couples for the moral commitments they assume in marriage (Atkinson, 1979).

Pastoral counselors serve at a unique intersection of societies' changing values of marriage and the personal decisions that constitute its moral obligation. Questions about the meaning of marriage and its intrinsic value are uniquely personal whether one is considering the decision to marry or the decision to divorce. In troubled relationships, eroding trust, diminishing rewards, and increasing pain often fuel the discontent and seeming inevitable demise of a marriage. Yet together, counselor and couple may also find faith in the promise of Christian marriage and its inherent claim to fidelity that itself anticipates, if not assumes, the reality of brokenness and a path toward redemption. Marriage understood in this light provides a means of sanctification, offering a crucible for transformation and a context for the personal growth of each partner (Branson, 1989).

Fidelity as Character in Marriage

The commitments that members of a couple make to each other embody the purpose each holds in marriage. Morally speaking, this purpose reflects the ultimate values they hold together as partners for the character of their relationship. In the Christian tradition the act of marriage is understood as an expression of fidelity or covenant partnership. This partnership is more than a social contract, rather marriage represents a covenantal relationship similar to the unconditional commitment of God to his people—the commitment of a God whose character is seen and known in a relationship of steadfast faithfulness that ultimately will outlast unfaithfulness (Anderson & Guernsey, 1985).

For couples, fidelity acts as the "mortar" (Smedes, 1986, p. 162) that holds together the promises that couples make to each other, often without fully knowing what they are getting themselves into. This fidelity is not simply an act of moral courage in the face of broken promises and disappointing relationships, instead this faithfulness is a way of being within the life of Christian community.

> It is fidelity that comes by being formed by a community whose life is sustained by a God who has proved faithful to us through the call of his people, Israel, and the establishment of the new age in Jesus Christ. Only people so formed are capable of the kind of promise we make in marriage, that of life long fidelity. (Hauerwas, 1985, p. 281)

It is within the covenant making and covenant keeping that the moral vision of fidelity takes hold. The struggle and the growth that results from living out these promises is an expression of God's creative purpose both in and through a relationship that serves as a source of belonging and as a basis for becoming more of what God intended. There is an intention of growth, sanctification, and discipleship assumed in both the commitment and blessing of living faithful promises in the light of God's "unbreakable faithfulness" (Hays, 1996, p. 371).

Stassen and Gushee (2003) conclude that Christ's teachings regarding the divine intent of marriage illustrate a further expression of Jesus's emphasis on the "inbreaking of the Kingdom of God" (p. 274). It is this vision of the kingdom that enables one to hold together the promise of transforming love along with the everyday realities and shortcomings of human intention and effort that are commonplace in marriage. The steadfast love and faithfulness of God provides an essential metaphor for the type of relationship that marriage was intended to be and the type of love it was to embody. Atkinson (1979) describes this covenant partnership as one that is faithful to a vow (i.e., one's "better or worse" promise), faithful to the calling to a vocation empowered by God, and faithful to a relationship of openness and growth. Fidelity is an expression of how one loves in a relationship. It is more a matter of practice than a result of the relationship. The practice of this vocation implies not only participation in a meaningful expression of one's chosen purpose but also participation in the purpose of God, which is seen in God's steadfast faithfulness (Brueggemann, 1979).

A pastoral psychology of marriage provides appreciation for the intrinsic connections between theological and human claims of faithfulness. Researchers have identified ways in which religious couples make explicit acknowledgment of the religious meaning of their marriage. Mahoney and colleagues (1999) describe couples who attached spiritual importance to marriage as sanctifying their relationship. These couples held as sacred the character and significance of their relationship (Pargament & Mahoney, 2005). These couples may describe their partner or relationship as a "gift from God" imbued with transcendent meaning and character. The effect of sanctification is expressed in their values and beliefs and the common practices that define their relationship.

Couples holding a more sanctified understanding of their relationship are more likely to seek pastoral counseling. These couples prioritize their relationship and seek to invest and preserve the sacred tie they share. Pastoral counselors who understand the implicit and explicit spiritual commitments partners share provide a unique context for exploring both the challenges and resources their faith provides. For some, their faith in God is a personal resource that can be drawn upon to strengthen their relationship (Pargament & Mahoney, 2005). For others, their religious beliefs may inhibit the couple's ability to adapt and respond to the changing needs and demands of family life. A pastoral counselor who responds to the meaning of these religious commitments, who remains emotionally present to the couple's experience, and who acknowledges the impact of the individual and collective experiences within a couple on their relationship provides partners with the ability to draw upon the resilience and adaptive aspects of their faith (Griffith, 2010).

The active presence of the counselor is required when partners must gather together that which has been scattered in themselves and their relationship through times of disillusionment and disorientation (Brueggemann, 1999). At other times the pastoral task includes gathering those aspects of self scattered through divorce. The loss of a marriage requires guidance toward a path for growth and transformation, making meaning of a different identity and changing role from what was known in marriage (Atkinson, 1979: Rice & Rice, 1986). Emotionally focused couple therapy provides a treatment model centered on a therapist's emotional presence. Empathic presence creates opportunities to be heard and offers a resource for couples desiring to regain contact with the heart of their relationship and the motivations that inspire what they have hoped for in marriage. Before

sacred ties   203

examining this approach it is important to weigh the costs and challenges
couples face when caught in patterns of distress.

Challenges of Couples in Distress

Marital distress is a common complaint found among adults seeking psychotherapy. Patterns of emotional dysregulation and disengagement present
unique challenges for couples and counselors alike. The imminent threat
of divorce or the enduring distance of eroding emotional sentiment often
prompts defining existential concerns, including the loss of personal significance, and insecurity in intimate relationships. Couples who profess a more
sacred view of marriage may find that the faith which often inspired love is
now a source of pain and confusion.

Sustained relational distress often results in a number of negative outcomes in family life. Amato (2000), summarizing research on distressed and
divorcing couples compared to other married individuals, found those in
relational distress more likely to experience decreased psychological well-
being, greater personal health problems, and increased isolation. For example, adults facing relational distress are at a greater risk for the symptoms of
depression (Whisman & Bruce, 1999), which may in turn reduce the quality
of their parenting in households with children (Hetherington et al., 1998).
The economic cost and systemic impact of relationship distress and divorce
has been estimated both in terms of lost productivity (Forthofer, et al. 1996)
and in terms of an estimated increased cost to the government of $30,000
per divorce (Caldwell et al., 2007).

In light of these costs it is striking that more couples do not seek help
in the early stages of their distress. Researchers suggest that as few as 10
percent of married couples seek help when confronting a relationship issues. Wolcott (1986) found that less than one in four couples will seek help
in the face of difficulty, either because they fail to recognize the problem, or
because they do not believe their partner will seek help. Many couples wait,
often several years, before seeking help (Notarius & Buongiorno, 1992, as
cited in Gottman & Gottman, 1999), increasing the likelihood of reduced
psychological investment in the relationship and a greater tendency to rely
on personal ways of coping with relational distress (Kayser, 1993).

In summary, relational distress and the impact of divorce pose significant challenges to couples and families. Pastoral counselors are more
likely to see couples who have struggled for some time with unresolved issues in their relationship and often are suffering personal and psychological
costs as a result. Escalating negative sentiment in the relationship generally

increases the likelihood of divorce among married couples (Gottman, 1994) and proves a primary challenge for the counselor, who is then employed to stem what appears too often as the inevitable end of a relationship.

The values and competence of the couple therapist influence the outcome of treatment for couples caught in distress. Doherty (1997, 2002) concluded that couple therapy can be hazardous to marital relationships when therapists lack essential skills in working with couples and operate from theoretical orientations that organize almost exclusively around individualistic values. Couple therapists who lack skill in managing couple sessions and escalated affect may default to individual sessions with partners as a means to manage the intensity or may give up on couple treatment as a reasonable approach to the couple's seemingly unmanageable escalations. Therapists who are trained and skilled in working with negative emotion provide a unique resource to couples lost in the hopelessness of their distress. Emotionally Focused Therapy (EFT) provides therapists with an empirically supported approach to conceptualizing and transforming patterns of negative affect in couples relationships, enabling partners to regain hope as a couple.

Exploring Emotionally Focused Therapy

Susan Johnson and Leslie Greenberg (1985) first introduced EFT based upon Greenberg's (2004) theories of emotional change and Johnson's (1986) interest in adult attachment bonds. Over time, Johnson's development of the EFT approach for couples emphasized adult romantic attachment as a means for understanding emotional dynamics of distress and healing (Johnson, 2004; Mikulincer & Shaver, 2005). For example, Johnson and colleagues (1999) highlighted how a couple's relationship, as an attachment bond, remains stable and secure when partners are emotionally accessible and responsive to one another. When a partner can reach for contact, care, or comfort in a time of need, the relationship provides a felt sense of security for each partner and this enables couples and partners to grow and strengthen in the character of their relationship.

Relationship distress disrupts security, leaving couples caught in rigid patterns of escalating negative affect. These destructive emotional patterns organize each partner's ongoing experience of the relationship. Changing these patterns requires a therapist to engage each partner's emotional experience, focusing on accessing, processing, and restructuring a couple's responses toward mutual accessibility and responsiveness. Couples then are better able to address specific issues in their relationship once they have regained a felt sense of security in their relationship. A couple's ongoing ability to express attachment needs and desires is adaptive and facilitates intimacy (Johnson, 2008).

EFT is a brief, systematic approach that incorporates an interpersonal and an intrapsychic focus. EFT treatment follows a nine-step process organized around three key stages of change: deescalating problematic interaction patterns, changing interactional positions, and consolidating and integrating new interaction patterns. These three stages may be completed in twelve to twenty sessions (Johnson, 2004). A central focus of this integrated model (i.e. humanistic, experiential, family systems) is the ability and capacity of the therapist to offer a collaborative therapeutic alliance. The therapist's active emotional attunement to each partner's emotional responses is critical to eliciting underlying emotions that hold the key to transforming the couple's negative pattern. EFT therapists promote primary emotional responses and lead the couple to enact more vulnerable sharing of emotion that in turn prompts more adaptive responses forming a new pattern of security. Typically the use of EFT is not appropriate with couples where risk of domestic violence, ongoing substance abuse, and active infidelity are aspects of a couple's presenting problem.

Overview of EFT Stages of Change

In the initial Stage of EFT the counselor helps a couple shift their focus from seeing their partner as the problem in their relationship to seeing a predictable pattern of negative interaction as basis for distress in their relationship. For example, a therapist may help a couple recast their common fights over household chores and infrequent sex as a negative cycle of pursuit and withdrawal. This problematic pattern is most apparent in times of distress. In Stage 1 EFT helps partners individually and together walk through the steps of their escalating conflict and identify the reactive emotions that drive this escalation. These negative experiences provide opportunities to access underlying hurt, fear, and sadness—often emotions that are deeply relevant to the arguments a couple has but are seldom shared because of the lack of emotional safety or attachment security in the relationship. The therapist encourages couple deescalation of their reactive pattern by helping each partner acknowledge underlying primary attachment emotions such as sadness about feeling alone, and reactive secondary emotional responses, such as numbing or anger that fuel their negative cycle.

In the second stage of EFT the counselor is more directly focused on promoting patterns of mutual accessibility and responsiveness—both keys to greater attachment security. As new experiences and new awareness are shared, the therapist promotes each partner's acceptance of the "softer" emerging vulnerability of the other. This gradually facilitates partners' taking more vulnerable positions where they can congruently reach for and respond to each other, creating a more secure bond. The partner's attunement and ability to respond with their partner to core emotional needs sets the stage for a deeper interpersonal and intrapersonal connection.

The final stage of EFT emphasizes the consolidation of new positions in the relationship by working through historical issues that remain unresolved. Critical to the process at Stage 3 is the counselor's ability to promote the couple's new patterns of engagement experienced in Stage 2 without falling victim to their historical negative interaction cycle of Stage 1. Partners at this stage actively take steps to foster greater trust and attachment security. These positive emotional experiences enable couples to "broaden and build" the resources that support a more resilient and flourishing relationship (Fredrickson & Losada, 2005; Mikulincer & Shaver, 2009). The following section reviews each of these stages in further detail through one couple's experience of EFT.

Case Example

Paul and Sharon struggled to regain the emotional momentum that had defined the early years of their relationships. After years of infertility, the birth of a child, and economic struggles, their carefree courtship appeared as a fleeting memory particularly in contrast to the disappointment and emotional distance that defined their everyday experience. The couple sought therapy after a series of arguments that ended in threats of divorce and enduring periods of silence. Sharon and Paul made explicit their commitment to their Christian faith and its importance to their marriage. Yet the years of hardship had left each questioning whether the commitment they shared was an empty emotional shell that no longer held hope for what they believed a marriage should be.

Sharon often felt Paul's distance particularly when she needed him most. Paul kept Sharon at arm's length emotionally particularly when he anticipated her disappointment. Either partner's action could instigate an escalating pattern of Sharon's complaint and demand and Paul's attempts to placate or withdraw from her concerns. Their patterns of arguing led to extended periods of emotional disengagement, which frightened both partners enough to seek help.

In their initial sessions, the EFT therapist engaged each partner about that partner's experience of their relationship during one of these arguments. Their sexual relationship was a common point of struggle. Following years of infertility treatment and the fatigue of childrearing efforts, both expressed concern about their inability to connect physically and emotionally. Paul described the path to their bedroom as a "minefield." Sharon shared that she often felt more alone after having sex and had become increasingly indifferent to Paul's concerns. Both expressed concern that they were failing at their marriage and that this was ultimately important to them and to God.

In session, the therapist walked the couple through this recent episode both acknowledging and validating each person's experience as the details of their fight unfolded. When Sharon described how lonely she felt in the face of Paul's criticism and emotional withdrawal, tears came to her eyes. The therapist slowed the session to focus on her experience in this moment:

> Therapist: "Can you tell me what's happening for you right now as you talk about this loneliness?" (Sharon moves more deeply into her emotion, now looking away from the therapist and Paul).
>
> Sharon: "It's really difficult, you know. I feel so alone, like we are in this marriage together but I am alone."
>
> Therapist: "Right. You are together but alone. And your tears?" (Therapist expands his focus on Sharon's more vulnerable emotion).
>
> Sharon: "Well, it hurts, you know. Not to feel wanted. Not to feel like I count to Paul. It's just so hard to feel this way."
>
> Therapist: "It's painful to feel so alone and unwanted, especially when you are with someone so important to you. You feel alone." Sharon nods returning her gaze to the therapist. "It is not what you want but it's where you find yourself in these moments." (Nodding again Sharon glances over toward Paul. He is now looking at her, his face showing concern.)

In cycle deescalation the EFT therapist helps a couple to identify the reactive patterns that drive the distress in their relationship. Paul developed a vigilant response to Sharon's criticism, and either withdrew from conversations or aggressively defended his position to ward away her anxious concerns. Sharon felt Paul's reserve and often felt like he was losing interest in her. She responded with demands or complaints as a protest to his emotional distance. Sharon found it difficult to disengage from this pattern as Paul's attempts to cope triggered her more anxious feelings.

The therapist focuses on Sharon's expression of more vulnerable emotion. By engaging and expanding this experience, the therapist helps Sharon more clearly see her own experience and with the therapist's felt presence begins to express the pain she often feels but never shares with Paul. Paul orients toward Sharon's underlying emotion and begins to see her experience also in a new way. It is premature for either to engage this level of vulnerability together, but in the context of the therapist's alliance the couple begins to explore their cycle and shift toward a more understanding stance toward each other. Together the couple begins to work against this pattern because they both understand and experience how their responses to vulnerability in the relationship have driven them apart. The therapist enables partners to see the shifts and moves they make when navigating the most important issues of their relationship. Offering more than a cognitive definition of their pattern, the EFT therapist engages couples in the emotional dynamics that drive this pattern, thereby expanding opportunities for partners to experience and explore the underlying emotions that fuel their reactive distress.

In the second stage of EFT, couples are able to recognize their patterns and begin to find ways to exit these fights together. "Negative cycle deescalation" enables partners to see this dynamic as one where no one wins and their relationship loses. As they begin to work together they feel better about the relationship and are better able to stay away from more reactive positions. However, neither partner is able to move effectively toward responding to the underlying emotional needs of the other. In Stage 2 the EFT therapist restructures the positions partners often take with each other in the context of the fears and needs they experience in this intimate relationship.

Typically Stage 2 begins with a focus on the partner who more often withdraws emotionally. The EFT therapist moves to expand and distill the emotional experience informing this partner's tendency to withdraw. This involves taking the partner deeper into their underlying emotions to access and expand the underlying attachment themes organizing their behaviors in times of threat or distress. At the same time the therapist is engaging the acceptance of the other partner in response to underlying vulnerability newly evident in session. As the couple moves between taking risks and being accepted, the therapist moves the couple toward sharing and receiving their attachment-related fears and needs. A new pattern emerges as partners are free to risk and reach toward one another in the most vulnerable areas of their relationship.

Paul recounted how he got triggered earlier in the week and had a hard time letting Sharon in on what was happening. In session the therapist asked Paul to take him back to the moment when he first started to pull away. He recalled a playful conversation he was having with Sharon and an indirect and admittedly awkward attempt to suggest they have sex. Sharon missed his cue and began to withdraw. Sharon recognized what happened, and in her attempt to reassure him Paul became more uncomfortable and left the room. He did tell Sharon that he was stuck and that they would talk about this in therapy. Paul began to talk about his embarrassment when the therapist mentioned that he seemed to be looking down in a way that suggested he did not want to be seen.

Paul: Yes. I hate this. (His tone a mix of frustration and sadness).

Therapist: You look down and say. "I hate this feeling."

Paul: (Slowly). Right, this terrible feeling. Like in that moment I felt exposed. Embarrassed. So . . .

Sharon: It's okay. I was fine with you asking. I just did not understand.

Therapist: (Interrupting). Sharon, I know you are trying to help Paul here, but can we go back to what he is saying here? (Sharon sits back). So Paul, . . . you said you were embarrassed and . . .

Paul: (Quietly). Ashamed. (Still looking down).

Therapist: And, you felt this terrible feeling. Embarrassed. Ashamed. And even now you are looking away. Almost like you are feeling it all over again.

Paul: Yes. It is so hard. After years of trying to conceive all the focus on having a baby and then all the fighting . . . sex was just my thing. Never about us. Sex just became a minefield for me. It was better to stay away than to take the risk.

Therapist: So you stayed away, but the other night you were feeling good with Sharon. You wanted to connect. You let her know, and it felt like you stepped on a landmine. That was devastating for you.

Paul: I know it shouldn't have. It was just a communication thing, but now it's too late. The damage is done. Inside it's like I just go to pieces. (His silence is followed by tears). I felt for so long like Sharon didn't want me. It was all about the baby, or all about my desires. It doesn't feel like she wanted to actually be with me.

Therapist: And that's what you felt in that moment. (Paul nods.) And now . . . this is what is happening now? (He looks away fighting to hold back his emotions and tears.) What would it be like for you right now to begin to let Sharon know what these moments are like for you? You know, these moments when you feel distant, alone, and unwanted? What would it be like to tell her what's in your heart?

The therapist begins to access Paul's fears of rejection and his negative view of himself. In Stage 2 these moments create new opportunities for partners to be seen and to respond. In this session, the therapist can follow Paul's risk to share his experience with Sharon if Paul chooses to, or can process and normalize Paul's fear if the risk of sharing this seems too great. The therapist will also explore the impact of Paul's sharing his fears, helping Sharon to both accept his response and share what it is like for her to have Paul begin to let her into his pain and fear. The restructuring for Paul culminates with him asking Sharon for reassurance and support when his fears take over. Stage 2 involves a similar process with Sharon, and the couple moves to Stage 3 once both are able to repeatedly engage new patterns of security. This couple's ability to risk and to reach for each other with attachment longings and desires provides the basis for a more secure bond, and acts as an antidote for the anxious responses that trigger their pattern of distress (Johnson, 2004).

For couples like Sharon and Paul, who have a more "sanctified" relationship, the EFT therapist may also engage their faith experience as a resource. In facing her fears of abandonment, Sharon expressed that in these moments it became hard for her to sense God's presence and grace. The EFT therapist would stay with Sharon's experience and invite her further into this moment of fear to share what this experience is like with Paul. In keeping with Sharon's more "sanctified" view of the relationship, the therapist could also ask Sharon what it is like for her to take these risks with her husband as an expression of her faith:

"When you face these fears of rejection and ask for comfort from Paul, it's like a step of faith for you. You are trusting Paul, but also trusting God with something so sacred. What is it like for you to trust God in this way?"

The EFT therapist can work with the couple's "sanctified" view of their relationship in a way that is first congruent with the couple's worldview but that also amplifies the meaning of the risks and reassurances they have made.

The final stage of EFT is focused on consolidating the couple's new patterns of emotional responsiveness. Paul and Sharon have built confidence that they can open up to each other and to share the fears that often triggered their pattern. Themes of insecurity can still be present in chronic problems the couple has faced. In Stage 3 the therapist helps the couple face these past difficulties with new solutions. In the later sessions of therapy this couple focused on communicating their hopes and desires for a more intimate sexual relationship. This was a "raw spot" in their relationship that required extra care (Johnson, 2008). They also explored how to recognize the triggers for their cycle and how they could work together to interrupt this destructive pattern before it escalated. Finally the therapist invited them to begin to see their sexual relationship as a gift from God, and a sacred place in their relationship where they could affirm the gift they are to each other. They discussed ways that regularly sharing affection could be an "attachment ritual," or sign of the investment they were making to affirm their commitment to each other. Attachment rituals provide ways for couples to intentionally symbolize their ongoing commitment and deepen the bond that they share (Johnson, et al. 2005). The therapist's work with emotion and attachment continues in helping couples to celebrate their successes and reflect upon the new connections they have made.

Conclusion

Couples like Sharon and Paul question the value of their marriage when it no longer meets (or, in some cases, when it competes with) the psychological needs it is meant to fulfill. Years of corporate struggle can devitalize a relationship, leaving couples entrapped in a progressive pattern of marital disaffection (Kayser, 1993). The pain of isolation and the hopelessness experienced by couples who increasingly rely on personal strategies of emotional survival propel couples toward dissolution of their relationship. The relationship no longer holds the purpose and meaning it was intended to embody. Pastoral counselors often meet couples at this point, when partners struggle with the moral constraints of commitment over against the negative emotional experiences each partner faces at a personal level (Guttmann, 1993). Helping couples at this precarious point in their relationship requires from a counselor both skill and sensitivity to the cognitive and emotional processes informing the decisions partners make to address their struggle. Sensitivity to differences in partners' moral and religious views about divorce, marriage, and commitment provides the pastoral counselor with an important resource for attending to each partner's unique emotional struggles.

This chapter has explored the use of Emotionally Focused Couple Therapy (EFT) as a relevant approach for pastoral psychotherapy. EFT is a leading empirically supported treatment for couple distress, based on the integration of humanistic, experiential, and systemic theories of psychotherapy. This chapter has demonstrated how an EFT therapist conceptualizes and intervenes with couple distress following the empirical guidance of attachment theory and a theological understanding of covenant fidelity. Practical examples have been used to highlight how the therapist guides an unfolding emotional process that enables couples to renew faith in their mutual commitment through the experience of the sacred ties that they seek to honor through love

References

Amato, P. R. (2000). The consequences of divorce for adults and children. *Journal of Marriage and Family, 62*, 1269–87.

Anderson, R. S., & Guernsey, D. B. (1985). *On being family: A social theology of the family.* Grand Rapids: Eerdmans.

Atkinson, D. J. (1979). *To have and to hold: The marriage covenant and the discipline of divorce.* Grand Rapids: Eerdmans.

Branson, M. L. (1989). Exploring a theological foundation for marriage. *Transformation: An International Journal of Holistic Mission Studies, 6*(1), 18–23.

Brueggemann, W. (1979). Covenanting as human vocation: A discussion of the relation of bible and pastoral care. *Interpretation: A Journal of Bible and Theology, 33*, 115–29.

Brueggemann, W. (1999). *The covenanted self: Exploration in law and covenant.* Minneapolis: Fortress.

Caldwell, B. E. et al. (2007). Preliminary estimates of cost effectiveness for marital therapy. *Journal of Marital and Family Therapy, 33*, 392–405.

Whitehead, B. D. (1996). *The divorce culture.* New York: Knopf.

Doherty, W. (1997). How therapists harm marriages and what we can do about it. *The Responsive Community, 7*, 31–42.

Doherty, W. J. (2002). Bad couples therapy: Getting past the myth of therapist neutrality. *Psychotherapy Networker, 26*(6) 26–33.

Fredrickson, B. L., & Losada, M. F. (2005). Positive affect and the complex dynamics of human flourishing. *American Psychologist, 60*(7), 678–86.

Forthofer, M. S. et al. (1996). Associations between marital distress and work loss in a national sample. *Journal of Marriage and the Family, 58*, 597–605.

Gottman, J. M. (1994). *What predicts divorce*. Hillsdale, NJ: Erlbaum.

Gottman, J., & Gottman, J. (1999). The marriage survival kit: A research-based marital therapy. In R. Berger & M. T. Hannah (Eds.), *Preventive approaches in couples therapy* (pp. 304–30). Philadelphia: Brunner/Mazel.

Greenberg, L. S. (2004). Emotion-focused therapy. *Clinical Psychology & Psychotherapy, 11*, 3–16.

Griffith, J. L. (2010). *Religion that heals, religion that harms: A guide for clinical practice.* New York: Guilford.

Guttmann, J. (1993). *Divorce in psychosocial perspective: Theory and research.* Hillsdale, NJ: Lawrence Erlbaum.

Hauerwas, S. (1985). The family as a school for character. *Religious Education, 80,* 272–85.

Hays, R. B. (1996). *Moral vision of the New Testament: A contemporary introduction to New Testament ethics.* New York: HarperCollins.

Hetherington, E. M. et al. (1998). What matters? What does not? Five perspectives on the association between marital transitions and children'sadjustment. *American Psychologist, 53,* 167–84.

Johnson, S. (1986). Bonds or bargains: Relationship paradigms and their significance for marital therapy. *Journal of Marital and Family Therapy, 12,* 259–67.

Johnson, S. M., (2004). *The practice of emotionally focused couple therapy: Creating connection* (2nd ed.). New York: Brunner-Routledge.

Johnson, S. M. (2008). *Hold me tight: Seven conversations for a lifetime of love.* New York: Little Brown.

Johnson, S. M. et al.(2005). *Becoming an emotionally focused couples therapist: The workbook.* New York: Routledge.

Johnson, S. M., & Greenberg, L. S. (1985). Emotionally focused couple therapy: An outcome study. *Journal of Marital and Family Therapy, 11,* 313–17.

Johnson, S. M. et al. (1999). Emotionally focused couples therapy: Status and challenges. *Clinical Psychology: Science and Practice, 6,* 67–79.

Kayser, K. (1993). *When love dies: The process of marital disaffection.* Perspectives on Marriage and the Family. New York: Guilford.

Mahoney, A. et al. (1999). Marriage and the spiritual realm: The role of proximal and distal religious constructs in marital functioning. *Journal of Family Psychology, 13,* 321–38.

Mikulincer, M., & Shaver, P. R. (2005). Attachment theory and emotions in close relationships: Exploring the attachment-related dynamics of emotional reactions to relational events. *Personal Relationships, 12,* 149–68.

Mikulincer, M., & Shaver, P. R. (2009). An attachment and behavioral systems perspective on social support. *Journal of Social and Personal Relationships, 26,* 7–19.

Pargament, K. I., & Mahoney, A. (2005). Sacred matters: Sanctification as a vital topic for the psychology of religion. *International Journal for the Psychology of Religion, 15,* 179–98.

Rice, J. K., & Rice, D. G. (1986). *Living through divorce: A developmental approach to divorce therapy.* The Guilford Family Therapy Series. New York: Guilford.

Smedes, L. B. (1983). *Mere morality: What God expects from ordinary people.* Grand Rapids: Eerdmans.

Stassen, G. H., & Gushee, D. P. (2003). *Kingdom ethics: Following Jesus in contemporary context.* Downers Grove: InterVarsity.

Whisman, M. A., & Bruce, M. L. (1999). Marital dissatisfaction and incidence of major depressive episode in a community sample. *Journal of abnormal psychology, 108,* 674–78.

Wilcox, B. W. (2002). *Sacred vows, public purposes: Religion, the marriage movement, and marriage policy.* Washington DC: Pew Forum on Religion and Public Life.

Wolcott, I. H. (1986). Seeking help for marital problems before separation. *Australian Journal of Sex, Marriage, and Family, 7,* 154–64.

----------- 14 -----------

From Systems to Narrative
Family Therapy

Suzanne M. Coyle

Happy families are all alike; every unhappy family is unhappy
in its own way.

—Leo Tolstoy, *Anna Karenina*

FAMILIES OFFER MANY CHALLENGES to the therapist—joy and triumph,
sadness and despair—often in the same counseling session. Working
with families is not for the faint of heart. The family therapist must engage the many worlds that each family inhabits, worlds that are tricky
to navigate. It takes an adventurous spirit and a plucky balance with
compassion to make a family therapist. In response to Tolstoy's quote,
some family therapists may contend that "dysfunctional" families share
common characteristics. Working with these kinds of families involves
making a systemic assessment of the family, creating a treatment plan,
and implementing interactional interventions that would ideally result
in less distress for the family. Foundational to this understanding is an
assumption that a normative standard of a healthy family exists.

The seemingly pessimistic note Tolstoy sounds about unhappy families offers us a counterstory. If we are able to discover the uniqueness of
each unhappy family's story and empower that family to create stories of
strength, then the isolation of that family is lessened. While the intent of

family therapy has historically been to alleviate the distress of families, at times theories of family therapy have unwittingly served to elevate a normative model of family that has proven to be just as oppressive as the original "dysfunction."

When I encountered narrative therapy in my journey as a pastoral counselor and family therapist, I was looking for an approach that would connect with my changing theological beliefs but that was not based on normativity. In addition, I was looking for creativity and meaning making. I discovered these qualities in narrative therapy.

Michael White, one of the codevelopers of narrative therapy, was quite fond of maps. Following his lead, I invite you to join me in beginning a journey to discover the richness of narrative family therapy in a theologically connected context. Our first stop will be an overview of family therapy and the development of narrative therapy.

Creating the World of Family Therapy

PSYCHOTHERAPY FOR DECADES MAINLY viewed families as an obstacle to a healthy outcome for distressed persons. The roots of this philosophy grew from the psychoanalytic emphasis on the intrapsychic processes that could best be explored through an intense relationship between therapist and client. Interference from other people, including the family, was deemed to be undesirable.

Despite the exclusion of family members in its early years, psychotherapy increasingly became intertwined with its clients' families. The first development was seeing children individually in a psychoanalytic setting while consulting with the parents in separate sessions. Then, with the advent of social work, whole families were seen in their homes through the modern invention of casework. No linear historical development can be drawn with these events. However, a ripple effect began that promoted interest in the family in various ways.

Prosperity in North America at the end of World War II changed the social context of families and communities. Houses could be purchased for a modest amount. Educational opportunities increased. New perspectives on family life focused on the role of the mother staying at home. As America became prosperous, families had more disposable income.

In the midst of this prosperity, psychotherapy produced other offspring. Interest in things psychological developed. The government provided large sums of grant money for projects that promoted public health. The theoretical offspring of individual psychotherapy often found themselves the recipients of these funds. Mental health clinics developed as part of hospitals or other institutions. Included in this outreach were child behavioral clinics where oppositional children were treated in sessions. Schools regularly referred obstreperous students to such clinics. In play therapy children were seen individually. Parents were seen separately for consultation. Detailed interpretation of the children's drawings and play activities further isolated children from the family context.

At the same time, therapists became interested in working with married couples. Any therapist who saw individuals recognized that a major portion of their clients' concerns focused on their family relationships, particularly their marriages. Work with couples and families sprang up across the country. The early pioneers of family therapy were primarily psychiatrists who were natural rebels disaffected with psychiatry. Salvador Minuchin (1974) was an Argentinean psychiatrist who worked at a school for delinquent boys in New York. Psychodynamic approaches did not work well with these young charges, whose families were largely from disadvantaged backgrounds. Minuchin's structural approach emerged from a desire to remedy dysfunctional family functioning.

Across the country in Palo Alto, the Mental Research Institute gathered people from different professional worlds to collaborate with anthropologist Gregory Bateson. Don Jackson and his team focused on interactional patterns of communication and the way families act within those patterns (Watzlawick et al., 1967). From this work sprang many schools of family therapy including the communications school, Milan systemic approach, and solution-focused therapy.

Another new approach, which bore the stamp of his large personality, was psychiatrist Karl Whitaker's experiential therapy (Whitaker & Bumberry, 1988). This approach saw the family as a collection of individuals whose dysfunction was caused by the lack of individuation and emotional expression. His work frequently involved three generations of family members so that the emotionality of the session could be expanded.

Continuing the practice of intergenerational work, psychiatrist Murray Bowen (1993) began his own family therapy journey with a presentation at a national psychiatric conference. His systemic focus sees the family as an organic entity whose balance is keenly affected by the interplay not only between members of the same family but intergenerationally. This beautiful theory is cast within a larger understanding of the natural systems of the universe of which human beings are a part.

Varying in orientation, these approaches share several assumptions about families. First, families are understood as systems that maintain balance. Thus, some theoretical intervention is necessary in order to disturb that balance and promote change. Second, these orientations are based upon mechanistic, biological, and linguistic models that are primarily concerned with how systems function. Third, they largely assume a normative understanding of families. Certain ways of being a family are considered preferable.

These various schools of family therapy enjoyed golden years of prominence. Then, in the mideighties, feminists began questioning the prevailing assumptions of family therapy. The first theory to be criticized was Minuchin's strong emphasis on a structure in which all parties equally contributed to its maintenance. Feminists argued that women were unfairly blamed in this understanding. Other postmodern voices joined in.

Harlene Anderson (1997) and Harry Goolishian explored social constructionist understandings in a joint project. Central to their discoveries was the understanding that language contains our self perceptions. The resulting collaborative therapy then endeavors to discover with the family ways of knowing that only the family can know. Closely related to collaborative therapy's world is narrative therapy—a family cousin to whom we now turn.

The World of Story Meanings

At this point in the development of family therapy, postmodernism's social-constructionist learning focused on meaning, interpretation, and the inter-subjectivity of knowledge. Family therapy repurposed insights from individualistic approaches to psychotherapy to address the relational aspects of human experience. Just as family therapy historically challenged the linear thinking of psychotherapy with the metaphor of the family as a system, so social-constructionist family therapies such as narrative therapy offered a new metaphor for the family.

Narrative therapy understands families as "interpretive communities" or "storying cultures" (Pare, 1995). Although there are many directions that postmodernism has taken within various disciplines, a direct contribution to the development of narrative therapy focuses upon where knowledge actually resides. In contrast to much psychotherapy, social-constructionist therapies understand knowledge to be "in between people" rather than inside an individual (De Shazer, 1991). This understanding draws from current debates among disciplines, especially the "hard science" of physics, that questions to what degree observation is ever objective. The assumption is that knowing a reality is impacted by the influence of the observer (Hawking, 1998).

Social constructionism is ultimately concerned with how meaning is arrived at in the community where the knowledge is learned. Knowledge is understood to be a function of how the community interprets the context (Pare, 1995). Thus, how something develops is secondary to the way things are perceived, interpreted, and constructed.

Beginning therapists often fret about whether what a client tells them is the objective reality. From a social-constructionist perspective, it is not really important whether what a mother tells you about her son's behavior is accurate. What is important is that it is her perception: that perception in turn interprets the world of the family both mother and son inhabit.

Into this philosophical world, narrative therapy, as codeveloped by Michael White, a social worker in Australia, and David Epston, an anthropologist and social worker in New Zealand, was born (White & Epston, 1990). Through their friendship and long conversations, postmodern effects were soon seen in their work with clients, grounded in two theoretical worldviews—a postmodern perspective primarily influenced by Michel Foucault (1984), and narrative metaphors derived from Jerome Bruner (1976). Narrative therapy was also heavily influenced by feminist theory through White's wife, Cheryl White (2009).

Narrative therapy understands that people make sense of their lives and give meaning to their lives through people and events, through the stories they tell others and that others tell them. Quite simply, people's narratives are their realities. Yet, we are not isolated storytellers. We are born into the dominant narratives or discourses of our cultures that are created by the powerful people in our culture. Freedman and Combs (1996) describe the worldview of the narrative therapist as a "way of living that supports collaboration, social justice and local, situated, context-specific knowledge rather than normative thinking, diagnostic labeling, and generalized (non-contextualized) 'expert' knowledge" (p. 18).

As we live in our own experiences we also take the dominant discourses of our culture as our own truths. Our lived experiences become oppressed by the narratives or discourses of our culture. Thus, the political and social agenda of narrative therapy becomes clear. The purpose of narrative therapy is to help people deconstruct their culturally influenced problem stories and then construct stories about themselves that open up the future. As part of this mission both clients and therapists need to look at ways culture profoundly influences their realities. Therapists need to make certain that they not impose their narratives upon their clients. We turn now to the specific practices of narrative therapy.

Practices of Narrative Therapy

Narrative therapy generally proceeds through asking specific kinds of questions that are designed to deconstruct the problem story of the family. Narrative questions are intended to influence the emergence of preferred outcomes. They are not asked purely for information or to explore a client's interpretation or understanding. In this theory questions serve to open up new possibilities for the client.

Let's say that a family comes to see you for counseling. Mary, age thirty-two, and Mark, age thirty-two, have a five-year-old daughter who cries uncontrollably when leaving for kindergarten. This distressing behavior has occurred for two months now, since she entered kindergarten. An approach to this challenge with modernist questions would be to explore the triggers to the behavior, what has been tried to extinguish it, and general exploration of the emotional distress for the family. A narrative question that deconstructs or explores the family's presenting problem in detail will focus on a rich description of the experience of the problem story.

So, the therapist might ask, "I'd like to explore the problem that brings you here by asking some questions. If the question sounds interesting to you, we'll talk about it." Then, the therapist might ask, "How does this problem make itself a part of your family?"

In response, the family members might say, "Kindergarten influences our entire life. We dread when school starts each day and look forward to the weekend."

The narrative therapist would then work with the family as they named the problem and recounted its effect on their lives.

At this point, it will be helpful to lay out some of the basic practices of narrative therapy. This explanation is intended as basic orientation to a narrative practice that will require additional training. Narrative therapy is a very different philosophical orientation from individual psychotherapy. Founder Michael White said that it takes three years to make a narrative therapist. So, enjoy your journey of curiosity.

A first step in most family-therapy approaches is the initial assessment. In general, narrative therapists are not predisposed to assessment given that assessment being driven by normative concerns. However, William Madsden has developed an assessment process that is narrative friendly, to which we now turn. The first step is a description of the family, which includes a description of the family network through a genogram or ecomap. Then the living environment along with recent changes and the family's hopes and preferred futures or dreams are identified (Madsden, 2007).

The next step is the presenting concerns. At this point, the family is asked to share their presenting concerns in the referral source's words. Then, the family's response to the referral, the family's definition of their concern, and finally the family's vision of life when the concern is no longer a problem are outlined. Basic to this approach are both a nonpathologizing exploration of the concerns that bring the family to therapy and respect for the clients' storying of the concerns.

The context of the presenting concerns is the next area of narrative assessment. At this point, the therapist engages the family in exploring situations in which the problem or problems are most and least likely to occur as well as the ways the family is affected by the problem. What are the family's beliefs about the problem? What are the interactions around the problem? And, important for the reauthoring of the problem story, what are the cultural supports for the problem?

The next area of assessment will vary widely, depending on the family's history with problems. This step focuses around the family's experience with helpers. The old cliché "Too many cooks spoil the stew" is true for the narrative therapist working with families.

It can be rightly argued that families attract more helpers since there are more people involved than with individual clients. Some families may be involved with larger systems such as social services, where for other families this may be the first foray into counseling. The narrative therapist will want to know the family's current involvement with helpers as well as past experience with helpers. Finally, the impact of the family's past experience on their view of helpers will be explored.

As these experiences and beliefs are explored, narrative interviews can make a place for relevant history. A multigenerational history is created with special attention to important themes about presenting concern, constraining interaction, beliefs and life stories, and experience with helpers. In gathering information about multigenerational history the purpose is not to identify a source of the problem for purposes of diagnosing as in many family therapies. The purpose is to explore the histories and knowledges of the family's landscape of life that they inhabit. This is an area that is currently being expanded by David Epston (2010), codeveloper of narrative therapy, in terms of what he calls genealogical inquiry.

After this information is gathered in a collaborative conversation with the family, basic information may be gathered, which will be necessary if you practice in a modernist setting such as in an accredited pastoral counseling center or clinic. This information includes medical information and risk factors as well as mental status. If you practice in a private pastoral counseling setting or church context, you will need to gather basics of this information in order to best serve the family. However, you may not need to gather as much information as you might need in a clinic setting.

Gathering information does not, however, adequately address the concern for narrative therapists' influence on the family in encouraging all the members to discover aspects of their identity as a family that can support or scaffold them as they reauthor their family stories into a story that can enrich their lives. At this juncture, protective factors that build the family identity are important.

These factors include personal, familial, and community characteristics, and "skills and knowledges" that protect the family from risk. At the same time, these factors help to promote resilience in the family. The therapist will also want to inquire about any improvements that the family has experienced since the first contact. In a real sense, assessment for a narrative family therapist involves the whole re-authoring process of family stories and is ongoing rather than fixed at the beginning of the counseling process.

As this information is gathered, the narrative therapist may need to make a diagnosis or diagnostic impression depending upon the state regulatory requirements. If a standard diagnosis is made, it is critical that the family understands the cultural expectations of mental health professions and insurance-company requirements. Further, the narrative therapist will want to deconstruct the meaning of the diagnosis in consultation with the family as to how it impacts their family story (Anderson, 2011).

Finally, a narrative assessment formulates a collaborative understanding of the family stories and life with the family. This formulation includes information that addresses biological, individual, family, and sociocultural factors. Based on these factors, narrative therapists then utilize several practices that help them deconstruct the problem story, liberate people from it, and construct a preferred story.

We now turn to a brief description of these narrative practices along with some examples of questions for a White/Epston type interview. The order of these questions does not determine a linear interview. One can start with externalizing, go back to it, or jump to some other practice. White (2007) refers to these practices as "maps" because much like a driver following a map, the therapist can get to the destination (the reauthored story) by a variety of routes—whether by the express highway or the scenic route.

Externalizing Conversations and Unique Outcomes

The purpose of externalizing conversations is to establish a context where people experience themselves as separate from the problem. The understanding is that people commonly find themselves unable to experience themselves as separate from the problem, which many times has become their identity. Through externalizing the problem, the person is able to reflect upon their relationship to the problem rather than to focus on a "problem person."

The narrative motto is repeated often as "the person is not the problem; the problem is the problem." A criticism of externalizing is that it absolves people from taking responsibility for their problems. But this is not the purpose of externalizing, nor does narrative practice promote irresponsibility. In fact, a concern for ethical positions is a huge part of its ethos. The intent of externalizing is to reduce guilt and blame so that people are better able to reflect more freely upon their problems and the impact of those problems upon them. Further, externalizing counteracts the effects of labeling upon families. As externalizing is practiced, the family is often given an option to name the problem. Through the naming of the problem, they then engage in conversation about its effects upon their lives.

The following are some possible questions that can develop rich externalizing conversations along with the four areas of inquiry that are non-linear in practice:

Naming of the Problem

When you say . . . , what do you mean?

Are there particular things that are happening when it occurs?

Does . . . arise more often when you're with particular people?

What tone does "it" use when telling you what to do?

Can you describe the shape and color of this character?

If you drew it, what might it look like?

Effects of the Problem

What do you notice about the way the problem gets in the way of what you're hoping for?

How is the problem causing you trouble in your life right now?

How have your concerns affected your relationship with others?

How does it affect the hopes and dreams you have for your life?

What impact does . . . have on the values that are important to you?

Evaluating the Effects of the Problem

What do you think about the effect . . . (name them) you have just described?

Do you think these effects you've just mentioned like . . . are helpful or un-helpful or maybe a bit of both?

What's all this like for you?

How do you feel about this problem?

Intentional Understandings of Experience and What Is Given Value

Why are you taking this position?

What does this position say about what is important to you?

What dreams do you get a glimpse of as you talk about this?

Who else knows these are important to you? (Roth & Epston, 1992, p. 1)

Asking these types of questions enables the narrative therapist to engage the family in fuller descriptions and understandings of their lived experience as a family. Through this type of questioning that is inductive rather than purely information gathering, the family develops thickened stories, which help them to stand up to the problems that are confronting them as a family.

In reflecting back upon these questions, one can see that narrative therapists use deconstructive listening and questions to help families trace the effects of the problems. As the process evolves, the family begins to dis-cover gaps in the problem story that has been adversely affecting them and begin to identify the dominant cultural discourse or story that has been af-fecting them. As the problem-saturated story becomes clearer to the family through these questions of relative influence (identified in the above ques-tions), the family begins to see themselves as coauthors of their lives.

It is at this point in narrative practice that the family, with the influ-ence of the therapist as the coauthor, see possibilities for a unique outcome as an alternative to the problem saturated story. At this point the therapist listens for and asks about times when the problem could have been a problem for the family but was not.

These types of questions invite the family to make sense of exceptions to the problem that they might not have recognized as important and to begin to use them as part of an emerging narrative that understands the family in a resilient way. Michael White offers the metaphor of mapping the problem in the landscapes of action and identity as a narrative practice that uses unique accounts to achieve the change the family desires. The landscape of action can be understood as the plot, events, sequences, and time of the story; the landscape of identity are the ways the family understands the landscape of action giving meaning to their identity (White, 2007).

Mapping in the Landscapes of Action and Identity

Mapping generally involves the following steps:

Identify a Unique Outcome

The therapist listens for a time when the problem could have been a problem but was not.

Have there been times when the problem was not a part of your life?

Ensure that the Unique Outcome is Preferred

Rather than assume, the therapist asks the family if the outcome is preferred.

Is this something that you want to happen?

Landscape of Action

The therapist begins to ask the family what occurred and in what order with specific details.

What did you do first?

How did other family members respond?

Was it easier than you thought?

Landscape of Identity

The therapist begins to map out with the family what happened during the unique outcome with the family's identity. This phase of mapping thickens the story associated with the unique outcome and thus helps the family develop more resilience.

What does this say about you as family?

What were your intentions behind these actions?

What do you value most about your actions?

What did you learn from this?

Does this change how you see life, God, your purpose, or your life goals? (White, 2007)

Other Narrative Practices

Narrative practice always tries to engage with the public dimension of both the problem story and the thickened story in working with families. By doing this, narrative therapists see themselves as not only advocating for the family but also coauthoring with the family different accounts of their identities that would not be possible in individual counseling. This approach is consistent with its acknowledgement of Foucault's analysis of power and knowledge being intertwined in the public arena, which will be discussed further shortly (1980).

These practices involve use of a reflecting team and outsider witnesses who may have experience with the problem and engage with the family to offer support as a "community of concern." These are ways of telling and retelling the story in order to acknowledge and sustain the new story.

Definitional ceremonies are another way to sustain the new story of the family. Any kind of ritual that can witness the change for the family is a possibility. Examples can be a certificate, an imagined public announcement, a song, and so forth. Writing letters are another example of acknowledging and supporting the changes made in therapy.

Narrative of a Theological Practice

As the practices of narrative therapy have been presented, the intent of narrative therapy is to position the family in a nonblame position, enable them to identify oppressive stories that form their identity as a family, discover cracks in the oppressive story that offer possibilities for a different story, and expand the meaning of the stories that form the family identity. At its very core, narrative therapy is about meaning making. And it is that value that offers some rich opportunities for conversation with theology.

Different approaches to practicing narrative therapy through a theological position have emerged. An almost automatic response to finding a theological fit with narrative therapy has been to connect it with narrative theology. On one level, this seems intuitively obvious. Narrative theology has a natural affinity with the essential quality of story as being central to Christian faith. In addition, it lifts up the biographical nature of our lives— our stories—as being worthy of theological reflection (Cook & Alexander, 2008). At the same time, narrative theology is certainly not a matched parallel for family narrative therapy. It primarily develops a single story whereas narrative therapy focuses on doubly listening and developing not only *an* alternate but multiple stories. Doubly listening involves listening to the flip side of a story as well as listening for an implied story.

Based upon this distinction, a theological approach that focuses upon the very approach or methodology of narrative therapy would be viable. Narrative therapy true to its postmodern worldview looks at deconstruction as an essential way to understand the true nature of stories. Stories contain the factors of one's identity. And, in turn, the stories that form a family's identity have power over the family as maintained by the stories that culture views as normative.

Power is then central to narrative therapy's method. Power grants privilege: the power to have one's story dominate another or to have one's own version of the truth prevail. The meanings from these stories are embedded in language that has a valence of what is normative and what is not normative.

Liberation and feminist theologies offer a way of looking at power in family narratives (Brown, 1993) to form a multistoried method similar to what occurs in narrative therapy. Liberation theology also looks critically at oppression from culture in the ways it blocks families from being able to create the stories that best enrich their lives. While liberation theologies are best known for critique of socioeconomic issues, it can be argued that power and the way in which it is managed lies at the core of socioeconomic issues. Further, the final result for families who experience the freedom that liberation theologies see for them is to have the power to create new stories for themselves.

Liberation theology then offers for narrative theology a way to deepen the meaning making of narrative by rooting it in a view of God that fits for the family and the lives they inhabit. Just as narrative understands the "story" of a family to be many stories, so liberation theology understands God to be the ultimate author of a family's story. By his involvement in the everyday experiences that often cause oppression, Jesus is understood as the liberator of people's lives. Woven together, human and divine stories are thickened into a richer narrative for the family.

A further delineation of a method in liberation approaches is found in the work of Paulo Freire. Freire's (2000) work is concerned ultimately with sharing knowledge with the masses and then engaging with them in reflection and action as method. In many ways, this approach matches with narrative therapy, which employs a deconstructive approach and gives the power of the process to those actually involved in the process.

Methods of Narrative Therapy and Liberation Theology

Let me now illustrate how liberation theology and narrative therapy can inform each other through a case study of the Lewis family. Alice, age forty, and Jerry, age forty, have been married for twenty years. Alice works in a nonprofit agency, and Jerry is a CPA. Alice calls to make an appointment with me. She indicates that Jason, age fourteen, has been expelled from school for interrupting the teacher and being disruptive. They bring Jason to the session. As they describe the problem, it is clear that Jason is identified as the problem. All the stories of frustration center on Jason. I ask Alice and Jerry to bring the whole family to the next session.

The next session has the other children, Jacob, age sixteen, and Ashley, age eleven. As the family begins to talk, the family begins to move from identifying Jason as the problem to naming the family as chaos. Chaos causes them to argue and explode. We then explore further what they mean by chaos. Through the practice of externalizing, the family describes the effect of chaos. As we begin to identify the unique outcomes that they would like for the family, it is determined that they would like to not have chaos overcome them.

Further deconstructing of chaos reveals that the family members have different relationships with the problem. Some run from it; others connect with it through yelling. As we further explore the story, the family names their motto, "Everyone must be responsible." We then trace the family's connection with their Protestant tradition, which is informed by a strict pietism. The Lewis family responds that you need to be responsible and that fun is not a good thing to have.

Through exploring the different stories of the family members, the Lewis family begins to challenge chaos. As they become more playful, chaos leaves the family for long periods of time. Then one day, Ashley talks about feeling that they are more of a family. We begin to explore the "unique outcome" of that experience. How does that experience of being a family change things for them as a family?

Soon a conversation emerges. Jason says that for a long time he has believed that the only way to be a member of the Lewis family is to live life responsibly. To deviate from being responsible and to have some fun would be to betray what it means to be a Lewis.

As the discussion among the family continues, it becomes clear that even Alice and Jerry have felt oppressed by the normative belief that responsibility really conveys who they should be as a family of faith. Alice says, "I always understood that God wanted us to do the right thing. For me, 'doing the right thing' meant being responsible. Having joy seemed to have little part of being Christian."

As one listens to the stories of the Lewis family, several stories are uncovered, according to their words, that undergird the identity of the family. As they talk, it becomes clear that they see the "rightness" of their faith contributing to their family story that a Lewis is responsible. So, when Jason did not act "properly" at school, it became clear that he had claimed a story that was counter to the dominant story of responsibility that the Lewises had come to believe was important.

The pastoral counselor can initiate a response to the Lewis family by pointing to a trait common to both narrative therapy and liberation theology. Both narrative therapy and liberation theology assume that power runs through lived experience and determines how people engage with their lives. The Lewis family has responded to the dominant discourse shaped by their faith, and specifically by the value of responsibility. The family has believed that shaping their lives any other way was impossible. So the Lewises storied their identity as a family in order to be compliant with this dominant discourse shaped by their faith and by the specific value of responsibility.

Unique outcomes emerge as liberation theology engages with narrative therapy. Narrative therapy's approach to introducing a new experience for the family and thus new "hopes and dreams"—a cherished narrative phrase for the future—rests with the family itself and also with outsider witnesses who are supportive persons. Power emerges from the human realm.

Liberation theology introduces God as powerful and at the same time compassionate, standing with families who experience oppression. Yet, the God of liberation as seen through Jesus the liberator is not the God of the status quo who upholds normative views for everyone. It is the God of freedom who sees the "hopes and dreams" of families to be experienced with family members and supporters as well as with God, who offers strength of a different quality than human beings.

Conclusion

Families struggle with many dilemmas when trying to identify the stories that engage all family members and that offer different future possibilities for their lives. Family therapy has sought to respond to this dilemma with many modernist, systemic approaches. Narrative therapy coupled with liberation theology offers fresh and generative stories to families, in which and through which families can find meaning and can discover new futures—both collectively (as family groups) and individually (as members of families). Supportive people empowered by the liberating God—whether friends or other family members—offer "hopes and dreams" that can guide the futures of all family members.

References

Anderson, H. (1997). *Conversation, language, and possibilities: A postmodern approach to therapy.* New York: Basic Books.

Anderson, H. (2011, August 25). Postmodern therapies. http://www.harleneanderson.com/.

Brown, R. M. (1993). *Liberation theology: An introductory guide.* Louisville: Westminster John Knox.

Bruner, J. S. (1977). *The process of education.* Cambridge: Harvard University Press.

Bowen, M. (1993). *Family therapy in clinical practice.* Lanham, MD: Aronson, Inc.

Cook, R., & I. Alexander. (2008). *Interweavings: Conversations between narrative therapy and Christian faith.* North Charleston, SC: CreateSpace Books.

de Shazer, S. (1991). *Putting difference to work.* New York: Norton.

Epston, D. (2010, December 4). Genological inquiry in narrative therapy. (P. o.-1. Work, Interviewer).

Freedman, J., & G. Combs. (1996). *Narrative therapy: The social construction of preferred realities.* New York: Norton.

Freire, P. (2000). *Pedagogy of the oppressed.* New York: Continuum.

Foucault, M. (1980). *Power/knowledge: Selected interviews and other writing, 1972–1977.* New York: Pantheon.

Foucault, M. (1984). *Foucault reader.* P. Rabinow (Ed.). New York: Pantheon.

Hawking, S. (1998). *A brief history of time.* New York: Bantam.

Madsden, W. (2007). Working with traditional structures to support a collaborative clinical practice. *International Journal of Narrative Therapy & Community Work, 2,* 51–61.

Minuchin, S. (1974). *Families and family therapy.* Cambridge: Harvard University Press.

Pare, D. (1995). Of families and other cultures: The shifting paradigm of family therapy. *Family Process, 34,* 1–19.

Roth, S., & D. Epston. (1992). (retrieved 2011, August 23). Framework for a White/Epston type interview. Narrative Approaches: http://www.narrativeapproaches.com/.

Watzlawick, P. et al. (1967). *Pragmatics of human communication: A study of interactional patterns, pathologies, and paradoxes.* New York: Norton.

Whitaker, C. A., & Bumberry, W. M. (1988). *Dancing with the family: A symbolic-experiential approach.* New York: Routledge.

White, C. (2009, December 2). History of narrative therapy. Lecture discussion, International Narrative Therapy and Community Work Training, Adelaide, South Australia.

White, M. (2007). *Maps of narrative practice.* New York: Norton.

White, M., & D. Epston. (1990). *Narrative means to therapeutic ends.* New York: Norton.

15

Group Psychotherapy as Metanoetic Liturgy

K. Brynolf Lyon

THE FLOURISHING OF HUMAN life significantly depends both on our ability to relate well to others in groups and on our group's ability to relate well to us as individual members of it. From our families of origin to our school, friendship, civic, church, and work groups, if we are genuinely to thrive we must learn to cooperate and compete with others justly and productively. We must learn to recruit and be recruited by others' care and concern fruitfully. We must discover how to deal with our own and others' aggression, love, shame, fear, disgust, and wonder in ways that protect, deepen and enrich our lives individually and communally, opening us to the depths of ourselves, others, and the world in vitalizing and, ultimately, morally and spiritually enriching ways. We must, in the words of theologian John Caputo (2006), learn to live in the *metanoetics* of the kingdom: to live in ways that open us up, unharden our hearts, make us vulnerable to the lost and the suffering around us and within us in a world rife with injustice and oppression.

Group psychotherapy, from a pastoral-psychotherapy perspective, seeks to be a means of *metanoia*. It is a practice offered to help transform our hearts of stone into hearts of flesh (Ezekiel 36:26) by creating a threshold into certain dimensions of the metanoetics into which we are called to live. Pastoral psychotherapy seeks to collaborate with God's persistent, patient transforming of the world by helping others to be open to their own transformation. Group psychotherapy from this perspective is, therefore, a therapeutic discipline with both emotional and spiritual registers. As emotional and spiritual practice helping to establish certain of the conditions or preconditions for *metanoia*, pastoral psychotherapy seeks to help us transgress those inner laws of our hearts and minds that have come to bind us to diminished and hurtful ways of living, that cut us off from relating well to our own and others suffering and joy.[1]

A Case Study

Bonnie and Steve were members of a seven-patient psychotherapy group. The group was facilitated by two cotherapists: one male and one female. The group met every week for one and one-half hours, attempting to help its members develop greater capacities to form and sustain healthy, emotionally intimate relationships.

Bonnie was an administrative assistant to a midlevel executive in the medical technology field. She was in her early forties, had been divorced and remarried, but entered the group at the point of the collapse of her second marriage. Bonnie had two teenaged children from her first marriage still living at her home. She grew up as the eldest of five children in a Roman Catholic household in which her father was an alcoholic and emotionally abusive. Her mother worked occasionally at a local grocery store to help make financial ends meet and was often absent (either physically or emotionally) when the father's tirades occurred. Bonnie had, perhaps not surprisingly, married two alcoholics, both of whom were also emotionally abusive to her and the children. She herself had difficulty regulating her emotions, either withdrawing or flaring dramatically in the face of complex emotional situations. She had been in individual therapy for two years before entering the group.

Steve was a successful businessman in his midforties. He had never married but had several long-term relationships with women who eventually left the relationship due to what they described as his controlling nature. While Steve knew that he had what he called "high standards," he felt that his former girlfriends had all overreacted and couldn't really appreciate him. Steve grew up in a large city on the East Coast, the eldest son of a domineering father and an emotionally chaotic mother, who frequently fought and, three years after the children had left home, finally divorced. Steve had been

1. Useful overviews of group psychotherapy include Ettin (1999); Garland (2010); Kleinberg (2010); MacKenzie (1997); Motherwell & Shay (2005); Rutan et al. (2010); Whitaker (1985); and Yalom and Leszcz (2005). *Metanoia* and *metanoetics* refer to a "change of heart and mind," a kind of freeing of ourselves from oppressive and diminishing ways of living.

referred to the group by a couples therapist who was seeing Steve and his latest girlfriend.

Steve and Bonnie both came into the group captive to deeply entrenched maladaptive patterns of experiencing themselves and others. In some respects, they were a perfect storm waiting to happen in the group: Bonnie had a well-earned reactivity to controlling men; Steve had a fear of the vulnerability and misrecognition evoked by less well emotionally regulated women. So little more than one year into the group, Bonnie and Steve began to bicker and fight with each other. Bonnie accused Steve of being another rigid and controlling male; Steve accused Bonnie of being "out of control" and demanding. For many sessions they seemed deadlocked, finding the situation increasingly impossible to bear. Other group members began to take sides, most joining Bonnie in the belief that Steve was "the problem."

Compounding this, as eldest children in chaotic households, Bonnie and Steve anticipated that parents were inept, dangerous, or both. Because Bonnie and Steve had so little experience of parents who could regulate their households, they unconsciously anticipated that the group therapists could not manage the group either. They entered the group with deep, unconscious expectations that they would have to rely on the ways of feeling and acting that had grown ingrained in them. Indeed, many other members of the group began to grow impatient with the therapists, who increasingly seemed to them like inept parents as well. Even though the group members came to the group hoping for change, their characteristic ways of experiencing the world were activated in the group, and the group, rather than serving as a respite from their outside lives, strangely seemed to mimic it.

The group was formed for the purpose of helping people like Bonnie and Steve have a living laboratory in which to feel and think about their characteristic patterns of relating and to experiment with alternative ways of relating. They were to do this with five other group members and two therapists. Both had been in individual therapy before, but neither had been in group therapy. Even before they began overtly to struggle with one another, they wondered, how was this going to work? What could they possibly get out of being with others in this therapeutic format?

The Distinctiveness of Group Psychotherapy

Bonnie, Steve, and the other members of the group were asking an important question. What are we to make of the most distinctive fact about group psychotherapy, that there are several patients in the room at the same time?

While the response we give to that question in the group-therapy context itself might be different from how we might address it in the process of learning about it in a training context, the question is nonetheless an important one. From the origins of group therapy in the earliest part of the last century, people working therapeutically with groups have struggled to understand the implications of the group context. For some, group therapy was simply an expedient necessitated by the limitation of professional personnel or money. It made therapy more cost effective and therefore more financially available for potential clients and/or it allowed a smaller number of trained professionals to treat a larger number of persons. Yet, to see this feature of group psychotherapy only from this perspective of technical rationality is to miss the emotional or dynamic significance of group treatment.

What I think is most distinctive about group psychotherapy is that the treatment takes place in the midst of three interacting vectors of influence. First, each person in the group (including the therapist) has their own intrapsychic life, the realm of meanings and forces that they bring with them from their particular histories. What happens in group life is inevitably influenced by the intrapsychic: the ways that feelings and behaviors of group members are energized or shaped by their own conscious and unconscious patterns of living formed throughout the course of their lives.

Second, the group is characterized by an interpersonal vector of influence. In other words, groups promote to varying degrees interaction between group members, not just interactions between a single patient and therapist. These interpersonal interactions are obviously influenced by the intrapsychic lives of the participants. Indeed part of the work of group therapy is understanding how our interpersonal interactions are distorted by the meanings and feelings we bring with us from our past. Yet, the interpersonal sphere is not simply the sum of two intrapsychic lives added together. The distinctiveness of our interpersonal exchanges derives from the reciprocal influences we have on one another over time.

Third, the group is characterized by the interactions of the "group-as-a-whole" or the group as a system. In other words, what is happening at any particular moment in group life is shaping and being shaped by the particular emergent emotional reality of the group itself as an evolving organic entity. Group psychotherapy in the fullest sense, from my perspective, takes the group context itself as dynamically central to the treatment.

Not everyone would agree with this perspective. For some, group psychotherapy is essentially a way to treat individual problems in the presence of others. The therapist basically "treats" the individual members while the group looks on, learning what it can as witnesses to the therapy happening somewhere else in the group. While I do not doubt that there can be therapeutic effect from this kind of treatment, this perspective misses a significant dimension of what is actually happening in the room by failing to address the group as a whole (see also Garland, 2010, p. 36). Therefore, in this essay I will be referring to group psychotherapy as a form of treatment that ideally addresses all three of the above vectors of influence.

What happens in group psychotherapy emerges from and within the above co-occurrent factors: the intrapsychic life of each participant; the particular interpersonal interaction unfolding in the moment; and the ways the emergent group as a whole is taking form, shaping and being shaped by member interaction. In one sense, we might say theologically that the group enacts a kind of liturgy in all this, a "work of the people." While it is not the kind of liturgy we associate with more usual congregational worship services, it is nonetheless a struggle to learn and practice with one another the metanoetics of wonder, love, and justice that call forth, lure, insist from the depths of our being together. And while God may never be mentioned, group psychotherapy is nonetheless an effort to engage with the faint but persistent insistence and lure that are God's presence in human life.

Of course, one might well imagine someone asking from a religious perspective if God should not be named straightforwardly as a vector of influence as well. Isn't God influencing what is happening in the group? Surely the answer is yes. However, theologically, I would suggest that God is not a separate vector of influence operating outside of or in addition to the vectors of influence we have discussed. God is not a separate actor among other actors. Rather, what we are referring to in speaking of God happens in and through the intrapsychic, interpersonal, and group-as-a-whole dimensions of group life. God is the lure (the insistence, as Caputo might have it) toward wonder, love, and justice that is found amid, not separate or apart from, the finite forces and meanings of group life (Caputo, 2013; Keller, 2008). God functions, as Tillich (1973) said, as a dimension of depth within all of life, not a separate dimension of life. Thus, in referring to God's influence on group life, one ought not to refer to a separate force or action, but rather to the dimension of depth within all such operative forces and actions in the group.

The metanoetic liturgy of group psychotherapy does not unfold through set or prescribed words. It is rather a deep procedural movement of the group's life, shaped by the therapeutic frame (McWilliams, 2004) of group psychotherapy and by the particular ways the emotional, moral, and spiritual registers develop within that frame.[2] The therapeutic frame refers

2. Though I have a different theological approach to cultural ritual, I am sympathetic here to the project of Smith, 2009, which seeks to interpret and explore "cultural liturgies."

to the task, boundaries, and ground rules of the therapy. Since the therapeutic frame can differ somewhat depending on the kind or task of group
psychotherapy in which one is engaged, it is important to think about these
issues.

Kinds of Group Psychotherapy

The therapeutic frame of group psychotherapy (and therefore the liturgy or
"work of the people" it makes possible) will vary depending upon the purpose of the group and the role of the therapist. Groups can serve a variety
of therapeutic ends.[3] For example, psychoeducational groups are characterized by the provision of psychological information to patients dealing with a
common concern. Psychoeducational groups might be formed around loss
and grief, parenting, coping skills for persons with bipolar disorder, or any
number of other issues. The central therapeutic action of psychoeducational
groups normally derives from two dimensions of the group: (1) the provision and sharing of information that the therapist has deemed useful to the
members and (2) group members sharing with one another their struggles,
successes, and failures, in the arena of their lives the group is meant to address. Psychoeducational groups will vary in terms of how much relative
importance is placed on either of those items.

Group psychotherapy can also take the form of support groups. Support groups may often have a psychoeducational component, but they are
primarily identified by their emphasis on the group providing ego support
for persons in difficult life circumstances. Support groups tend to address
conscious and preconscious material but not material that is dynamically
unconscious.[4] Persons dealing with life-threatening or life-altering physical illnesses, adult children supporting parents with Alzheimer's disease,
trauma survivors, and adolescents with behavioral issues are all populations
that have been treated with support groups. In both psychoeducational and
support groups, the group therapist tends to be active, often directing or
structuring the conversation according to an agenda the therapist has developed, often following a protocol, and often providing handouts or other
psychoeducational material.

---

3. See, for example, the discussions of Yalom and Leszcz (2005); MacKenzie, (1997);
and Ettin (1999) on the variety of kinds and purposes of group psychotherapy.

4. Material that is "dynamically unconscious" refers to aspects of our psychic life
that we are unconsciously motivated to keep from our awareness or from formulating
into recognizable experience.

Psychodynamically oriented groups are groups in which the clinical emphasis is on the preconscious and unconscious dynamics that shape the emotional and spiritual processes within and between group members. At the further extreme of psychodynamically oriented groups are process groups: groups that are focused on no other task than that of helping members explore and understand the dynamics of the group itself and the roles members take in relation to those dynamics. Psychodynamically oriented groups in general illuminate the connections between, on the one hand, members' feelings and behaviors in the group and, on the other hand, their problematic patterns of feelings and relationships outside the group. Such groups, it might be said, are more fully focused on the here-and-now in the group: exploring what is happening in the moment as it unfolds in the group process. Psychoeducational and support groups are different in that members tend to spend more time talking about the "there-and-then" (i.e., talking about things occurring in the members' lives outside the group). Although, as Ettin (1998) and others have observed, all psychotherapy groups have dimensions of here and now and there and then, they differ in their respective emphases on these dimensions of group life. The role of the therapist in psychodynamically oriented groups tends to be significantly less active and structuring of the group interaction. The therapist's role, in effect, is to be with the group in a way that allows it to explore its evolving ways of being together such that the characteristic processes through which members individually and interactively regulate themselves and others emerge in the group and become available for exploration in the here-and-now of group life.

Different kinds of groups have, therefore, different tasks or purposes and, subsequently, different leader and member roles. Therefore, they address different dimensions of human experiencing in groups and invite different kinds and processes of human change. In addition to the task of the group, the therapeutic frame of group psychotherapy also concerns the agreements, contracts, or covenants that bind members and leaders together in that task.

The Group Agreements

The metanoetic liturgy of group psychotherapy is shaped by the group contract or group agreements that form the commonly understood boundaries and rules of group life. These boundaries and rules promote the basic values that serve as the therapeutic envelope (Cohen, 2005) of the group. While different kinds of groups will have different agreements, it may be helpful to use the example of a psychodynamically oriented group to get a feel for the nature and role of these agreements.

The group contract[5] will usually include a number of items. For example, group members normally agree to arrive on time and stay for the entire group session. This may seem straightforward. Many group members join a group hoping that it will be a relief from the burdens and pains of their relationships in their lives outside the group. Inevitably, members find it is not so simple. The problem people or issues from whom or which they sought escape begin to appear in simulacrum in the group itself. Members begin to feel the urge to miss sessions, to arrive late, or to engage in other resistances or fall into unrepresented or unformulated gaps in their internal and interpersonal worlds.

A second common agreement involves confidentiality: the group members and leaders agree to protect the confidentiality of the other members of the group. Confidentiality, however, presents different problems in group psychotherapy than in individual therapy. While group members agree to confidentiality, the therapist cannot guarantee that members will in fact abide by this agreement. This cautionary clause is part of the boundary itself. While confidentiality is expected, group members cannot in fact be assured in a professional or legal sense that it will be followed by anyone other than the therapist.

A third common agreement is that members agree to share their feelings in words, not actions. Many of the emotional difficulties that members come to group therapy to work on are precisely instances where they unconsciously act out rather than reflect on the anxieties or vulnerabilities that motivate their behavior. Sharing and reflecting on feelings members have about themselves and toward one another, therefore, is a critical dimension of group life. Enriching the capacity to "mentalize" (that is, to hold one's own and others' minds in mind) is a central part of the therapeutic action of group psychotherapy.[6] In another sense, this agreement is also meant to protect the safety of the group: members can talk about difficult issues but agree to keep the group space safe from actions or behaviors that might otherwise be threatening or traumatizing.

A fourth part of the contract or covenant of group psychotherapy is that members agree to use their relationships with others in the group for therapeutic rather than social ends. In most cases, this means that members agree not to have contact outside the regular group meeting itself. As

5. Many of these examples are drawn from Rutan et al. (2010) and Cohen (2005).

6. The literature on the importance of the capacity to mentalize in regulating or containing emotion is growing rapidly. For an overview, see Bateman and Fonagy (2012).

Caroline Garland (2010) has noted, if the group is to be an alternative to the social worlds from which its members come, the group must be clearly demarcated from that social world. Attempts to pull the group back into the familiar patterns of relationships and meanings from which the members originally wanted relief (however appealing it may begin to feel in face of the discomfort of the therapeutic culture of the group) is to be avoided if at all possible.

Finally, members agree to give sufficient notice of their intent to leave the group for the group to work through their feelings about the loss. On the one hand, members sometimes feel the urge to leave rather than deal with difficult issues. This agreement is meant to enable members to reflect with one another about urges to leave in order to discern the complex meanings that may be at stake. On the other hand, as we will see below, the loss that leaving creates in a group is itself a dense emotional and spiritual event, one that would benefit from careful consideration.

Beginning therapists are often distressed when group members violate the group contract or the therapeutic frame more generally: by coming late, forgetting to pay, meeting other members outside the group, or threatening to leave prematurely. Yet, given the emotional challenges of group therapy, therapists should anticipate that members will sometimes resist or attack the group norms and agreements that structure the group. Such events are expectable occurrences and are important for the group to reflect on and understand. Group members should come to expect that the group will help them wonder at times what is happening in the group member and what is happening in the group as a whole. How might transference and countertransference phenomena be involved? In order to understand these developments, it can be useful to see them in the context of the overall development of the group and in terms of the emotional dynamics that commonly occur in group life.

Group Development

While every group is unique in important ways, nearly all groups have common developmental trajectories. There are various ways to understand these developmental stages or phases (Agazarian, 2004; MacKenzie, 1997; Rutan et al., 2010; Wheelan, 2004). I will use the terminology of Rutan et al., (2010) for this discussion. Groups begin their lives dealing with problems of joining. In particular, members face dilemmas regarding their emotional boundaries. To join a group means that the boundaries around the self must be permeable enough to allow real connection with the group and its members to occur while also being sturdy enough to keep the self safe. Group members will come to this dilemma at the formative stage of the group with varying strengths and weaknesses from their developmental histories. Through trial and error (a process sometimes joyful, sometimes painful), members learn which experiences and behaviors are invited or welcomed and which are received more coldly, harshly, or ambivalently. Group members often spend their time talking about or addressing commonalities among the members, the ways "we are alike." The group is developing at this early stage the group's culture and norms. The role of the therapist is to model the group norms most conducive to therapeutic effect: respectful listening, encouragement of "mentalizing" (i.e., thinking about feelings in increasingly complex and nuanced ways, and about the things that happen that close such thinking down), and curiosity about the ways groupwide events can illuminate interpersonal and intrapsychic issues.

A second stage of group life is called the reactive stage. In the reactive stage, the group tends to focus more on differences within itself and the emotional reactions to belonging to a group with those differences. As Rutan et al. (2010) observe, emotional reactivity is high during these periods, with questions often emerging about commitment to the group, threats of leaving, and other resistances to the group contract. Group members start to notice that the group, which they had hoped would be different from the problematic groups in their lives (family or work groups), is really "just like them." Members often feel like the group isn't helping or is making things worse. Remember, for example, the case of Bonnie and Steve in their therapy group. What is happening, in effect, is that after the romantic period of the formative stage, maladaptive patterns of relating to others are starting to emerge. From a therapeutic standpoint, of course, this is precisely the opportunity on which group therapy is meant to capitalize. The problems about which people have been talking are no longer simply "out there," but are now in the here and now of the group's life, where they can be empathically listened to, their meanings explored, and alternative ways of experiencing and behaving opened up and reinforced.

In the mature stage of group life, both commonalities and differences are appreciated, and the group has enough of a rupture/repair history with one another that intense affect can be tolerated and worked through. The suffering of others is appreciated and responded to more in its own right, as less a projection of others' fears or of dissociated parts of the self. In this stage, the group is focused almost entirely on the here and now of the group experience. It has also developed a more collegial relationship with the therapist. In other words, in a larger sense, the group itself has become the therapist, the group doing the emotional work of therapy with less chronic interference from group destructive forces.

The termination stage of group life occurs either when the group itself is concluding its work, or, if the group is ongoing, when a member chooses to terminate. We often don't think of this, but when a member leaves the group, the group has in some significant way ended, even if other members continue. The group is no longer the same. Likewise, when a new member enters a group, a new group must in some sense be formed. In termination, grief and mourning processes dominate: feelings of sadness, pining, anger, guilt, shame, and fear arise and are available to be worked through. The group often struggles with the guilt, shame, or secret delight that they have somehow caused the member to leave. Of course, loss in the group produces memories of prior losses in members' lives, so the group is always dealing not only with the present loss but also with the history of meanings around difficult losses evoked by the current loss. Even at its ending, the intrapsychic, the interpersonal, and the group-as-a-whole are deeply intertwined.

Group Dynamics

The therapeutic frame constitutes the envelope within which (and in relation to which) the metanoetic liturgy of group psychotherapy unfolds. The liturgy itself happens through complex group dynamics that develop inside the envelope or that attack or undermine the envelope. For this brief introduction to group therapy, we will look cursorily at four such dynamics: *group-as-a-whole, projective identification, scapegoating,* and *enactments.*

There are many versions of *group-as-a-whole* perspectives on group psychotherapy (Dalal, 1998; Horowitz, 2014; Lyon et al., 2012; Stone, 2009). For illustrative purposes I will focus on Wilfrid Bion (1961). Many years ago Bion developed a perspective on what he called "basic-assumption" behavior in groups that remains important today. Basic-assumption behavior is a kind of group-as-a-whole phenomenon in which the anxiety within the group propels it to act as if its task is something other than it is. For example, in the basic assumption of dependency, the group acts as if its task is to find a leader on which it can depend to help it deal with the distress and vulnerability of the group therapeutic environment. The group wants someone who knows, someone who will tell it what to do or how to be in order to be safe and secure in the face of the anxieties of being in a group. Likewise, in the basic assumption of fight or flight, the group looks for an enemy to explain the group's distress and subsequently, either to attack and defeat, or to escape from. The group hopes that in either defeating or escaping from the perceived enemy, it will be relieved from its distress. Finally, Bion observed that sometimes groups operate on the basic assumption of pairing in which the group attempts to connect two of its members or leaders, in the hope that in their relationship hope will be generated and the group's despair overcome. Bion's basic-assumption behaviors exemplify ways that groups try to avoid or vanquish their disappointment with their therapists or leaders rather than finding ways to contain and better metabolize the underlying emotions that give rise to the distress. The recovery of the group's ability to think its feelings rather than simply act them out becomes part of the therapeutic action of group therapy. In any event, what happens in group life always takes place, in part, within a broader group dynamic that should be part of the therapist's attention.

Think, for example, here about Steve, Bonnie, and the therapy group described above. We have spoken about it so far as if the dynamics that were created were produced solely through the intrapsychic and interpersonal vectors of influence. We might wonder, however, to what extent the group as a whole was enacting something here. Perhaps the group unconsciously focused on a man and a woman, in part, as a substitute for (pairing) the male and female therapists. In other words, perhaps the group was not simply responding to two members in conflict but was also using (and maybe encouraging) that conflict as a way to make visible or enact a deeper struggle for which it had no words.

One of the emotional mechanisms that produce group-as-a-whole phenomena in group psychotherapy is called *projective identification*. Developed originally by Melanie Klein and refined and transformed by many others subsequently, projective identification is a two-person defense. That is, it is a way of protecting ourselves from unbearable feelings and thoughts that involves the use of another person or subgroup (Shay, 2011). This feature of projective identification is what makes it important in group therapy. The basic process of projective identification involves one person (or subgroup) feeling threatened with the potential intrusion of an unbearable feeling. In order to protect the selves of those so threatened, the feeling is then projected onto someone else (or another subgroup) in the group who has a particular valency to enact that feeling. The feeling is thus vacated from the projector or projectors and identified with by someone else in the group, who then proceeds to act it out in the group.

One of the most common ways projective identification occurs in group life is through the scapegoating process (Lyon, 2010). In scapegoating, an individual or subgroup is made to bear what is unbearable by other members of the group. Some part of the self that is felt to be too painful to recognize within oneself is seen only in someone else. Held captive in the other, the scapegoating process seeks to drive the painful feeling deep into the heart of the other and to protect the rest of the group from what is felt to be its disturbing and toxic effects. Such group dynamics frequently use the markers of race, sexual orientation, gender, or other social categories distinguished by power differences to work the scapegoating process (McRae & Short, 2009; Shah & Kosi, 2012). The therapeutic work involved in situations of scapegoating (as in projective identification more generally) is to enable those disowning and projecting the disturbing feelings to recognize these feelings in themselves and to work to understand and contain them in more fruitful and just ways.

A final group dynamic important to note has to do with the place of transference, countertransference, and *enactments* in group therapy. As observed earlier in this essay, group members often repeat (transfer) relationship patterns within the group that are similar to the problematic patterns they came to address in the first place. For some this might seem discouraging. For Steve, for example, it seemed like a defeat: first, that the therapists would admit someone (Bonnie) to the group who was so clearly like the girlfriends with whom he struggled; and second, that for some time he couldn't seem to find a way to respond to her differently. Bonnie felt much the same way. She responded to Steve's rigidly controlling defenses from the feelings and meanings that shaped her own history of relationships. From a psychodynamic perspective, of course, the fact that group members find themselves enacting familiar, troubling patterns of relationships in the group itself is precisely the setting within which therapy must work. Helping members use the group as a living laboratory allows them to explore the emotions and meanings involved in relational patterns as they unfold. Observing these patterns allows group members to mentalize more fully and contain intense feeling states better so that they do not have to repeat the wounding behaviors that have so painfully distorted their relationships.

In even more complex situations, enactments occur. *Enactments*, as I will use the term here, refer to situations where dissociated (unformulated) aspects of the clients, the therapists, or both coalesce to produce events in the therapy that repeat painful, often traumatizing, situations from the pasts of all parties involved (Lyon et al., 2012; Stern, 2009). Enactments may seem like situations one would prefer to avoid. However, again from a psychodynamic perspective, they are often the only means through which nonverbal, procedural dimensions of our experience can be accessed. It is sometimes only through an enactment that what otherwise has no words can be known.

How Group Therapy Helps: Metanoetic
Liturgy and the Already/Not-Yet

Bonnie, Steve, and other members of the group eventually began to interact with one another differently in many respects. They began to see how the unhelpful ways they were experiencing each other and their therapists were being perpetuated by the expectations they brought with them from their own experiences in their families of origin. They began to be able to see and understand their own emotions and desires and those of the others in the room in richer, more accurate, and more thoughtful ways: that is, they grew in their capacity of mentalization. They also gained more confidence that their lives could be better and that they were less alone, less idiosyncratic in their struggles. In the classic descriptions of Yalom and Leszcz (2005), they made good use of the interpersonal learning experience provided by the group; gained self-understanding, a deepened sense of hope; and found greater self respect in being able to be helpful to others in the group.[7] They found ways, we might say, to struggle with the haunting, persistent Insistence toward that wonder, love, and justice fragmentarily disclosed within and between them (Caputo, 2013). They responded to the Murmurings at the margins and the depths of group life.

Pastoral psychotherapy represents a somewhat unruly family of perspectives on the clinical disciplines. In this essay I have offered an outline of a pastoral-psychotherapy perspective on group psychotherapy. It makes visible its distinctive orientation where the therapeutic frame and the group dynamics that characterize group psychotherapy shape and are shaped by those places where the edges of desire reach into that final mystery that surrounds our experience. It is that place where we are sometimes met within and between us by a More, an Other that insists or lures us toward the wonder, love, and justice that we have so long resisted but that nonetheless characterizes what Christian and other faith communities have pointed toward as *metanoia*.

Of course, the kingdom can only be known or realized in part, not in full. It is already present in a fragmentary way but not yet present in its fullness. However much Steve, Bonnie and the other members of the group productively grapple with the patterns and structures that tie them to diminished ways of living, they will only know the relief they seek in part, not in full. And while partial relief can be a great relief indeed, perfect or complete release from the things that bind us is not possible. Yet God calls

7. For fuller descriptions of how group psychotherapy helps, see Yalom and Leszcz (2005); Rutan et al. (2010); Garland (2010); Billow (2003); and Harwood and Pines (1998).

us toward what is perhaps yet possible amid it all: to participate in a wonder, love, and justice that we might better creatively embody. Said another way, the metanoetic liturgy of group psychotherapy, when it is faithful to the insistence or lure it seeks to disclose, enacts and invites something of the deeper wonder, love, and justice (that to which the name *God* refers) to which it can but point in fragmentary ways (Caputo, 2006).

While this brief outline cannot hope to encompass the complex issues involved, it is meant to invite readers to consider their own perspectives, to find ways to lean into the discipline and practices of group psychotherapy so that the spiritual dimensions of life become visible and compelling. This is an increasingly complex task, given the challenges to religious and spiritual life in our time. But it is an important task, I would argue, in that it discloses and illuminates dimensions of our experiencing otherwise unformulated and unseen but nonetheless persistently present.

References

Agazarian, Y. M. (2004). *Systems-centered therapy for groups.* London: Karnac.

Bateman, A. W., & Fonagy, P., (Eds.). (2012). *Handbook of mentalizing in mental health practice.* Washington DC: American Psychiatric Publishing.

Billow, R. M. (2003). *Relational group psychotherapy: From basic assumption to passion.* International Library of Group Therapy 26. London: Jessica Kingsley.

Bion, W. R. (1961). *Experiences in groups, and other papers.* London: Routledge.

Caputo, J. D. (2006). *The weakness of God: A theology of the event.* Indiana Series in the Philosophy of Religion. Bloomington: Indiana University Press.

Caputo, J. D. (2013). *The insistence of God: A theology of perhaps.* Bloomington: Indiana University Press.

Cohen, B. R. (2005). Creating the group envelope. In L. Motherwell and J. J. Shay, (Eds.), *Complex dilemmas in group therapy* (pp. 3–12). New York: Brunner-Routledge.

Dalal, F. (1998). *Taking the group seriously: Toward a post-Foulkesian group analytic theory.* London: Kingsley.

Ettin, M. F. (1999). *Foundations and applications of group psychotherapy: A sphere of influence.* International Library of Group Analysis 10. London: Kingsley.

Garland, C., (Ed.). (2010). *The groups book: Psychoanalytic group therapy.* London: Karnac.

Harwood, I. N. H., & Pines, M. (Eds.). (1998). *Self experiences in group: Intersubjective and self psychological pathways to human understanding.* International Library of Group Analysis 4. London: Kingsley.

Horowitz, L. (2014). *Listening with the fourth ear: Unconscious dynamics in analytic group psychotherapy.* New International Library of Group Analysis Series. London: Karnac.

Keller, C. (2008). *On the Mystery: Discerning divinity in process.* Minneapolis: Fortress.

Kleinberg, J. L. (Ed.). (2012). *The Wiley-Blackwell handbook of group psychotherapy.* Oxford: John Wiley and Sons.

Lyon, K. B. (2010). Scapegoating in congregational and group life: Practical theological reflections on the unbearable. In K. Greider et al. (Eds.), *Healing wisdom: Depth psychology and the pastoral ministry*. (pp 141–56). Grand Rapids Eerdmans.

Lyon, K. B. et al. (2012). Unbearable states of mind in group psychotherapy: Dissociation, mentalization, and the clinician's stance. *Group: Journal of the Eastern Group Psychotherapy Association 36*, 267–82.

MacKenzie, K. R. (1997). *Time-managed group psychotherapy: Effective clinical applications*. Washington DC: American Psychiatric Press.

McRae, M. B. and Short, E. L. (2009). *Racial and cultural dynamics in group and organizational life: Crossing boundaries*. Thousand Oaks, CA: Sage.

McWilliams, N. (2004). *Psychoanalytic psychotherapy: A practitioner's guide*. New York: Guilford.

Motherwell, L., and Shay, J. J. (2005). *Complex dilemmas in group psychotherapy: Pathways to resolution*. New York: Brunner-Routledge.

Rutan, S. et al. (2010). *Psychodynamic group psychotherapy* (4th ed.). New York: Guilford.

Shah, S. A., and Kosi, R. (2012). Diversity in groups: Culture, ethnicity, and race. In Kleinberg, J. L. (Ed.), *The Wiley-Blackwell handbook of group psychotherapy* (pp. 667–80). Oxford: Wiley.

Shay, J. (2011). Projective identification simplified: Recruiting your shadow. *International Journal of Group Psychotherapy 61*, 238–61.

Smith, J. K. A. (2009). *Desiring the kingdom: Worship, worldview, and cultural formation*. Grand Rapids: Baker Academic.

Stern, D. B. (2009). *Partners in thought: Working with unformulated experience, dissociation, and enactment*. Psychoanalysis in a New Key 12. New York: Routledge.

Stone, W. (2009). *Contributions of self psychology to group psychotherapy*. London: Karnac.

Tillich, P. (1973). *Systematic theology, Vol. 1*. Chicago: University of Chicago Press.

Wheelan, S. A. (2010). *Group processes: A developmental perspective* (2nd ed.). Upper Saddle River, NJ: Harlow, Pearson Education.

Whitaker, D. S. (1985). *Using groups to help people*. International Library of Group Psychotherapy and Group Process. London: Routledge.

Yalom, I. D., with Leszcz, M. (2005). *The theory and practice of group psychotherapy* (5th ed.). New York: Basic Books.

16

Coda: Self-Care for the Least of These

Ann Belford Ulanov

The Least of These

WE ARE USED TO interpreting Matthew 25:32–45 in relation to our less
fortunate neighbor and quite rightly hear Jesus tell us, insofar as you give
food to the hungry, water to the thirsty, clothe the naked and visit the
imprisoned, you give this to me. Jung reminds us that we, ourselves, may
be the least among us, but then we do not extend that kindness. We do
not feed hungry parts of ourselves, shelter our vulnerable nakedness of
defenses, visit parts of us imprisoned in anxiety or depression. Instead,
we "condemn and rage against ourselves," hide our lowly nature from
others. If God appears to us in this "despicable form," we would deny
any knowledge of this other, cross to the opposite side of the road (Jung,
1933, p. 235).

This chapter takes up the crucial issue of self-care for the clinician who
approaches work from a pastoral departure point. What sustains our seeing
the other as also within ourselves? How do we stay alive, and glad to be so,
in this work of therapy? What sustains vitality and balance over decades of
pastoral clinical work? Are there practices we find and that find us that we
might share for our mutual aliveness?

Because we stand with a foot on both sides of the frontier of psyche
and soul, we can ask outright, what goes on feeding our soul in doing this
work? Who or what, then, feeds the feeder (Ulanov & Ulanov, 1991/1999)?
And what is the work, the nub of it? It is not curing the client. If that is the

stated goal we end up eating our clients as well as feeling devoured by them. Hovering, to see how they are doing as evidence of our success imposes a needy hunger of our own into the center of the work. Like Cronos, who eats his children to secure his ruling position, we can use our clients to prove we are effective in our job, and thus make a meal of their suffering and growth. And in that process, we neglect our own hungry parts that need our attention. Blurring those with the clients' needs delivers us up as the meal to be eaten, feeling we are endlessly giving and giving and worn out by the work, indeed devoured by it because we ignore self-care. Responses to what is the work and what methods help us not just survive its perils but thrive in the joy of it, come in psychological and religious ways.

The Work

It helps to have ideas, images, even myths about what this work is that we do, especially over many years. Freud (1964/1973) says his myth is the instincts. Jung (1953) talks about the alchemy of transformation of the individual, from the depths up, so to speak, and through the individual into transforming society. Melanie Klein (1948/1975) finds a place for guilt over destructive aggression in igniting our efforts to repair, make amends, and create. D. W. Winnicott (1971) and Marion Milner (1952/1987) find the necessity of illusion to foster self and symbol in living creatively. Philip Bromberg (1998), of the relational analysts, talks about our standing in the spaces between different self-states within us, getting them talking to each other, not segregated by dissociation. Kohut (1997) talks about the method of empathy to restart growth of self- esteem (narcissistic energy) on its path of healthy development toward, ultimately, humor, wisdom, compassion. Sue Grand (2010) finds connections between self-growth and justice toward others, lessening the force of evil in the world. George Atwood (2012) finds in the intersubjective space between us our life themes emerging in how we find, endorse, or traumatize each other, into fullest expression of self.

All these theorists, and many more, circle around the mystery of self and other, the core of us that cannot be defined exactly and that depends on others to come into being at all. The pastoral psychotherapist adds the linking of that core with ultimate reality, a transcendent presence named God, the All and the Vast in this life and the next, "from the ages to the ages" (to cite a Christian orthodox phrase). It is this linking that lends to psychotherapeutic work conversation at the deepest place of the particular person's wounds and secret hope.

Whatever our theory, it behooves us, I suggest, to gain and gain again a sense of the background that orients us to the work. What theories stand out for each of us as the lenses through which we perceive what we do in the sessions with our clients? From what countries do we hail? What God presides over our work? (Ulanov, 1992/2004a). Ongoing awareness of this orientation protects our clients from being fit to our theory instead of the other way around. None of us wants to be fit to someone's theory. As Wittgenstein reminds us, the person is not an item in the world.

We are subjects who go on unfolding until dead, unless terrible hurt or abuse interrupts, or we fall into sloth. From whence do we see and hear the hungry, thirsty parts of ourselves and of our clients? We share this life, this fear of rigid imprisonment, of being pushed away. We are the same in our different experiences; we just sit in another chair in our consulting room, and the focus stays on the client's story. We need to find our myths that orient us to the work, to name what we believe in, so that after our therapy ends, our training completes, we go on growing our theory in lively ways (Ulanov, 2001/2004c).

Our ideas of what the work is foster livingness in it. For, after all, we work in the precincts of psyche, a human process made up of conscious and unconscious ways of thinking and imaging; of modes of gender and sexuality; of feminine and masculine symbolizing; of body breathing, sweating, weeping, and yelling in sessions; as well as quiet dwelling together in something larger that holds us both. And, after all, we in our pastoral capacities know and name this something larger as God and discover ways unheard of how it communicates, always from the muck of the stable; or as Nicholas of Cusa (1997) says, truth shouted in the street.

Methods of Self-Care

From the psychological side, to take care of ourselves, we need to engage in constant interview with the reality of psyche, having a theory about it (a metapsychology), using our consciousness, even if inevitably muddled, to reflect, articulate, communicate with each other about our human psyche, and its relation to the mystery of existing in this world. We wish to be in touch with what originates and sustains us in life as a person. Here we use our minds and imaginations to inquire into what we live for finally in the most everyday tasks.

We need an ongoing interview with the psyche. Such investigation leads directly to that interior well, that reservoir without which we die. This is not constructing a scientific formula that can be fastened down and then imposed on each client, or applied to each client's material in precisely the same way. But there is a principle involved that we all circle around in this work, or better yet, an image. A good one is the image of the well. In such imagining, we represent in words and picture, what exists in each of us and between us: a well of being that supports our becoming, the event of going on as persons, together and alone.

The power of this image gets projected into the work of connecting in ourselves and with our clients through a resource that feels like a source of livingness. If we consider theories of personal history, they go further and further back into time—from oedipal layers to preoedipal layers, to earliest months of infancy, to neonatal life, as if these theories that hold numinous power for many will carry into articulation our meditations on the mystery of becoming a person at all.

Being trained in religion as well as in psychological disciplines delivers us to the simple but profound truth that health is not and cannot be our first commitment as professionals. We know deep within us there is an important difference between being functional and feeling alive and real, between adjusting and living with a sense that our life is worthwhile. Despite being fractured and hurt, we know from Blues singers, from painters, how important it is to live fully engaged, present, taking all that is there, named in scripture as the abundant life. Our psychological training tells us that our ability to gain and sustain a self depends on psychological development. Our religious tradition tells us psychic development is not enough to give us that precious sense of value, that our living from a unique center matters. Religion tells us bluntly (regardless of which faith or denomination) that the good life is the life lived in relation to God, to mystery at its core, to a truth that we can never capture and sum up.

The soul is another center in our pastoral-psychotherapeutic work. We might liken the soul to that space within us, within our psychosomatic self that is embodied in our living, where God can put a paw on us at any time. Responding from soul can happen anytime in our lives, even if we have neglected our soul, and even up to the last moments before our death. Soul brings a willingness to respond, to become the person we are, to reach to others, to a longing toward God. This readiness to be and become, to want to live within these central relationships moves us to say yes to life, to engage, to be there in aliveness. This willingness sustains our psychotherapeutic practice silently in its background, like a quiet humming that is just present in the work.

Useful Options of Self-Care

As we go on working over decades, specific methods can help us. For example, in the constant interview with our self, the psyche and soul in us, we depend on others. Some like periodic peer groups for reciprocal supervision of cases. Some like reading groups to keep feeding the necessity for knowledge of how to work with dreams, with devastating collapse, with psychological issues in aging.

With the enlargement of the circle of consciousness of what we know, bringing more light into the work, the circumference of darkness also grows bigger. Can we accept that we fall through the holes in our theories, to wait and watch with our client for what emerges in the turmoil? Does our faith in the integrative forces of psyche sustain us in dark periods of not-knowing?

Some of us return to analysis, initiated by rough patches in living, blows of fate that knock us flat. Changing our seat in the consulting room, joining our clients' perspective in the work, benefits them. We are in the soup, in the well firsthand with our own unfolding stories, giving space to our own narratives, refreshed in how important it is to have that space. Such experiences protect our clients from our smuggling our story into theirs, because ours demands our attention and will get it one way or the other.

Thought must be given to how we review our work with each client each year, and over the years. Do we read over all our notes? Do we take each client's work into periodic review? This is time-consuming. In such labor we can learn a little something—something we never saw, something hidden (or sometimes out in the open) that speaks the whole arc, the whole point of this person's work with us. Some of us take notes during sessions; some of us take notes after sessions; some review monthly because we keep no notes. To mull, to think over what has happened, what has emerged, what has failed or gotten stuck impresses into our work a sense of alignment with what this person's psyche circles round, aims toward, and with what this person's soul longs for, arrives at, leaves behind.

In addition, we see with some clarity our own demons and can track our countertransference rhythms using its usual types of our normal, abnormal, induced, archetypal reactions to gauge our response to our clients (Ulanov, 1997/2004b). This keeps us alert to what the work with each client introduces into our own growing.

Practices of Self-Care

Specific practices suggest themselves to me, to care for ourselves over years of this fascinating and strenuous work we do. We need exposure to otherness, other worlds, other perspectives than our own. Take up a completely different activity—start running or walking regularly, into different neighborhoods or landscapes. Listen to all of Bartok's music. Learn Japanese. My favorite example comes from a student of many years ago, an older woman developed spiritually and sophisticated in her dress and manner. She took up tap dancing. She joined a class of children and even participated in their end-of-year recital. Being the tallest, she was in the back row of the performance, complete with outfit and snazzy tap shoes. What daring!

We need food for our spirits. Augustine says when he prays, he talks to God; when he reads spiritual writers, God talks to him. We must be on the hunt for the authors that touch our soul, open our heart. We must keep alert for methods of quieting down, opening attention, styles of meditation and prayer that draw us into that well of Source beyond source.

We need help with our own problems, work with our own psyches, knowing concretely where the potholes exist, and we fall in. We know from our training the usual signs of complexes taking over our perceptions. We get edgy, take offense too easily; we get caught and only notice our unconscious fall into identification with this splinter personality in us by the fact we are yelling or red in the face. We discover we cannot let the issue go. We must repeat it still another time to the one who will listen. Such signs signal something important is pushing its way into consciousness. Who is the stranger at the door? Can we greet her or him with hospitality or at least with curiosity, even if also with alarm tinged with hostility? (Kearney, 2010).

We depend on friends who love us enough to tell us we are full of baloney, and who ask, as Simone Weil (1951) asserts, the one important question: what are you going through? The best prevention of all is love, to have it and live it, coming in and going out of us, between us, and around us, with a mate, a dog, a child, a painter, a teaching, a poet, God. Even if love does not appear in a form we long for, it still exists. We can witness to it as well as live it. It enlists our sexual being, includes aggression and an endless stirring us up from the bottom, composting our fears and troubles, releasing us into unfolding.

One particular care we must take in our peculiar profession addresses the weight of pain we hear in sessions. If the work goes well, unbearable pain may find a voice to be spoken. No longer mute, a person may build with us a space in which the unsayable can find words. We want this to happen, but its cumulative weight can become overwhelming. We must find ways to live in this intensity of experience and not be crushed by it.

Our other foot in religious tradition proves the most helpful, I suggest. For there we have a comforter and Wonderful Counselor (Isaiah) in whose presence we participate. We do not have to carry all the weight, nor fix all the pain, nor can we whisk it away, transform it so it is no more. There is an Other who already has come to enter that person's pain, who suffers the worst death dealing we inflict on each other and rises from its suffering.

Our job is space making, engaging the intensity of a person's experience so that she or he can experience the awful that has happened to them, to feel its impact and not go out of existence. Thus we all come to bear the scars of suffering but to carry it within instead of being held hostage to its engulfment. In addition, we have the knowledge of prayer, to confide our clients to God's care, and to entrust ourselves and our limits to God's care, to give over the pain of our sessions into the God who says, "Behold, I make all things new" (Revelation 21:5). I understand this to mean, not that suffering magically disappears, but that we grow firmer flesh around the wound. We carry the bleeding place, are not lost in it or defined by it.

What sustains us above all in this work is the privilege, with all its perils of burnout, of the excitement of living close to the well, to the unknown as it touches us. Each person's journey is an adventure, with its own idiosyncrasies of symptom and symbol, its own weirdness that surprises, its unique path that inspires awe. We cannot make up events and characters that appear in dreams, in a person's new opening to life, in a still deeper suffering. An accompanying danger, of burnup from being close to the fire, must instill our practices of quieting, waiting, trust that in the human connection of understanding and hearing, space not only enlivens but anchors, grounds us in the ongoing work.

Those New Testament women come to mind who recognize that it is God at the door. They respond by pouring out tears, wiping his feet with their hair, anointing the one they love with costly ointment, surrounding the foot of the cross together in a gaggle of Marys. These women see, they stay, they let go their projections, to see who is in fact come to bring the new.

References

Atwood, G. E. (2012). *An abyss of madness.* Psychoanalytic Inquiry Book Series 37. New York: Routledge.

Bromberg, P. M. (1998). *Standing in the spaces: essays on clinical process, trauma and dissociation.* Hillsdale, NJ: Analytic.

Freud, S. (1964). *Anxiety and instinctual life.* In J. Strachey (Ed. And Trans.). *The Standard Edition of the Complete Psychological Works of Sigmund Freud,* (Vol. 22, pp. 81–111): London: Hogarth Press. (orig. publ. 1933).

Grand, S. (2010). *The hero in the mirror: From fear to fortitude.* Relational Perspectives Book Series 41. New York: Routledge.

Jung, C. G. (1933). *Modern man in search of a soul.* (W. S. Dell & C. F. Baynes, Trans.). A Harvest Book. New York: Harcourt, Brace & World.

Kearney R. (2010). *Anatheism: Returning to God after God.* Insurrections. New York: Columbia University Press.

Klein, M. (1975). On the theory of anxiety and guilt. In *Envy and gratitude & other works, 1946-1963* (pp. 25–43). Writings of Melanie Klein. New York: Delacorte/ Seymour Lawrence. (Orig. publ. 1948).

Kohut, H. (1984). *How does analysis cure?* A. Goldberg (Ed.), with the collaboration of P. E. Stepansky. Chicago: University of Chicago Press.

Kohut, H. (1977). *The restoration of the self.* New York: International Universities Press.

Milner, M. B. (1987). The role of illusion in symbol formation. In *The suppressed madness of sane men* (pp. 62–84). New Library of Psychoanalysis 3. London: Tavistock. (Orig. publ. 1952).

Nicholas of Cusa. (1997). *Nicholas of Cusa: Selected spiritual writings.* (H. L. Bond, Trans.). Classics of Western Spirituality 89. New York: Paulist.

Ulanov, A. B., & Ulanov, B. (1999). *The healing imagination.* Einsiedeln, Switzerland: Daimon. (Orig. publ. 1991).

Ulanov, A. B. (2004a). Unseen boundaries, dangerous crossings. In *Spiritual aspects of clinical work* (pp. 225–56). Einsiedeln, Switzerland: Daimon. (Orig. publ. 1992).

Ulanov, A. B. (2004b). Countertransference and the self. In *Spiritual aspects of clinical work* (pp. 353–91). Einsiedeln, Switzerland: Daimon. (Orig. publ. 1997).

Ulanov, A. B. (2004c). After Analysis What? In *Spiritual aspects of clinical work* (pp. 455–75). Einsiedeln, Switzerland: Daimon. (Orig. publ. 2001).

Weil, S. (1951). *Waiting for God.* (E. Craufurd, Trans.). New York: Putnam.

Winnicott, D. W. (1971). *Playing and reality.* New York: Basic Books.